To
Rebecca

**Luther's
Catholic
Christology**

Luther's Catholic Christology

ACCORDING TO HIS JOHANNINE LECTURES OF 1527

Franz Posset

NORTHWESTERN PUBLISHING HOUSE
Milwaukee, Wisconsin

Library of Congress Card 87-63002
Northwestern Publishing House
1250 N. 113th St., P. O. Box 26975, Milwaukee, WI 53226-0975
© 1988 by Northwestern Publishing House. All rights reserved
Published 1988
Printed in the United States of America
ISBN 0-8100-0275-2

TABLE OF CONTENTS

Part Three

PREFACE

The origins of this historical-theological dissertation lie in the seminar on Luther's hermeneutics
conducted by Professor Kenneth Hagen of Marquette University. I found out that Luther lectured
on a Johannine text in the year 1527, on the First
Epistle of St. John; and I learned that St. John was
Luther's favorite evangelist. I realized there is a gap
in modern Luther research; the Johannine Luther is
neglected, while the Pauline Luther dominates. At
the same time, the celebrations of Luther's five-hun-
dredth birthday were under way at Marquette University and around the world. In addition, the results
of the U.S. Lutheran — Roman Catholic Dialogue on
"Justification By Faith" were being promulgated in
Milwaukee. During that time, the question began to
fascinate me: What if Luther's doctrine of Christ
could be demonstrated as being Catholic? This question and those events are the *Sitz im Leben* of this
work.

For the friendly support and expertise, special
thanks go to my dissertation director and member of
the Lutheran — Catholic Dialogue, Professor Kenneth Hagen, and to the Doctoral Committee, Dr. Pa-
trick Carey, Dr. Daniel Maguire, Dr. Paul Misner,
and Dr. Oliver Olson.

To Dr. William McCutcheon of Beaver Dam, I owe
my thanks for shaping my English; and to Ms. Mary
Mayr of Mayville, I am greatly indebted for coping
with the time pressure and for her skill in producing
a neat manuscript in due time for the public defense
of this thesis on October 31, 1984.

I am very grateful to Northwestern Publishing House for accepting this study in the scholarly publication program, and to its associate editor Rev. John A. Trapp, for his thorough review of the English, French, Latin, and Luther-German texts, and of the Greek and Hebrew terms which had to be interspersed occasionally. As for the translations, anyone familiar with rendering Luther texts of the given macaronic (German/Latin) kind into modern English will understand that the translator can only hope that if Luther were able to read his texts or student lecture notes, he would not find occasion on every page to refer to this ancient epigram, slightly paraphrased:

The work you recite is mine, O translator,
But when you recite it badly it begins to be yours.

Last, but not least, I am happy to acknowledge that this enterprise could not have been carried through without concessions made by the members of my family, for which I am most grateful to my wife Beverly, and to Martin and Rebecca, and my in-laws.

Franz Posset
Beaver Dam, Wisconsin
January 1, 1988

ABBREVIATIONS OF
BOOK TITLES AND JOURNALS

ARG	*Archiv für Reformationsgeschichte*
CR	*Corpus Reformatorum*
EvTh	*Evangelische Theologie*
Festgabe 1983	Helmar Junghans. *Leben und Werk Martin Luthers von 1526 bis 1546. Festgabe zu seinem 500. Geburtstag.* Berlin: Evangelische Verlagsanstalt; Göttingen: Vandenhoeck & Ruprecht, 1983.
KD	*Kerygma und Dogma*
PL	*Patrologia Latina*
ThLZ	*Theologische Literaturzeitung*
ThStKr	*Theologische Studien und Kritiken*
TRE	*Theologische Realenzyklopädie*
ZKG	*Zeitschrift für Kirchengeschichte*
ZkTh	*Zeitschrift für katholische Theologie*
ZST	*Zeitschrift für Systematische Theologie*
ZThK	*Zeitschrift für Theologie und Kirche*

INTRODUCTION

Nam in corde meo iste unus regnat articulus, scilicet Fides Christi, ex quo, per quem et in quem omnes meae diu noctuque fluunt et refluunt theologicae cogitationes.

> — Martin Luther's Preface to the Commentary on Galatians (1535)[1]

Christological Focus

Luther, in the preface to his Galatians commentary, indicates the significance of the Christological question for life. He declared that in his heart there rules one article, namely, faith in Christ; from it, through it and in it all his theological thoughts flow and return day and night. It has become almost a tradition in Luther research to use this quotation as an epigraph or an overture.[2] In continuation of this

---

[1] WA 40$^\text{I}$: 33, 7-9 (LW 27:145). On the abbreviations, see below n. 10.

[2] Cf. J. A. Rust, "Luthers Christusglaube," *ZST* 1 (1923): 453; "Die Christusverkündigung bei Luther," *Peregrinatio: Studien zur reformatorischen Theologie und zum Kirchenproblem* 2d ed. (Munich: Kaiser Verlag, 1962), 30 (first published in 1936); cf. Albrecht Peters, "Luthers Christuszeugnis als Zusammenfassung der Christusbotschaft der Kirche," KD 13 (1967): 1; cf. Hans Küng, *Menschwerdung Gottes: Eine Einführung in Hegels (!) theologisches Denken als Prolegomena zu einer künftigen Christologie*, Ökumenische Forschungen II. Soteriologische Abteilung 1 (Freiburg: Herder, 1970), 18; cf. Marc Lienhard, *Luther: Witness to Jesus Christ. Stages and Themes of the Reformer's Christology*, trans. Edwin H. Robertson (Minneapolis: Augsburg Publishing House, 1982), 11; cf. Gerhard Müller, "Martin Luther als Autorität für die lutherische Kirche?" *Luther Sendung für*

"tradition," I place this reference at the beginning of my investigation as well, because it is the proper approach for a study on Luther's Christology, which is at the center of all his work, and because it symbolizes the close connection of Luther's life with his theology. This emphasis on Christocentric concern has not always been normative in Luther research. Karl Holl understood Luther's theology as theocentric with the assumption that Luther's Christology was modalistic and subordinationist.[3] Several critics of Holl came forth with their stress on Luther's Christocentrism.[4] It is not the place here to review

Katholiken und Protestanten, ed. Karl Lehmann (Freiburg: Katholische Akademie; Zurich: Schnell and Steiner, 1982), 57; cf. James Atkinson, Martin Luther: Prophet to the Church Catholic (Exeter: The Pater Noster Press; Grand Rapids: William B. Eerdmans Publishing Company, 1983), 173.

[3]Cf. "Was verstand Luther unter Religion?" Gesammelte Aufsätze zur Kirchengeschichte vol. 1: Luther (Tübingen: Verlag Mohr, 1948), 72 (This was a talk given in 1917, first published in 1921, quoted here from the seventh edition 1948).

[4]Carl Stange wrote in 1928 against Holl, that each thought in Luther's theology contains already his Christology, cf. "Die Person Jesu Christi in der Theologie Luthers," ZST 6 (1928):450. In the following year 1929 Erich Vogelsang observed his contemporary scene and declared that Luther's Christology is heavily controversial: "Hart umstritten ist Luthers Christologie in der Forschung," Die Anfänge von Luthers Christologie nach der ersten Psalmenvorlesung insbesondere in ihren exegetischen und systematischen Zusammenhängen mit Augustin und der Scholastik dargestellt (Berlin and Leipzig: Verlag von Walter de Gruyter & Co., 1929), 1. Hans Joachim Iwand also takes the Christocentric view, cf. Rechtfertigungslehre und Christusglaube: Eine Untersuchung zur Systematik der Rechtfertigungslehre Luthers in ihren Anfängen, third ed. (Darmstadt: Wissenschaftliche Buchgesellschaft, 1966), 94-99 (first edition in 1930). Ernst Wolf published his critique of Holl in 1936. Erich Seeberg's works corroborated the Christocentric position, cf. Luthers Theologie, vol. 2: Christus: Wirklichkeit und Urbild, reprint (Darmstadt: Wissenschaftliche Buchgesellschaft, 1969), 278-298 (first published in 1937). All these authors must be considered

adequately the paths of Luther reseach in the twentieth century. However, an additional note of introduction is in order for the purpose of clarifying the acute problem of Luther's Christology according to the interpretation of recent Catholic theologians. What is their precise charge against Luther's Christology? The decisive one was formulated by Yves Congar in his "Regards" on the 1500th anniversary of the Council of Chalcedon in 1951. In the tracks of K. Holl and E. Vogelsang, Congar thought to have noticed that Luther had a monophysite Savior image of Christ,[5] while he admitted that Luther always has

as members of the school of thought of Theodosius Harnack, whose book on *Luthers Theologie* had been reprinted in 1927: *Luthers Theologie mit besonderer Beziehung auf seine Versöhnungs-und Erlösungslehre*, vol. 2 (Munich: Kaiser Verlag, 1927); it appeared originally in 1862-1886 in Erlangen.

After the Second World War, the Christocentric position prevailed. Gerhard Müller pointed out that Holl must be corrected, cf. "Luthers Christusverständnis," *Jesus Christus: Das Christusverständnis im Wandel der Zeiten*. Eine Ringvorlesung der Theologischen Fakultät Marburg, ed. Hans Grass and Werner Georg Kümmel (Marburg: N. G. Elwert-Verlag, 1963), 41-50. It is M. Lienhard's declared goal to invalidate Holl's thesis, cf. *Luther: Witness to Jesus Christ*, 13. Theobald Beer, *Der fröhliche Wechsel und Streit: Grundzüge der Theologie Martin Luthers*, second revised edition (Einsiedeln: Johannes Verlag, 1982), 443, joins as a Catholic author the predominantly Protestant debate and also maintains the Christocentric view. Otto Hermann Pesch contributes much to the clarification of the debate in " 'Um Christi willen': Christologie und Rechtfertigung in der katholischen Theologie: Versuch einer Richtigstellung," *Catholica*, 35 (1981):17.

[5]Cf. "Regards et réflexions sur la christologie de Luther," *Das Konzil von Chalkedon: Geschichte und Gegenwart*, ed. Aloys Grillmeier and Heinrich Bacht (Würzburg: Echter Verlag, 1954) 457-486, here page 485: "Et comme sa christologie est essentiellement sotériologie, cela lui donne, malgré son affirmation très sincère de la realité des deux natures, une saveur monophysite qu'on a dénoncée plus d'une fois avant nous." And on page 586: "Luther, en un mot, a la christologie de l' 'Alleinwirksamkeit Gottes.' "

professed the dogma of Chalcedon.[6] Thirty years later Congar came out with "New Regards" on Luther's Christology, and he revised his position by emphasizing, in 1982, that Luther made room for the divine Christ's activity in his humanity in regard to the work of salvation.[7] In the meantime, Theobald Beer, another Catholic theologian dealing with Luther's Christology, relied on Congar's old "Regards" on Luther's Christology. In 1974 he published his thesis that Luther's idea of the "holy exchange" was not orthodox (revised edition, 1980, reprinted in 1982).[8] But Congar himself, in his latest publication on Luther, defended the reformer against Beer's accusation, which maintained that Luther was in contradiction to the Councils of the Church. Congar pointed out (in 1982) that Luther's intention was to teach the same matter of faith in Christ but in a new

---

[6]"Luther, a toujours professé le dogme de Chalcédoine," ibid. 457.

[7]Cf. "Nouveaux regards sur la christologie de Luther," *Revue des Sciences philosophiques et theologiques* 62 (1982):180-197. Reprinted in Congar's, *Martin Luther: Sa Foi, sa réforme* (Paris: Les Editions Du Cerf, 1983, 105-133); Congar referred to the unpublished thesis of Constantini di Bruno, Le rôle salutaire de l'humanité du Christ a la lumiére des grandes thèmes de la christologie (1979), Congar, *Martin Luther*, 43.

[8]Cf. *Der fröhliche Wechsel und Streit*, 114 and 393. There are several recensions written on Beer's book, which would require careful reviewing. But this would mean presenting a rather extensive *Literaturbericht*, which is not possible here. Two Catholic Luther scholars deserve mentioning for their criticism of Beer's interpretation: Jared Wicks, "Revision des katholischen Lutherbildes? Zu Theobald Beers Grundzüge der Theologie Martin Luthers," *Theologische Revue* 78 (1982): 1-11, points out that it is mistaken to see Luther ground the antropological *simul* in the Christological *simul*. Erwin Iserloh, "Der fröhliche Wechsel und Streit. Zu Theobald Beers Werk über Grundzüge der Theologie Martin Luthers," *Catholica* 36 (1982):101-114, criticizes Beer for his misleading quotations, which let one believe that in Luther's Christology, the human side is only added to the divine nature.

language. My own study's results lean toward Congar's latest "Regards," and I can hardly find common grounds with Beer's interpretation. The primary concern of this study, however, is Luther's Christology in mid-career according to his lectures on John, which are not taken into consideration by Beer's interpretation of Luther's Christology. In a preliminary way, at the beginning of the investigation, I tend to share the position of the Christocentrists in their interpretation of Luther's theology. Such an orientation and description of one's standpoint is in order when one takes into consideration what famous Luther scholars have said from their experience with the study of Luther's theology: Whoever approaches the work of the Reformer enters an "ocean,"[9] i.e., ca. 100 volumes of critically edited works.[10] Without a standpoint, one runs the risk of drowning in these waters. For navigation on this "sea" of Luther's works and of the interpretations of them, I found no better guide than the quotation from the preface,

---

[9]"Luthers Theologie ist ein Ozean." Paul Althaus, *Die Theologie Martin Luthers* (Gütersloh: Gütersloher Verlagshaus, 1963), 8. In Gerhard Ebeling, *Luther: Einführung in sein Denken* (Tübingen: J. C. B. Mohr (Paul Siebeck), 41, this image is repeated: "Man gerät auf ein Meer, wenn man sich in das Studium seines Schrifttums begibt."

[10]The critical edition *Weimarer Ausgabe* (= WA) is the basis for our study: *D. Martin Luthers Werke. Kritische Gesamtausgabe* (Weimar: Hermann Böhlaus, 1883-). For Luther's correspondence, the abbreviation WA Br is used; for his Bible translations it is WA DB, and for his table talks is is WA TR. When quoting, the volume and page are separated by a colon such as WA 20:600, which refers to volume 20, page 600. The number after the page signifies the lines of the given page such as in WA 20:600, 10, which means line 10 of page 600 in volume 20. An elevated Roman numeral after the volume means the part I, II, or III of that volume. When works which are included in the American edition, are referred to, volume and page are indicated as LW 30:200 for volume 30 and page 200. A reference without the indica-

which is in agreement with the table talk: "Christ is the subject of theology."[11] Throughout our expedition on the "sea" of Luther's works, the fixed star to which our sight is attached will be that of Christology. On the "ocean" of Luther's theology, we may sail without land in sight, i.e., we may study without limitations and forever, unless we make certain provisions to limit ourselves. Therefore, we will anchor at a particular place which is not explored much, if at all, in modern Luther research: Luther's course on 1 John.[12]

---

tion of lines refers normally to WA's editors' pages in their respective introductions to the edited sources.

[11]"Christus est subiectum theologiae," WA TR 2:242, 4 (No. 1868) referring to Rom 1:2 (autumn 1532).

[12]A survey of exegetical studies with the purpose of elaborating on Luther's Christology, reveals that, indeed, the anchor place at the course on 1 John in 1527 is unexplored territory; included here are also studies which focus on Christology at a particular point in Luther's career. For Luther's lectures in 1513-15 on the Psalms (*Dictata*), there is E. Vogelsang's work on the beginnings of Luther's Christology: *Die Anfänge von Luthers Christologie* of the year 1929; Friedrich Huck carried on the investigation of the years 1515-16 with his study on the development of Luther's Christology from the lectures on the Psalms to the course on Romans: *Die Enwicklung der Christologie Luthers von der Psalmen zur Römervorlesung, TSK* 102 (1930):61-142. For the year 1517, we have the study by Bernhard Lohse on Luther's Christology during the controversy over indulgences: "Luthers Christologie im Ablasstreit," *Lutherjahrbuch* 27 (1960):51-63. Luther's Christology in the lectures on Hebrews of 1517-18 is included in Kenneth Hagen's book *A Theology of Testament in the Young Luther: The Lectures on Hebrews*, Studies in Medieval and Reformation Thought, 12 (Leiden: E. J. Brill, 1974). The young Luther's Christology is summarized by Dorothea Vorländer, *Deus Incarnatus: Die Zweinaturenchristologie Luthers bis 1521*, Untersuchungen zur Kirchengeschichte, 9 (Witten: Luther-Verlag, 1974) and by M. Lienhard, *Luther: Witness to Jesus Christ*, 17-151. As far as I can see, there is no monograph on Luther's Christology in Galatians (1516-17) or on the second course on the Psalms (1518-21), but these lectures are taken into consideration by Vorländer, and in part, by Lienhard. Strangely, Lienhard does not deal with the lectures on Galatians. For the 1520s, the christological monographs became more scarce. On Luther's Christology in the con-

Focus on 1 John

With the anchor lowered here in 1527, we will observe the situation around this anchoring place by taking into consideration the original *Sitz im Leben* of these lectures and their interrelation with other works and sayings of Luther. This study focuses on Luther's Christology, fully aware that his doctrine of Christ contains more than one problem. Much research has been done on the topic of Christology, but only seldom has Luther's Christology been worked out in monograph form, as a leading European researcher stated recently.[13] This study will fill some of the gaps in Luther research by tracing Luther's doctrine of Christ in the Reformer's mid-career, specifically in his course on 1 John.

Focus on Mid-life

In Luther's mid-career, the focus of study will be on Luther's life and work after the year 1521. In Luther

text of the Eucharistic controversy with Zwingli, there is the Inaugural-Dissertation of Paul Wilhelm Gennrich, *Die Christologie Luthers im Abendmahlsstreit. 1524-29* (Königsberg: Otto Kümmel Druckerei, 1929). Luther's Christology in his hymns is studied by K. Burba, *Die Christologie in Luthers Liedern* (Gütersloh: 1956). For the years 1535-40, there is the essay by Carl Heinz Ratschow, "Christologie und Rechtfertigung: Luthers Christologie nach seinen Disputationen," *Iustificatio Impii. Festschrift für Lauri Haikola zum 60. Geburtstag am 9.2.1977*, ed. Iussi Talasniemi (Helsinki: 1977), 204-26. Luther's understanding of Christ in his postilla of 1544 is presented by R. Frick, "Luthers Christusbild in der Hauspostille," *Monatsschrift für Pastoraltheologie*, 26 (1930):16-19 and 76-82. Reinhard Schwarz observed the difference between Luther's doctrine of the person of Christ and the one of the Occamists: "Gott ist Mensch. Zur Lehre von der Person Christi bei den Ockhamisten und bei Luther," *ZThK* 63 (1966):289-351.

[13]Cf. O. H. Pesch, *Hinführung zu Luther* (Mainz: Matthias-Grünewald-Verlag, 1982), 253.

research, the period of the so-called "young Luther" ends with that year. Also, until 1521, Luther's guide and mentor seems to have been Erasmus.[14] With a classical biography on the "young Luther" we concur that "when the gates of the Wartburg closed behind him for the first time," a period ended, a decisive turning point occurred in his career. "It may be said that now the period of his youth was definitely closed."[15] In following Boehmer's biography, H. Bornkamm presents Luther in mid-career, 1521-30. The beginning and ending of Bornkamm's account of Luther's mid-career are set in the solitude of two hilltop castles — the Wartburg (1521) and the Coburg (1530), where he lived between the ages of thirty-seven and forty-six, or, in the "middle of his life," as the German title reminds us.[16] With H. Junghans[17], it is

---

[14]Cf. Bernhard M. G. Reardon, *Religious Thought in the Reformation* (London and New York: Longman, 1981), 31.

[15]Heinrich Boehmer, *Martin Luther: Road to Reformation*, trans. John W. Doberstein and Theodore G. Tappert, 3d ed. (New York: Meridian Books, 1960), 432.

[16]Heinrich Bornkamm, *Martin Luther in der Mitte seines Lebens; Luther in Mid-career 1521-1530*, edited and with a forward by Karin Bornkamm, trans. E. Theodore Bachmann (Philadelphia: Fortress Press, 1983); see the noteworthy preface by the translator.

[17]Helmar Junghans, "Interpreting the old Luther (1526-1546)," trans. Inge Forssmann, *Currents in theology and mission*, 9 (1982):271-81. H. G. Haile, *Luther: An Experiment in Biography* (Garden City: Double Day, 1980), covers the years after 1530 of the old Luther, including his sojourn at Coburg in 1530, but erroneously believes that Rörer was at Luther's side there (cf. p. 32). According to the biographers H. Bornkamm, *Luther in Mid-career*, 674-5, Joachim Rogge, *Martin Luther: Sein Leben — Seine Zeit — Seine Wirkungen. Eine Bildbiographie* (Gütersloh: Gütersloher Verlagshaus, 1982), 251, Gert Wendelborn, *Martin Luther: Leben und reformatorisches Werk* (Vienna: Hermann Böhlaus Nachf., 1983), 314, Rörer was at Wittenberg, and Veit Dietrich with Luther at Coburg. This is not unimportant because of Rörer's significance; see under Part One.

preferable to speak of the "unfolding" of Luther's theology, because the formidable work by the later man is not simply a repetition of what he had written before 1526. At the same time, the expression "development" is to be avoided, because it could easily be misunderstood that Luther had worked a theological system out of a definite theological insight, from which everything else was derived. One must understand Luther's theology no more to be a uniform system, than the biblical tradition can be considered as one uniform system. The concept of "unfolding" implies, of course, that there are fundamental insights of the professor's theology, while at the same time, there is essentially no disagreement between the young, the old and, as we may add, the middle-aged Luther.

Although Lienhard's book title might insinuate the concept of "development," he states clearly that it is important to note that the theme of the Incarnation, for example, never ceases to recur in Luther's works and also that the theology of the cross may not be confined to a special period in his work. There are no fundamental modifications in Luther's Christology.[18] Lienhard himself speaks, then, of "The Unfolding of Christology"[19] in his third chapter. Lienhard and Junghans confirm earlier observations by E. Wolf on Luther's Christ-proclamation. Wolf notes that the Luther scholarship of his time was unable to dissolve apparent contradictions in Luther's writings via "developmental" explanations. Wolf continues, that the distinction of "young" and "old" is

---

[18]M. Lienhard, *Luther: Witness to Jesus Christ. Stages and Themes of the Reformer's Christology*, 50-51, 65, 249.
[19]Ibid. 153.

being replaced by the concept of discovering the "young" in the "old" and the "old" in the "young" Luther.[20] The same methodological insight is reflected by R. Prenter, who also relies on Wolf.[21]

In terms of the historical context, our range will be the year 1527. The time of our selected academic course on 1 John happens to be the year of the tenth anniversary of the "crushing of the indulgences," as well as the year of Luther's greatest depression.[22] His life situation (*Sitz im Leben*) at the time would roughly equal our popular "mid-life crisis."

Method

So far, the scope of this study has been clarified, as setting its course through the midst of troubled waters. The goal also has come into sight: Luther's doctrine of Jesus Christ. Is it "catholic" or not, in the sense of the Christological dogma of the Council of Chalcedon?

As mentioned above, the investigator's own position in regard to the ebb and flow of Luther interpretations over the years opposes that of Karl Holl insofar as the evaluation of the significance of Christ for Luther's life and work is concerned. Luther's Christocentrism, his "Christ alone" principle, is of utmost importance as the foundation upon which to build. Still, more must be said about the manner of procedure and standpoint with respect to current Catholic Luther studies.

---

[20]Cf. Ernst Wolf, "Die Christusverkündigung bei Luther."

[21]Regin Prenter, *Spiritus Creator*, trans. John M. Jensen (Philadelphia: Muhlenberg Press, 1953), xv-xvi.

[22]Cf. Roland H. Bainton, *Here I Stand: A Life of Martin Luther* (New York: Abdingdon-Cokesbury Press, 1950), 359.

It seems best to use a method of analysis similar to the method used in the interpretation of the Bible. First, the relevant texts must be examined, i.e., the available sources have to be evaluated in terms of the grammar, various textual readings and scribal emendations. This task will be undertaken in Part One. Secondly, the life setting (*Sitz im Leben*) must be taken into consideration in regard to the circumstances of the texts, i.e., their context. This historical-theological approach will be carried out in Part Two. Thirdly, the interpretation of the most precise available source or sources will be presented, once the context is elaborated, by following the *leitmotif* of Luther's understanding of Christ. When dealing with the "standpoint" and "method," one must be aware that this way of proceeding is "dangerous." It is exposed to scholarly criticism which observes that "in Roman Catholicism they continue to give great importance to the person of Luther as an aspect of the Reformation. . . . The interpretation of the Reformation and judgment on Luther's person are closely connected."[23] I can see the validity of this criticism, but I still maintain that Luther's texts must be studied in context, including the context of his career. Therefore, it is impossible for a historical-theological study such as this one, to separate the context from the text.

Focus on Catholicity

When departing from previous Catholic Luther research in particular, I break away from a typical

---

[23]M. Lienhard, "La place de Luther dans le dialogue protestant-catholique actuel," *Positions lutheriennes* (Paris: 1965), 69, as found in Richard Stauffer's, *Luther as seen by Catholics*, trans. Mary Parker and T. H. L. Parker (London: Lutterworth Press, 1967), 7.

Catholic approach of presenting the Reformation as stemming from Luther's subjectivism and his lack of being a "hearer in the full sense" of the word of God:

> This is the all-important fact: he[24] who desires to render himself without reserve to God's word has never been a hearer in the full sense of the word. We shall see that this fact overshadowed Luther's path until the very end. Down to his very roots, Luther was cast in a subjectivistic mold.[25]

Lortz's judgment was accepted by Hans Küng and is still maintained by Otto Hermann Pesch, each of them a leader of the avant-garde of the ecumenical movement.[26] The work of these scholars has great significance; nevertheless, one must depart from their opinion in this regard. One must insist that, first of all, the charge of subjectivism is a psychological one.[27] Furthermore, the typical Catholic objec-

---

[24]i.e. Luther.

[25]Joseph Lortz, *The Reformation in Germany*, trans. Ronald Wulfs, based upond the revised edition of 1949 (London, New York: Darton, Longman & Todd, Herder and Herder, 1968), vol. 1, 184.

[26]Hans Küng declared in the tracks of Lortz, that Luther did not understand the Word of God in its fullness, and that the Reformation was "essentially a revolution," one man's "personal, subjective" exegesis having eclipsed the teaching office of the Church, *The Council, Reform, and Reunion*, trans. Cecily Hastings (New York: Sheed and Ward, 1961), 74. Otto Herman Pesch presents in his recent introduction to Luther for Catholics this same judgment that Luther was not a full hearer (*Vollhörer*) of the Scriptures, and one may very well admit with Lortz that indeed, he was not: "Man darf unbefangen zugeben: In einem inhaltlichen Sinne ist Luther tatsächlich kein 'Vollhörer der Schrift' (Joseph Lortz) mehr." *Hinführung zu Luther*, 68.

[27]Cf. Erwin Mülhaupt, *Luther im 20.Jahrhundert* (Göttingen: Vandenhoeck & Ruprecht, 1982), 43.

tion is unfair in the light of the wide range of exegetical works on both the Old and the New Testament done by Luther, and also in the face of Luther's cherished hermeneutical principle of "scripture interpreting scripture,"[28] which on principle requires listening to all of scripture and interpreting one passage by means of another one. With my emphasis on the professor's Johannine lectures, I wish to challenge the notion that Luther was not a full hearer of the word. Another similar Roman Catholic interpretation is that Luther was a "revolutionary" or "rebel," titles given by Catholic biographers.[29] If Catho-

---

[28]"sui ipsius interpres," WA 7:96,4—101,9 (1520).

[29]These "titles" for Luther show up especially in Catholic books: Michael Meisner, *Martin Luther: Heiliger oder Rebell* (Lübeck: 1981); Hellmut Diwald, *Luther: Eine Biographie*, 3d ed. (Bergisch Gladbach: Gustav-Lübbe-Verlag, 1982) uses the concept of "revolutionary," in his text, but not in the title. Another recent book whose author's denomination is unknown to me (Anglican?) speaks also of Luther as "religious revolutionary," Bernard M. G. Reardon, *Religious Thought in the Reformation*, 47. More adequate is the title used by Horst Herrmann, *Martin Luther Ketzer wider willen* (Munich: Bertelsmann, 1983) (Luther: Heretic against his will). In a preliminary way, I join Gottfried Maron's description of the Catholic image of Luther, in which Maron states that Diwald and others are not reckoned as representative for Catholic Luther research in Germany. With Maron one may take the following authors of the twentieth century as having made decisive contributions to Luther research on the Catholic side: Franz-Xaver Kiefl, Adolf Herte, Johannes Hessen, Joseph Lortz, Erwin Iserloh, Peter Manns, Otto Hermann Pesch, Daniel Olivier, Stephan Pfürtner, Albert Brandenburg, cf. *Das Katholische Lutherbild der Gegenwart*, Bensheimer Hefte, ed. Evangelischer Bund, vol. 58 (Göttingen: Vandenhoeck & Ruprecht, 1982). The names quoted by Maron represent the Catholic revaluation of Luther up to 1983, as also James Atkinson agrees, cf. *Martin Luther, Prophet to the Church Catholic*, 21-39, where French and Anglo-Saxon authors are included. Walter Brandmüller, "Die Reformation Martin Luthers in Katholischer Sicht," *Münchener Theologische Zeitschrift* 35 (1984):32-46: "Martin Luther — Reform oder Umsturz," 36-40.

lic Luther research maintains this view uncritically, it will find itself ironically in the same boat with the traditional Marxist interpretation of Luther, according to which Luther is the "reformer and rebel" as part of the early bourgeois revolution.[30]

In contrast to the virtually identical use of titles by traditional Catholic and Marxist biographers (although from different perspectives), most evangelical Lutheran authors refrain from labels and prefer rather neutral descriptions or do not use any "titles" at all.[31]

On the grounds of Luther's Christocentrism and of his profession as a Bible professor, it is preferable to speak of Luther as a "classic of theology"[32] and to

---

[30]Cf. Wolfgang Landgraf, *Martin Luther: Reformator und Rebell. Biografie.* 2d ed. Berlin: Verlag Neues Leben, 1982).

[31]Heinrich Boehmer, *Martin Luther: Road to Reformation*; Heinrich Bornkamm, *Luther in Mid-career 1521-30*; Gerhard Bott, Gerhard Ebeling, and Bernd Moeller, *Martin Luther: Sein Leben in Bildern und Texten* (Frankfurt: Insel Verlag, 1983); Martin Brecht, *Martin Luther: His Road to Reformation*, trans. James L. Schaaf 1483-1521 (Philadelphia: Fortress, 1985); Richard Friedenthal, *Luther: His Life and Times*, trans. G. J. Nowell (New York: Harcourt, Brace, Jovanovich, 1970); Helmar Junghans, ed., *Leben und Werk Martin Luthers von 1526 bis 1546*; Festgabe zu seinem 500. Geburtstag (Berlin: Evangelische Verlagsanstalt; Göttingen: Vandenhoeck & Ruprecht, 1983); Marc Lienhard, *Martin Luther: Un temps, une vie, un message* (Paris: Le Centurion; Geneva: Labor et Fides, 1983); Hanns Lilje, *Martin Luther: In Selbstzeugnissen und Bilddokumenten* (Reinbeck: Rowohlt, 1981 — first printing in 1965); Walther von Loewenich, *Martin Luther: Der Mann und das Werk* (Munich: List Verlag, 1982); Bernhard Lohse, *Martin Luther: Eine Einführung in sein Leben und sein Werk*, 2d ed. (Munich: Beck Verlag, 1982); James Mackinnon, *Luther and the Reformation* (New York: Russell & Russell, Inc., 1962); Hans Mayer, *Martin Luther: Leben und Glaube* (Gütersloh: Gütersloher Verlagshaus G. Mohn, 1982); Joachim Rogge, *Martin Luther: Sein Leben — seine Zeit — seine Wirkungen. Eine Biographie*; Gert Wendelborn, *Martin Luther: Leben und reformatorisches Werk*; Heinz Zahrnt, *Martin Luther in seiner Zeit für unsere Zeit* (Ulm: Süddeutscher Verlag, 1983).

[32]Johannes Brosseder, "Martin Luther (1483-1546)," *Klassiker der Theologie*, vol. 1, ed. Heinrich Fries and Georg Kretschmar (Munich: C. H. Beck, 1981).

accept the balanced vision of the Catholic scholar Peter Manns (a student of Lortz).[33]

The question of titles for Luther is as old as the Reformation. It should be noted that Luther himself hardly used the title derived from his "Reformation"; he himself spoke of *eine reformation* only in 1528 and mentioned "reforming" again six years later.[34] In 1523 and in 1530, he preferred to call himself "prophet."[35] In 1531, he is "by God's grace evangelist in Wittenberg" and "Jesus Christ's unworthy evangelist."[36] In our Johannine lectures here, he spoke of himself as "servant of God" as he adopted this title a decade earlier in Greek form.[37]

[33]Peter Manns and Helmuth Nils Loose, *Martin Luther: An Illustrated Biography*. Text by Peter Manns, photographs by H. N. Loose. Introduction by Jaroslav Pelikan, trans. Michael Shaw (New York: Crossroad, 1982).

[34]"Ich meine ja, ich hab ein Concilium angericht und eine reformation gemacht . . . ": WA 26:530, 7-8 (Preface to the book by Stephan Klingebeil on married priests (1528); in a letter of 1534 on private masses Luther wrote that he has done more reforming with his gospel than five councils: "Ich hab, Gott lob, mehr reformiert mit meinem Euangelio, denn sie villeicht mit fünff Conciliijs hetten gethan," WA 38:271, 2-4.

[35]" . . . yhr habt ewrn Propheten gehort," said Luther at the end of his sermon on keeping children in school (1530), WA 30II:588, 2 (LW 46:258). See E. Mülhaupt, *Luther im 20.Jahrhundert*, 90 and 245.

[36]"Martin Luther von gottes gnaden Euangelist zu Wittenberg," WA Br 3:5(1523). "Jhesu Christi unwirdiger Euangelist," WA 30III:366, 9 (LW 34:91).

[37]"servus dei," WA 20:649, 7 (1527). In 1517 Luther in the manner of contemporary Christian Humanists, signed his letter of November 11 with "F. Martinus Eleutherius, imo dulos et captivus nimis" WA Br 1:122,56. In this signature, the paradox of Luther's personality is enclosed in the contradictory self description of being Martin "the Free" (Eleutherius) and the negation of it as expressed in the Greek version δοῦλος for servant together with "all too captive" (captivus nimis). On Luther's name see Bernd Moeller and K. Stackmann, *Luder — Luther — Eleutherius: Erwägungen zu Luthers Namen*, Nachrichten der Akademie der Wissenschaften in Göttingen I. Philologisch-Historische Klasse Nr. 7 (Göttingen: Vandenhoeck & Ruprecht, 1981).

His adversaries, of course, called him different names, such as "enemy of the church."[38] Pope Leo X elegantly alluded to Psalm 80:14 when writing the Bull against Luther and then referred to him less elegantly as the "wild boar in the vineyard of the Lord."[39] Others gave him a rather tame title: "Dr. Exaggerator" (*doctor hyperbolicus*).[40]

Catholic Luther research has come a long way. The "enemy of the Church" of the sixteenth century is now *doctor communis* — the most fascinating change I have found in my title-search for Luther. This title was conferred on Luther by Cardinal Willebrands, President of the Vatican's Secretariate of Christian Unity. In German, *gemeinsamer Lehrer*[41] also means "shared teacher," i.e., shared by the denominations. When this title is translated into the ecclesiastical language of Latin, it is *doctor communis. Doctor communis* is the traditional name given to the prince of scholasticism, Thomas Aquinas! In 1970, Luther is like Thomas Aquinas — the "shared," the "common," the "general" and the "ordinary" teacher of the universal Church. At least as honorable a title is given to Luther a decade later by one of

---

[38]*Enchiridion of Common Places of John Eck against Luther and other Enemies of the Church*, trans. Ford Lewis Battles (Grand Rapids: Calvin Theological Seminary, 1978). On J. Eck, there is now the biography available by Erwin Iserloh, *Johannes Eck (1486-1543): Scholastiker, Humanist, Kontroverstheologe*. Katholisches Leben und Kirchenreform im Zeitalter der Glaubensspaltung 41 (Münster: Aschendorff, 1981).

[39]W. von Loewenich, *Martin Luther*, 169.

[40]J. Lortz, *The Reformation in Germany*, vol. 1: 172.

[41]Cf. O. H. Pesch, *Hinführung zu Luther*, 272.

the leading Catholic Luther experts of the Lortz-school, Peter Manns, who calls Luther "Father in Faith."[42]

This Catholic interest in Luther is grounded in Luther's catholicity, which he claimed in his disputation against the scholastic theologians on September 4, 1517, in thesis 99, namely that these theses are "all good Catholic."[43] The Abbot Valentine of Lehnin delivered to Luther a letter from Bishop Jerome Schulze of Brandenburg, in which the bishop informed Luther that he had found no error in the *Resolutiones*, that in fact he had found them to be "good Catholic."[44]

Luther was considered so Catholic that the red hat for him to become a cardinal was not out of the question at all, but, of course, within the political power game of the day. To prove the pope's sentiments, a nuncio alluded to the "state secret," namely, that Pope Leo X would be ready to bestow the cardinal's hat on Frederick the Wise's protégé to honor the elector who was a candidate for the imperial throne and at the same time to bring the Lutheran question to a conclusion.[45] Besides all these mentioned indicators of Luther's catholicity, Luther said in 1533 that all his Christocentric teaching stemmed from his superior, Staupitz:

---

[42]Peter Manns, "Ketzer oder Vater im Glauben?" *Vorlagen* No. 4 (Hannover: Lutherhaus-Verlag, 1980).

[43]Cf. W. von Loewenich, *Martin Luther*, 102.

[44]Cf. H. Boehmer, *Martin Luther*, 199 (Resolutions concerning indulgences).

[45]Cf. P. Manns and H. N. Loose, *Martin Luther*, 116.

However, my good Staupitz said, "One must keep one's eyes fixed on that man who is called Christ." Staupitz is the one who started the teaching (of the gospel in our time).[46]

In the disputations in the late 1530s Luther explicitly spoke of his "catholic faith," as C. H. Ratschow pointed out.[47] It is then quite in agreement with J. Lortz when we start this study where the master ended, with his conclusion that Luther seems to be the best representative of an authentic catholicity among his contemporaries.[48] Albert Brandenburg asks whether it is not the Catholic Church which is the *Heimat* (home) of and for Luther.[49] If Brandenburg's question is answered positively, one may very well examine Luther's witness to Christ — as we intend to do in this study — for its catholicity or un-catholicity, in terms of the early Church dogma which is shared by Christians in the East and West, and in terms of the medieval tradition of St. Augustine and St. Bernard of Clairvaux. Thus the specific *leitmotif* is the question of the catholic Christology in the "conservative Reformation"[50] of Luther. If

[46]WA TR 1:245 (No. 526) (LW 54:97).

[47]"Christologie und Rechtfertigung: Luthers Christologie nach seinen Disputationen," *Iustificatio Impii. Festschrift für Lauri Haikola zum 60. Geburtstag am 9.2.1977*, ed. Jussi Talasniemi (Helsinki: 1977), 204-26.

[48]Cf. J. Lortz, Wie kam es zur Reformation? (1955), as referred to by E. Mülhaupt, *Luther im 20.Jahrhundert*, 43.

[49]Cf. *Die Zukunft des Martin Luther. Luther, Evangelium und die Katholizität. Eine These* (Münster: Aschendorff; Kassel: Johannes Stauda Verlag, 1977). See also Gerhard Müller. "Der Katholizismus als Heimat Martin Luthers," *Luther*, 52 (1981):78-80.

[50]Charles Porterfield Krauth, *The Conservative Reformation and its Theology*, reprint (Minneapolis: Augsburg Publishing House, 1978).

this examination can demonstrate that this is the case, must we hesitate then to confer on Luther not only the label of "conservative rebel," but also the honorific title of *doctor catholicus* in regard to the central article of faith in Jesus Christ?

Outline

Part One will evaluate the available and critically edited sources of Luther's lectures on 1 John. There are two major issues to be covered. First, which of the sources can be used in a historically responsible way for theological investigation on the central Christian doctrine of Christ's person and work? Secondly, the question will have to be whether Luther used for his academic work his own German Bible translation or the Greek-Latin edition of Erasmus, and if so, which one of the several editions? Or, did he take the Vulgate as his starting point for his interpretation? This Part One is most necessary, because these textual questions have not been dealt with previously. It is hardly known that Luther gave a course on a Johannine text.

The second question, of the biblical foundation in Luther's lectures, will lead us to Part Two — the historical context, which begins with the position of Luther's Johannine lectures within his academic work as a professor of the Bible. This also offers an opportunity to correct the mistaken view about the

---

In this work of 1870, Krauth understands the "reformation" as a conservative effort to preserve the one, holy, apostolic and Catholic Church against "conservatism" in the form of the "Romish" and the "Greek" types of the Church and also against "progress" without "conservatism" as in Protestant sectarianism. With Zwingli's words Krauth was convinced that Luther has brought forth nothing novel.

alleged interruption of his lectures on Isaiah and their replacement with the course on 1 John. We will take an overview of Luther's weekly lecture plan and explain its irregularities as much as it is possible. Next to this *academic* context, the *biographical* one will focus on Luther's correspondence about his personal situation before, during and after the course on 1 John. Thirdly, we will consider the *world political context* (the "Sack of Rome" in 1527) under Luther's eschatological perspective, as the Johannine text led him to his conclusions about the Antichrist. Connected with this is the *local historical context* of the fortification of Wittenberg. Fourthly, we will deal with the *theological-historical context* and give priority to Bernard's influence on Luther's exposition of 1 John.

Since we will have entered much unexplored territory in dealing with Luther's mid-career lectures, Part Three will corroborate the thesis about Luther's catholicity, first, by establishing that Luther's favorite evangelist is John, whom he considered the *summus evangelista* and the highest authority among Christians. Thus we will dispense with the questionable accusation that Luther was a "Paulinist," and thus only a "partial hearer." This introductory Chapter 7 of Part Three will prepare the reader for the presentation of Luther's doctrine of Christ's person and work as it found its precipitate in the lectures on 1 John.

In Chapter 8 we will examine Luther's opening lecture on 1 John 1:1, with special reference to the catholic dogmatic foundations for the doctrine of the *person* of Christ in two natures. Here, in Luther's dealing with the notion of "God's flesh," we will see how strongly he emphasized the real humanity of Christ and also the divinity of Christ when he interpreted the "mercy seat" as being occupied by Christ.

In Chapter 9 we will concentrate on Luther's German-Saxon phrases in which he expressed his understanding both of the *person* and of the *work* of Christ for the salvation of man.

Chapter 10, then, we will dedicate exclusively to the topic of Christ's *work* as Luther explicated it in a Christocentric mysticism nurtured by images of the medieval tradition, namely of St. Augustine with the image of *Christus medicus*, which is also found in St. Bernard. On this *fundamentum* of the Western Catholic tradition, and precisely in this perspective, we will be confronted with Luther's sentence that sin and being born of God do not stand simultaneously together. This means a challenge to the principle of *simul* in Luther's theology,[51] a provocative text which so far has not been pointed out in Luther studies. It is as catholic as Luther's dogmatic doctrine of the person of Christ in two natures. The grounds for Luther's *Non Stant Simul* will be further explicated in the subsections of Chapter 10 on Christ as the resident and purger in the heart of man, Christ as the Sun of Righteousness and on Christ as *exem-*

---

[51]Cf. K. O. Nilsson, *Simul: Das Miteinander von Göttlichem und Menschlichem in Luthers Theologie* (Göttingen: Vandenhoeck & Ruprecht), 1966. Nilsson does not include Luther's commentary on 1 John and thus he was not confronted with the challenge of Luther's *Non Stant Simul*. — O. H. Pesch, in his *Hinführung zu Luther*, gave an excellent summary of the present state of research in regard to this issue of *simul iustus et peccator* (in Chapter 11) from his Catholic point of view. However, Pesch also does not mention Luther's lectures on 1 John, and thus he ooverlooked Luther's *Non Stant Simul*.

plum. Luther's Christological-soteriological construction leads to the consequence that man must be seen by nature as being good at the day of judgment, while he was bad before.

In the first subsection of Chapter 11 we will see Luther's conservative position against the Anabaptists of his time on the one hand, and against the monastic "mistreatment" of Christ's blood on the other hand. Then our attention will be directed to Luther's Christocentric reinterpretation of Erasmus's "Christian Soldier" when Luther pointed to the War Lord Christ and the Victor Christ rather than to the *Miles.*

In this study we will constantly encounter Christocentrism and with it we are right at the kernel of Luther's mental world because, as he said, it is Christ who reigns in his heart. This is observed throughout his lectures on 1 John.

PART ONE

THE TEXTS FOR LUTHER'S LECTURES
ON THE FIRST LETTER OF JOHN

INTRODUCTION TO PART ONE

When studying Luther's exegetical works, we deal with him primarily as professor of the Bible. This concentration on Luther as Bible-scholar was not always possible during the history of exegesis in general, and of Luther research in particular, because the sources were not always available in a critical edition. For instance, such famous lectures as the ones on Paul's letter to the Romans (1515-16) were published for the first time only in this century (1908),[1] and they were accepted in the critical edition of the *Weimarer Ausgabe* as late as 1938.[2] Also, the Reformer's lectures on Hebrews (1517-18) which contain Luther's initial use of the key phrase "theology of the cross,"[3] and which survived as two sets of student lecture notes, were published only in 1929 for the first time. A decade later they appeared in a critical edition.[4]

Luther researchers always had the printed version of the 1 John lectures at hand since the beginning of the eighteenth century. It was based on a source which we will examine. The critical edition, which

[1]Cf. W. von Loewenich, *Martin Luther*, 91.

[2]WA 56:1-528 (LW 25:1-524).

[3]Cf. W. von Loewenich, *Martin Luther*, 97.

[4]WA 57III:97-238 (LW 29:107-241). See Kenneth Hagen, *Hebrews Commenting from Erasmus to Bèze 1516-1598*, "Beiträge zur Geschichte der Biblischen Exegese," ed. Oscar Cullmann et al., vol. 23 (Tübingen: J. C. B. Mohr (Paul Siebeck), 1981), 8 n. 15.

did not appear until 1904, includes this printed version as one of several sources of Luther's commentary on 1 John. Three sources are edited there: R, W, P.[5] P stands for the printed version based upon lecture notes of an anonymous student, collected by the Augustinian Jakob Propst, whose initial P serves for the designation of the source.[6] Propst was Prior of the friary at Antwerp, an influential evangelical center. Friars from Antwerp studied at Wittenberg. Propst was among those who received their doctorate from Wittenberg University. After persecution by the Inquisition, he fled to Wittenberg in 1522, while his friary was destroyed in 1523 and two friars were burned at the stake.[7] R stands for Georg Rörer's lecture notes,[8] which will be discussed shortly below. W is the abbreviation for the manuscript extant at Wolfenbüttel under the name *Scholia ex praelectionibus D. Martini Lutheri anno 1531, die Augusti 17*, together with annotations on Timothy and Titus.[9]

Almost a quarter of a century later, in 1927, a fourth source came to light, which the editor calls *In primam epistolam Iohannis scholia*,[10] and which I name for practical purposes with the abbreviation S

[5]WA 20:599-807.

[6]This abbreviation is given by the editor, cf. WA 20:597. On J. Propst, see now Ortwin Rudloff, *Bonae Litterae et Lutherus: Texte und Untersuchungen zu den Anfängen der Theologie des Bremer Reformators Jakob Propst* (Bremen: Hauschild, 1985).

[7]Cf. *Ein Brief an die Christen im Niederland, 1523*, WA 12:73-80. See H. Bornkamm, *Luther in Mid-career*, 100-02.

[8]Cf. WA 20:597; this abbreviation also stems from the editor of WA 20.

[9]Cf. WA 20:592-93.

[10]WA 48:314-23.

when evaluating it in Chapter 1. Thus, our investigation of Luther's lectures on 1 John begins with four available sources which have to be examined in regard to which one is the most precise, most complete and closest to Luther's wording, and also which one is uncontaminated by a redactor or printer. This one will then furnish the textual basis for our further studies. Connected with this evaluation of the sources is the question of the biblical textual foundation on which the lectures were based.

CHAPTER 1

SCHOLIA, LECTURE NOTES, PRINTED VERSION, TRANSLATION

Scholia (S)

Is S actually what the editor claims it to be? Is S to be taken as Luther's preparation notes for the lectures or is S better characterized as a student's lecture notes? The answer to this question will influence the ranking of this source S among the four sources. The term *scholia* is used ambivalently: Among our four sources, two are called *scholia*, i.e., in Greek, "lectures." There is W, which contains *scholia* and "sermons" on the First Letter of John and "annotations" on Paul's letters to Timothy and Titus.[1] There is S, which the editor calls *scholia* but by which he does not mean lecture notes by a student, but preparation notes by Luther himself; as the subtitle says: Luther's written preparations for the lectures on the First Letter of John in summer 1527.[2] The editor declares W as a copy based upon student lecture notes.[3]

---

[1]*Martini Lutheri Scholia et Sermones in primam Iohannis epistolam atque Annotationes in epistolas Paulinas ad Timotheum et Titum. Ex codicibus manuscriptis Bibliothecae Academicae Helmstadiensis nunc primum edidit D. Paulus Iacobus Bruns . . . Lubecae, impensis Ioh. Fried. Bohn. MDCCXCVII.* On pages 1-154, W is found with the title "*Scholia ex praelectionibus . . .* "; cf. WA 20: 592-93.

[2]WA 48:313.

[3]WA 20:593.

S in manuscript form does not carry the title *scholia* as given by the editor. It only says, "On the First Epistle of John," as the introduction indicates.[4] When the edition and print of the source actually begins, the WA includes only this title, but the whole text is found under the title *scholia*.[5] The editors of WA regard S as preparation notes of Luther and W as student notes. Clearly, S is declared by its editor as a copy of notes from Luther's hand because it is found together with *scholia* on Titus, which forbids by its character to be taken as student notes.[6] While the *scholia* W mention 1 John first, and then the annotations on Timothy and Titus, the source S is placed after the *scholia* on Titus within the original manuscript,[7] thus deviating from the chronological sequence in which the lectures had been delivered: First 1 John, then at the end of the year 1527 the lectures on Titus.[8]

S is extant in Latin, but contains one proverb in German with the meaning: "The learned, the turned."[9] This proverb appears also in R.[10] It is part

---

[4]*In primam epistolam Ioannis fol 62*, WA 48:314.

[5]*In primam epistolam Iohannis Scholia*, WA 48:313.

[6]"Wie beim Titusbrief, so verbietet auch hier die Eigennart der Scholien die Annahme, als handle es sich um eine Nachschrift der Vorlesung." WA 48:313. It must be noted, however, that the *scholia* on Titus and on 1 John differ in length. The notes on one biblical verse of Titus take (on an average) fewer lines than those on 1 John. This observation makes one cautious. Are they really *scholia* by the same author?

[7]Cf. WA 48:314.

[8]Cf. H. Bornkamm, *Luther in Mid-career*, 707.

[9]"et verum fit proverbium: Die gelarten, die verkarten," WA 48:317,23. The modern German equivalent is "Die Gelehrten, die verkehrten," with the meaning that the learned scholars turn things up-side-down or around, and thus make them come out wrong.

[10]WA 20:613,11-12. P does not have it but instead gives the explanation of it in German: "je klüger, je thörichter" (the wiser one gets, the more foolish he becomes), WA 20:613,29.

of Luther's collection of proverbs and appears in the Table Talks.[11] The orthography varies as follows:

Luther's collection : *"Die gelerten die verkereten"*
R   : *"Die gelerten die verkerten"*
S   : *"Die gelarten die verkarten"*
Table Talk (no. 7030): *"Die gelehrten,*
die verkehrten"
Table Talk (no. 7122): *"Die gelerten die vorkerten"*

Luther's original and R are more similar than the odd version of S. This observation makes one cautious in considering S as stemming from Luther's pen. While R has a very sharp ear[12] and would have noted Luther, the Saxon, pronouncing German *a* instead of *e* (as Rörer was from Bavaria[13] and as such pronounced *e* clearly in his own Bavarian dialect), he in fact wrote down in his notes "die gelerten die verkerten" as he heard Luther pronouncing it, even though the peculiar Saxon accent leans toward an *a*. A Saxon very easily may have understood Luther as saying, " ... *die gelarten die verkarten,*" as it appears in S. This would be then an indicator that S is notes by an anonymous Saxon student. This argumentation is, course of, not sufficient in the light of the uncertainties of orthography during Luther's times. But adding this argument to others, it may count. Therefore, the proofs pro and contra S (as preparation notes by Luther himself) must be evaluated.

---

[11]Cf. WA 51:645,7. — Also WATR 6:345,5 (no. 7030) and WA 48:692,5 (no. 7122).

[12]"Rörer fasste das Gehörte scharf auf." WA 20:VII.

[13]Cf. Bernhard Klaus, "Georg Rörer, ein bayerischer Mitarbeiter D. Martin Luthers," *Zeitschrift für bayerische Kirchengeschichte* 26 (1957):113-145.

The rest of the source S is extant in Latin in precise
expressions which to the editor prove that the text
cannot be classified as student notes.[14] This argument is invalid if one judges R as the most precise of
Luther's stenographers, as R is recognized to be in
today's Luther research.[15] The precision of expression could very well point to a similarly gifted student like R. An examination of S results, however, in
several imprecisions which makes one wonder about
the editor's judgment on S. In support of the editor's
thesis of S being preparatory notes by Luther himself, we are referred to S's biblical quotation of
1 Peter 1. The argument is this: the 1 Peter 1 quotation is of a peculiar kind and is taken from Luther's
revised Vulgate.[16] Against this argument one must
maintain that first of all S mistakenly refers to
1 Peter while the editor himself silently corrects the
mistake on the margin: 2 Peter 1:4.[17] Could Luther
have made this mistake? Regardless of the answer,
this source's "precision," as praised by the editor, is
lacking here. The offered explanation of the peculiar
version of 2 Peter 1:4 as being taken from the revised edition of the Vulgate collapses because this
quotation is identical with the Greek-Latin edition
which Luther used, and in which Erasmus's Latin
version says the same as S, which happens also to be
identical with the finished revision of Luther's

---

[14]" ... eine solche Prägnanz des Ausdrucks, wie sie keinem Nachschrei-
ber möglich gewesen wäre," WA 48:313.

[15]See below on Rörer.

[16]"Dazu kommt eine Reihe eigentümlicher Schriftzitate die Verwen-
dung des Bibeltextes der von Luther damals vorbereiteten Vulgata
recognita. . . . " WA 48:313.

[17]WA 48:316,31.

Vulgate edition of 1529, in which he maintains after all the old Vulgate version.[18] Thus, the reference to 2 Peter 1:4 does not necessarily point to Luther's Vulgate revision. However, it remains puzzling that the rest of the lecture notes of R, W and P report Luther as having said *"participes"* of the divine nature. Further comparison of biblical references in S with Luther's *Vulgata recognita* shows discrepancies in 1:3,5,8; 2:1,2,4,8,11; and 5:7,8. These variations exclude Luther's *Vulgata recognita* as a text basis for S, and thus, as an argument for S as being Luther's preparatory notes. S uses Latin quotations which are not found in Luther's *Vulgata recognita*. These quotations are not always in Erasmus's edition either, nor in the original Vulgate. This imprecision in regard to clearly unidentifiable Latin Bible references disproves the "precision of expression" argument used as proof that S represents Luther's preparation notes. Imprecisions in regard to the Latin Bible quotations may be attributed either to an anonymous Saxon student or to Luther as the preparer of the lecture notes.

The editor of S furthermore argues, in support of the assumption that S is Luther's preparatory notes, that S contains historical examples which are not found in R.[19] But interestingly the examples are indeed found in R under the date of September 3, 1527. The first is the story of the Lord Jesus appearing to a certain Cyprian. Christ wept when things did not go

---

[18]Original Vulgate: "divinae consortes naturae"; Luther's revision (WA DB 5:744,34): "divinae naturae consortes"; Erasmus' version and S: "consortes divinae naturae."

[19]Cf. WA 48:313.

right.[20] It is the same as the example in S: Cyprian imagined Christ sitting with his hand under the head, saddened that people do not want to accept him. The other example pertains to Dionysius and is also found in R.[21] The editor of S is therefore mistaken. He simply overlooked the given examples in R. The fact that the two examples appear in R as well as in S indicates that both are probably student lecture notes.

The "fragmentary character" of S is brought forth as further evidence that S represents Luther's preparatory notes and not a later excerpt or reworking of the lectures.[22] This fragmentary character as such indicates nothing one way or the other, however. The pieces that are extant might very well have come from a student who was unable to attend regularly, especially during the plague in Wittenberg. In fact, only from the following lecture days do we have S's notes: August 19,20,21,26 and September 2,3,9 (the lecture from September 4 is missing); the last lecture which S covers is the one from October 30.[23] In contrast to this, we possess the complete notes made by R. In the discussion of the fragmentary character of S, the argument is brought forward that Luther had prepared notes for September 9 on 1 John 2:7-14, but actually lectured only up to v. 11 (according to R). First of all, as demonstrated in footnote 26, S pre

---

[20]Cf. WA 20:639,16-17.

[21]Cf. Wa 20:640,1-5.

[22]"Auch die Lückenhaftigkeit der Scholien wehrt der Annahme, dass sie ein späteres Exzerpt oder eine Bearbeitung der Vorlesung darstellen," WA 48:313.

[23]This means that only the following verses of 1 John are dealt with in S: 1:1-10,2:1-12 (not as the editor claims 7-14 cf. p. 313); and 5:6-8 (with the irregularity that vv. 6 and 8 are dealt with first, then v. 7). In addition to this, the given dates in S are taken from R's notes!

sents notes only for 2:7-12, and not up to v. 14. Secondly, the edited text of S contains but two lines of 2:12.[24] That the shortness of the notation, the editorial introduction and the actual edition contradict each other, does not make S more trustworthy in support of the editor's thesis. However, how can it be explained that S has notes on 2:12 for September 9 while R has not? If it is not a mistake by the editor who erroneously assigned S's two lines on 1 John 2:12 to September 9 instead of the lectures of September 10, then I offer the following explanation: R, being aware of the end of the lecture of September 9, anticipated Luther's continuation with reference to 2:12, which called for a new paragraph. Luther called the forthcoming verses an *excursus*.[25] Indeed, Luther on the next day of lecturing (September 10) began afresh with 2:12,[26] as R must have anticipated. Therefore he did not write notes on it on the previous day. R has eighty-three lines in comparison to S, who took down two lines on this text. With this explanation, it is pointless to refer to Luther's illness of more than two months earlier (July 6, 1527) and its consequences, namely, the gap of notes between the ninth and the twenty-fifth lectures.[27]

Having exposed the weakness and invalidity of the arguments that S represents Luther's preparation notes (in copied manuscript form), one must resist the temptation of interpreting R, P and W in the light of S. We are justified in interpreting S with-

[24] WA 48:323,11-12.
[25] WA 20:653,14
[26] WA 20:653,16-657,18.
[27] Cf. the editor's argumentation, WA 48:313.

out this preference. We should deal with it, at best, as being on equal ground with P and R.

S differs from P and R regarding Luther's comments under 2:9. S reads, "Who simply has the light, cannot be without hate," i.e., he who has the simple light has hate.[28] P reads, "He who is not in the true light cannot love his brother,"[29] i.e., he who has the light, can love his brother. R reports Luther as saying, "Therefore, whoever is not in the light, simply cannot be without hate,"[30] i.e., he who is in the light, can "be without hate," or, as P says, "can love." Interpreting S in the light of R and P, one must state that S is missing the point by leaving out the negation in the first part of this sentence, while R has preserved it. The improved reading of S would say then: "Who simply *does not* have the light, cannot be without hate." Such a person must have hate. So here S makes sense only when improved by R and P. This demonstrates that S, in need of obvious mending, is an unreliable source.

In another reference, to Psalm 139:22,[31] S and P (not R) do not help anyone understand the passage better. Maybe it is a later interpolation after the discovery of the obscurity of the notes. Psalm 139:22 justifies hate against the wicked as God's enemies, and is needed only to allay misunderstanding if the clear text of R is not at hand. Apparently P and S are

---

[28]"Qui habet simpliciter lucem, non potest esse sine odio." WA 48:322,26.

[29]"Qui non est in lumine vero, non potest diligere fratrem." WA 20:649,37 (LW 30:242).

[30]"Qui ergo non est simpliciter in luce, non potest sine odio esse." WA 20:650,1-2.

[31]Cf. WA 48:322,24 (S); WA 20:649,33 (P)

related; but this is a question which does not primarily interest us here. The fragmentary notes of S are best considered to be pieces of lecture notes, probably taken by a Saxon student who was unable to attend classes on a regular basis because of the plague at Wittenberg. Another explanation would be that these are incomplete notes, partly lost in the course of time, if they have ever been complete at all. The S source with its nine-and-a-half edited pages is inferior to the R source which is complete. As we have seen, not only the brevity and fragmentary character, but also the poor quality of S, speaks for itself. The arguments given by its editor do not withstand critical examination. Therefore we conclude that S is an anonymous Saxon student's Latin notes with the addition of a German proverb from Luther's collection.

Lecture Notes (W, P, R)

After concluding that S represents student lecture notes, one has to go into detail concerning the other three sources — R, P and W. The lack of textual criticism may lead to an indiscriminate use of the sources.[32]

To answer the question as to which is the best of the sources edited in *WA* 20, it is logical to pay attention to the opinion of the American editors of *LW*. In an evaluation of the sources, it also will be necessary to deal with the linguistically macaronic nature of Luther's lectures, as well as the possibility that the writers of these notes made mistakes. Unlike the

---

[32]This can be observed in the otherwise most valuable work on Luther's Christology by Jan D. Kingston Siggins, *Martin Luther's Doctrine of Christ*, Yale Publications in Religion, 14 (New Haven: Yale University Press, 1970), 61, n. 88; 131,119.

case of S, where we could not follow the editor's observations, in the case of R, P and W we do not have any problems in the historic ranking of the sources. As the arrangement in the *WA* indicates, priority is given to R. In support of this, editor Koffmane makes the following observations which compelled him to consider R as superior:

R's manuscript on 1 John is similar to that of the Rörer notes on Ecclesiastes. Both of the above are preserved in their original form as a manuscript at the University of Jena, Germany.[33] Koffmane relates that Mathesius made a copy of the 1 John lectures from R. According to Mathesius, Luther lectured on the Epistle of John in 1527 to those students who remained with him; Georg Rörer later had given Mathesius a copy of his own notes. The copy itself is not extant. Just this remark about it is known to us. It is possible that this Mathesian copy served as the text basis for a second source, namely W, which is preserved under the title *scholia* and dated August 17, 1531 — a date which is derived from a sermon included with the lecture notes. However, the correct date for this sermon is the following year, 1532. W is, thus, a composition of lecture notes and sermon notes. This compilation is accompanied by a liberal redaction which is evident in W from the fact that biblical verses and classical citations are fully quoted, as well as from the fact that German phrases are

---

[33]Cf. WA 20:1 and 592; see also Irmgard Kratzsch, "Quellenmaterial zu Martin Luthers Leben und Werk in der Universitätsbibliothek Jena," *Wissenschaftliche Zeitschrift der Friedrich-Schiller-Universität Jena*, Gesellschaft- und Sprachwissenschaftliche Reihe, 32 (1983):229-248.

almost completely eliminated. The style is made even and flowing. When these redactor's elements are subtracted, only those matters remain which we find in R. The editor debated about referring to W at all in the critical edition. He included parts of it in smaller print than R and P in order to give the reader the opportunity to examine the low quality of W.[34] With Koffmane we conclude that W stemmed from a copy which was produced in 1531 with R as its basis.[35] We are, therefore, left with the texts P and R.

Printed Version (P)

Georg Neumann published in 1708, in Leipzig, the source we call P.[36] Because of an appendix to the manuscript containing some of Luther's letters to Jakob Propst in Bremen, it was concluded that Propst is the student who took the notes from Luther's mouth, although the original notes have been lost.[37] However, Propst was not at Wittenberg in

---

[34]"Man konnte schwanken, ob die Wolffenbütteler Handschrift überhaupt zu berücksichtigen sei.... Nur um den Leser in Stand zu setzen, unser Urtheil über den Unwerth dieser Handschrift nachzuprüfen, haben wir unter R einzelne Abschnitte als Proben in kleiner Schrift mitgetheilt." WA 20:597.

[35]"So stammt offenbar die Wolffenbütteler Handschrift aus einer Abschrift, die 1531 aus Rörers Heft gemacht wurde." WA 20:593. It is suspected (cf. ibid. 593-4) that Flacius is the redactor of W. This sounds reasonable, since Flacius would not have any interest in the German passages of the original text, himself being from the Balkans. On Flacius, see Oliver Olson, art. Flacius Illyricus, Matthias (1520-75), *TRE* 11:206-14.

[36]See above note 6 on p. 40.

[37]Neumann remarks that the print follows the notes taken "without doubt from Luther's mouth": "sub initium Ms. leguntur haud dubie quoque ex ore Lutheri notata," WA 20:599, n. to lines 27-30. About the lost original, the editor plainly states that the manuscript is lost, WA 20:594.

1527 at the time of the lectures on 1 John. Therefore the printed version we have in P goes back to an anonymous student. The fully quoted Bible verses in P are most likely the work of the editor/printer Neumann.[38] The same must be the case for certain explanations which have been added to the text.

An examination of P's Bible quotations reveals a puzzle similar to the one in S. The biblical references are not based on one single Latin version. At times P follows the version of Erasmus in regard to *sermo* instead of *verbum* in 1 John, also in regard to 1 John 1:4,6,8,; 2:3,13,28; 3:7. At other times P's references to the Bible are identical with the traditional version of the Vulgate, as, for example, in 1 John 1:2; 2:10,14,16-18; 4:3,14; 5:2,16,18,20. The printer's version does not seem to know of Luther's revised text of the Vulgate. When comparing P and R further differences arise. P notes on 3:1, "The reason why the world does not know *us* is that it did not know him."[39] In contrast R reads "you" instead of "us." Luther had lectured that "us" is not in the Greek original,[40] an annotation which is neglected by P. P naively follows the traditional Vulgate version and ignores Luther's annotation. P, on 3:7, reads with Erasmus "he who exercises justice,"[41] while R has the Vulgate version "he who makes justice."[42] P, on 4:2,3, gives the traditional Vulgate version, "And every spirit that *severs* Jesus,"[43] while R quotes the phrase as "does not con-

---

[38] Cf. WA 20:594.

[39] "non novit nos," WA 20:694,34 (LW 30:266).

[40] " . . . non novit vos. 'Nos' non est in greco," WA 20:694,14.

[41] "Qui exercet iustitiam," WA 20:703,37 (LW 30:271).

[42] "Qui facit iusticiam," WA 20:703,16.

[43] " . . . qui solvit Iesum . . . "; WA 20:729,27.

fess."[44] Luther lectured on how the Greek differs from the Latin *solvit* (he severs),[45] an annotation ignored by P. These comparisons between P and R demonstrate the inferiority of P to R, because P does not seem to know about Luther's remarks on the difference between the Greek and the Latin versions.

To further exemplify R's superiority over P, let us take a closer look at 1 John 3:4. P preserves the following text: "A difficult passage. For John distinguishes sharply between sin (ἁμαρτία) and lawlessness (ἀνομία)."[46] R reports the opposite: "This verse is obscure. It needs interpretation: for John does *not* distinguish, [but] to guess is dangerous. I, meanwhile, distinguish as follows. ... "[47] We must correct P, and consequently, we must improve the English version as follows: "A difficult passage. For John does *not* distinguish sharply between sin and lawlessness." The alternative would be to read R as corrected by P, which would end in the absurdity: "This verse is obscure. It needs interpretation: for John does distinguish sharply, [but] to guess is dangerous. I meanwhile distinguish as follows." The course of correcting P with the superior R makes sense.

In the light of these observations, and with the knowledge that P is only a copy of a lost original

---

[44]" 'Non confitetur' das ist der recht Antichristus," WA 20:729,10. Here Luther seems to have interpreted the Bible verse in German.

[45]" 'Solvit' In Graeco aliter," WA 20:725,7-8.

[46]WA 20:699,38-700,25 (LW 30:269).

[47]" 'Iniquitas' iste locus est obscurus. Indiget interpretatione: nam Iohannes non distinguit, divinare est periculosum. Ego sic interim distinguo," WA 20:699,17-18.

which underwent redaction in 1708,[48] one must agree with the editor, Koffmane, that R remains the superior source over P and, as we have noted, also over S and W.

Translation

The editors of LW chose P as the basis for their translation of Luther's unique Johannine Lectures of 1527 into the English language. One would have expected, because of the clear evaluation by Koffmane, that the LW editors would have given preference to R as a source. This was not the case. The LW editors claim that "a good case could be made for the adoption either of the Rörer or of the 'Propst' version."[49] The American edition of 1 John is based on the inferior P, simply because of the editor's general principle of taking a printed version, "whenever this is editorially defensible."[50] I am unable to share this conviction in view of the demonstrable weaknesses in the printed version as detailed above.

A further review of the American edition shows another weakness in dealing with the critically edited source materials. The American translator makes inconsistent use of the WA editors' apparatus. In regard to 1 John 3:7 he accepts the improved reading of the Latin *exserit* in place of *exerit*, while he ignores the greater probability, indicated by the WA editor,

---

[48]The printer, Neumann, influenced the text on 3:11, on 4:11 and on 5:16, cf. WA 20:708, n. to line 32; 746, n. 1 to line 33; 794, n. 1 to line 35. In P there is a misplacement of the beginning of the September 18 lecture on 1 John 2:23, which had to be corrected by the editor, cf. WA 20:683,14 — 684,31, in the light of R.

[49]LW 30:xi.

[50]Cf. ibid. What are the criteria for such a defense?

that it should read *exercet*.[51] The translation into English, therefore, reads, "for he *shows* righteousness and imitates Him who is righteous,"[52] thus adopting the Latin verb *exserit*. However, the textual critical evidence drawn from the comparison of the biblical references of P and R must lead to the option of the Latin verb *exercet*, which the Erasmian version uses for 1 John 3:7 and to which P alludes at the end of the exposition of 3:7.[53] The translation of the improved P version should not read "he *shows*," but instead, "for he *practices* (*exercet*) righteousness and imitates Him who is righteous."

Also, in regard to the interpretation of 1 John 4:11 and 5:16 as given in P, the translator ignores the WA editor's suggestion to replace *perpetuum* with *proprium* because the printer was probably mistaken in reading the abbreviation as he did.[54]

The use or non-use of the WA apparatus by the editors of LW corresponds to their unfortunate decision to prefer P over R as the basis for their translation. In addition to that, the S source, in dealing with the lectures on 1 John, plays no role for the editors of LW. A historical-critical approach to Luther's lectures, then,

---

[51]WA 20:704, n. 1, reads: "*exerit* kann = *exserit* 'macht offenbar, zeigt' sein, wahrscheinlicher ist *exercet* zu lesen." LW 30:271, n. 6, refers to this WA-footnote.

[52]LW 30:271.

[53]The Latin version given by Erasmus reads, "Qui exercet iustitiam, iustus est." P reads in its exposition of this verse, "quia exerit iustitiam" (WA 20:704,23), which is probably a printing mistake and, therefore, should read *exercet*, which the editors of WA suggest as the most probable solution.

[54]Cf. WA 20:746, n. 1: "Neumann's *Perpetuum* beruht vielleicht auf falscher Auflösung einer Abkürzung von *Proprium*." LW 30:296, cf. WA 20:746, n. 1. On 1 John 5:16, see LW 30:324 and WA 20:794, 3 with n. 1.

must work out its own translation based on S and R, in order to pursue a theological study about Luther' doctrine of Christ. The basic text for our purposes, therefore, will be R. Thus we will be accompanied and supported by the heretofore unanimous, scholarly judgment about Rörer as conservator of Luther texts.

Superiority and Significance of R-Notes

The eminent Luther scholar, Gerhard Ebeling, points out the significance of R-notes in general. Rörer's labors in preserving Luther's sayings and writings are of utmost importance from a linguistic point of view, because these notes are some of the earliest direct notes in German.[55] Other scholarly opinions on R take the same direction and may be summarized briefly as follows: Rörer's achievements are no longer debated.[56] He has gained great credibility in preserving and transmitting Luther's lectures. Rörer's most trustworthy notes exist in stenographic form.[57] B. Klaus notes that a comparison of R with others' notes demonstrates that Rörer was the most gifted of Luther's students. All Luther researchers agree unanimously that R's stenographic notes are

[55]Cf. Gerhard Ebeling, *Luther: An Introduction to his Thought*, trans. (Philadelphia: Fortress Press, 1970), 52.

[56]"Rörer's Verdienste um die Überlieferung von Luther-Texten sind heute nicht mehr umstritten," Hans Volz, *Martin Luthers deutsche Bibel. Entstehung und Geschichte der Lutherbibel.* Introduction by Friedrich Wilhelm Kantzenbach, ed. Henning Wendland (Hamburg: Friedrich Wittig-Verlag, 1978), 91.

[57]"Am zuverlässigsten sind die von Rörer in Schnellschrift aufgenommenen Nachschriften," Siegfried Raeder, "Luther als Ausleger und Übersetzer der Heiligen Schrift," *Festgabe 1983*, 258; cf. also E. Mülhaupt, *Luther im 20. Jahrhundert*, 264, n. 7.

of unique value for the tradition of Luther's work and for the whole of Luther research.[58]

The person most familiar with Rörer's manuscripts, I. Kratzsch, declares that his notes are the most important ones of their kind within the handwritten sources of Luther's thoughts; they are second to none.[59]

Today's Luther scholars simply confirm what Luther himself had noticed when, in 1540, he compared students' lecture notes on Isaiah; after Veit Dietrich had published Luther's lectures on Isaiah, the professor is reported to have said to Justus Jonas that Veit's notes were too dry and meager, and that Magister Georg (Rörer) had more.[60]

---

[58]"Der Vergleich mit anderen Nachschriften zeigt übrigens, dass Rörer als der geschickteste unter allen, die zu Luthers Füssen sassen, angesehen werden muss. Über den geradezu einzigartigen Wert der Rörerschen Nachschriften für die Lutherüberlieferung vertritt die gesamte Lutherforschung eine einhellige Auffassung," B. Klaus, "Georg Rörer . . . ," 137.

[59]"*Rörers* unmittelbare Nachschriften der Vorlesungen und Predigten *Luthers* stellen Quellen von erstrangigem Wert dar . . . "; "Quellenmaterial," 239, cf. 238; her Appendices I and II show R's notes as they are published in WA.

[60]"de Esaia, quem excepit Vitus. Doctor: Er ist gar zu dirre und mager; Magister Georgius hatt mehr", WA TR 4:564 (no. 4869).

On Rörer, there is so far no scientific biography written which would elaborate his significance and function on Luther's side. He was for instance the first person ordained by Luther for the ministry at Wittenberg; he was the one who baptized Luther's first child; he was the secretary of the Bible commission for the German translation. Cf. H. Bornkamm, *Luther in Mid-Career*, 200.473.561. See also Hans-Günter Leder, "Luthers Beziehungen zu seinen Wittenberger Freunden," *Festgabe 1983*, 438. Luther called Rörer his *imperator* and together with wife Katie "Moses," who both apparently often told the professor what to do. Cf. Leder, 439. On Luther's Bible translation, see Karl Heinz zur Mühlen, "Luthers deutsche Bibelübersetzung als Gemeinschaftswerk," *Die Bibel in der Welt*, 18 (1978):90-97, where the team work in this work is pointed out with Rörer's central role. See also

There are, however, a few minor uncertainties and mistakes to be reported, as we take up our evaluation of R. There are errors which crept into the otherwise careful stenographer's notes who was so faithful to what he heard that he even wrote down Luther's exclamation, "Ah." When it was impossible for R to stenograph Luther's words in full length, he indicated this by his characteristic sigil for "etc."[61] R developed his own shorthand system in Latin, and when Luther spoke German, we know that R translated as much as possible according to this Latin shorthand system. Where the German expression was so impressive or too difficult to translate instantly, R preserved the original German. For the German, there was no shorthand system developed at that time. His contemporaries complained about the difficulties of deciphering his notes.[62] R's code is described in the editor's preface to WA 20, where the editor points out that R used also traditional abbreviations such as *pr* for *pater* (father), i.e., used, the first and last letter of a word; or with an additional letter in the middle such as *sba* for *substantia* (substance). Beyond that, R employs 800 abbreviations.[63] It does not take much imagination to anticipate that there are ex-

---

Hans Volz, *Martin Luthers deutsche Bibel. Entstehung und Geschichte der Lutherbibel.*

[61]"Ah," WA 20:770, 20. — The abbreviation "etc." is always kept in the direct quotations (when given in this study).

[62]Cf. Paul Pietsch, Vorwort, WA 20:V.

[63]Cf. ibid. p. VI — A list of R's abbreviations and sigla is given in WA 29:XVI-XXIV. Here are some examples: *ec* = *ecclesia* (church); *va* = *vanitas* (vanity) or *varietas* (variety); *ga* = *gratias agere* (to give thanks); *c* = *caput* (chapter or head); *E* = *Euangelium*; *p* = *peccatum* (sin); *P* = *Paulus*; *ss* = *summa summarum* (the sum of it all); a sigil X stands for *crux* (cross), and *Xfigere* then means *crucifigere* (to crucify).

amples which are difficult to solve and that there are often two or three possible meanings for one abbreviation.[64] In our specific text on 1 John there are several instances where the problem is evident.[65] Concerning the issue of Christology, one must ask whether the abbreviation *hu. .tem* used in the exposition of 1 John 2:20 means humility or humanity.[66] Here, the context requires the option for humanity: "Therefore the orders and status, which are established to achieve the salvation, are nothing. So far he [John] explains his [Christ's] humanity in relation to the Christians."[67] Whether Luther spoke German at this point cannot be determined; there are only two German fragments in the immediate context.[68]

At another point, namely, on 1 John 3:20, there is an error to be corrected which is done on the basis of P. In R one reads: "If idleness of life or a work against

---

[64]For instance, the sigil *v* may be *vult* (he wants), or *vita* (life), or *verbum* (word).

[65]Cf. For instance WA 20:622, 15: is it *cogitationem* or *cognitionem*? Consideration or insight? Thought or knowledge? In this case I tend to *cognitio* as insight, while the editor prefers *cogitatio*, for the abbreviation *cog*. In the following line 16, the abbreviation could mean *fideli* (dativ of *fidelis*) or *fide*(m) (by faith or through faith); the first reading is unlikely.

On the next page (623), the abbreviation *iust. .*a may read *iustificata (fides)* or *iusticia*, justified faith or righteousness? The first reading is favored.

In WA 20:784,19, we read in the edited version: *faciunt deum mendacem et deum* (they make God a liar and God), which does not make sense, because the abbreviation *di. .*um is read as *deum* (God accusative form) but it could also be *diabolum*, as the editor suggests, and which makes more sense: "(the enthusiasts) make God a liar and a devil." The printed version used the smoother remark, "they make God the Father a liar," WA 20:784,34.

[66]WA 20:679,20.

[67]ibid. lines 19-21.

[68]Cf. ibid. lines 16,17, and 23.

love bothers you, you will *not hope* because it is a command (not a counsel) that you should hope for the Lord. . . . Desperation is prohibited. . . . "[69] Where R has the negation of hope, P has the negation of despair, which alone makes sense.[70] In Latin the prefix *de-* is missing. When the prefix is added in R as it is in P, the reading is this: " . . . you will not despair because it is a command (not a counsel) that you should hope in the Lord. . . . Desperation is prohibited."

Next to this error of omitting the prefix *de-*, which caused an absurdity, there is an error found in R which probably stems from the student's lack of historical knowledge. However, it must be emphasized that R alone contains the name Nicolaus, while the rest of the sources on 1 John do not mention it. R's error is to call this Nicolaus *papa*.[71] He did this by adding *papa* to his manuscript at a later point as the editor recognized and noted in the footnote. Apparently R thought the name Nicolaus must be a pope's name because in the same sentence Luther spoke of

[69]"Si vexaverit te ignavia vitae vel opus contra charitatem, non sperabis, quia praeceptum est (non consilium), ut speres in dominum. . . . Desperatio est prohibita . . . ," WA 20:716,14-19.

[70]"Site reprehenderit vitae ignavia, adhuc tamen non *de*sperabis. Euangelii enim summa est, ut credas et speres," WA 20:716,31-32 (emphasis added). The syllable *de* makes all the difference here. R did not hear the *de-* or became confused with the negation. Otherwise though, as noted above, his ability of noticing any detail is unsurpassed.

[71]"Statuta Romanae ecclesiae aequipollent Euangelio, ut sit salus servantibus. Econtra Nicolaus papa, tamen recedere a Papatu adeo difficile etc. nisi dederit spiritus sanctus hanc cogitationem," WA 20:622,13-15. Our interest at this point concentrates on the textual criticism.

the papacy. With the editor one must take Nicolaus not as *papa*, but as Panormitanus, a medieval representative of the conciliar movement, who is known for his critical attitude toward the papacy as the immediate context indicates as well. Thus, it turns out that R's attempt at improving his lecture notes when reviewing them and adding *papa* created a mistake which would not have happened if he would have left the words as he heard them, i.e., without *papa*.

Lecturing in Latin and German, Luther's Saxon pronounciation of Latin words may have something to do with mistakes such as in regard to *dum* and *tum* (during and then), because the Saxon dialect (even today) tends to soften the German *t* toward *d*. So, when Luther lectured *tum*, R wrote down what he heard: *dum*.[72] Thus, it may have been Luther's pronounciation which led to writing mistakes such as this one. When Luther lectured *interpellator* he pronounced its *p* like a *b* as the Saxons do, and that is apparently why R's notes contain the mistake *interbellator*.[73] This observation of Luther's Saxon pronounciation of Latin words demonstrates that he actually lectured at least partly in Latin, which would mean that a suggestion of Luther lecturing exclusively in German altogether is in error.

So far we have been occupied with the Latin text. However, it must be seen clearly that R actually is a

---

[72] WA 20:615,3. Also, see WA 20:685,24: *decum*, instead of *tecum*.

[73] WA 20:637,17. On this issue see WA 20:VII, where the editor points out that R understood correctly what he heard: namely Luther's Saxon pronounciation, which led him to mistakes: *b* instead of *p*; *d* instead of *t*.

macaronic composition of Latin and Saxon-German with occasional transliterations of Greek terms.[74] The first lecture on 1 John 1:1, August 19, 1527, contains more than a dozen German expressions in the basically Latin text; in comparison, P's notes have only one, but not one identical with R. What P preserved in German is absent in R.[75] This means that a combination of the German elements of R and P would enable us to reach the historical Luther's original German, untainted by Latin translations.

The German expressions often are strong verbs indicating forceful activity or feelings, such as during the first lecture:[76]

setzt er uns hin	he places us there
sind eingerissen	they have broken into
auffghet	rise
reizt uns	irritates us
geht die gantze person an	concerns the whole person
nimmt die gantze person mit	takes along the whole person
mochten des nicht	did not like it
ful ich prot und wein	I feel bread and wine
erwegt euch mit gantzem hertzen drauff	deliberate over it wholeheartedly
weis nicht was er redt	does not know what he is talking about

---

[74]WA 20:726, 10.16.17 (*energian*) et al.
[75]Cf. WA 20:604,29-30 (P).
[76]Cf. WA 20:599-606.

The point is not to present a complete linguistic study; our primary goal is to reach the historical Luther and his teaching by means of the historical-critical method and its textual criticism. The above observations aim to give additional support to the argument that R is superior to P as the most authentic textual basis for the Christological investigation. In Part Three there will be the opportunity to refer again to this issue, where we will emphasize those German elements which bear Christological significance.

During our seafaring on the "ocean" of Luther's works, we have come across some primordial rocks of Luther's original Saxon brogue in the Bavarian Rörer's lecture notes. The historical significance of Luther's amanuensis Rörer, with his most precise sense of hearing and his excellent shorthand system, can hardly be exaggerated. When one compares, for instance, Calvin's secretaries with Luther's student Rörer, one realizes the greatness of the latter's role more fully. More than one secretary tried to take notes on Calvin's sermons, but none of them was competent to do more than capture the main headings until a professional was found who had a system of shorthand.[77] In conclusion, in regard to Luther's lectures on 1 John, R's notes are superior to the rest because of their accuracy in Latin and German and because of their completeness and precise dating with reference to each lecture day. S, with its fragmentary character, should be considered as an ano-

---

[77]Cf. Thomas Henry Louis Parker, *John Calvin: A Biography*, (Philadelphia: The Westminister Press, 1975), 91.

nymous Saxon student's notes rather than a copy of lecture preparation notes from Luther's pen. As far as the printed version is concerned, it ranks after R and above W and S. As the basis for the LW translation, it received more attention than it deserves.

CHAPTER 2

WHAT BIBLE VERSION
DID LUTHER USE
IN HIS ACADEMIC WORK?

The question is not as simple as it might seem at first. In 1521-22 Luther worked on the translation of the New Testament into his native German. Does that mean that he used his own translation also in his academic lectures? Considerable attention is given to the question of the sources of Luther's translation. In regard to the letter of Paul to the Galatians, Heinz Bluhm studied the translation and concluded that Luther used Erasmus's Greek-Latin edition of 1519, and that he followed mainly the Greek and only six times the Vulgate version.[1] In contrast to Bluhm, Heinrich Bornkamm tells us that the German translation of Romans is proof that Luther repeatedly made use of two Latin helps. He claims that at times Luther followed the Greek text, but that the Vulgate remained his mainstay. The first essential reference he used for his translation at the Wartburg castle was the Vulgate. He was quite aware of this

---

[1]Cf. Heinz Bluhm, "The Sources of Luther's September-Testament: Galatians," *Luther for an Ecumenical Age*, ed. C. S. Meyer (St. Louis: Concordia, 1967), 144-171.

Latin Bible's deficiencies; Erasmus's edition was the second reference for his German translation.[2]

The issue of Luther's New Testament translation is only indirectly related to the question we pose here: Which Bible version did Luther use in mid-career in his academic lectures? In the previous chapter it has been indicated from the source material that Luther lectured in both German and in Latin, and that it is virtually impossible to determine which language was dominant. The student notes and the alleged *scholia* from Luther's pen were done in Latin via shorthand. It has been observed that the young Luther used German and Latin in his lectures. This is the testimony of John Oldekop of Hildesheim. The editor Paul Pietsch remarks that Luther must have given whole passages in German. But this does not give a direct answer to our question, because our question only deals with the lectures and the comments on a biblical text. Our problem here is: What Bible version did he use in his academic work? In the best available source (R), all the Bible references are in Latin. This fact rules out any attempt to find out whether Luther used his German Bible translation.

---

[2]Cf. H. Bornkamm, *Luther in Mid-Career*, 44-46. Bornkamm has revised his position of 1953, when he was opposed to the thesis that Luther's translation is based upon the Vulgate. Cf. *Luther's World of Thought*, trans. M. H. Bertram (St. Louis: Concordia, 1958). Bornkamm confirms now the thesis of Hermann Dippelt that Luther translated chiefly from the Latin almost without the Greek text: "Der Vulgatatext ist seine Grundlage geblieben," 326., i.e., the Vulgate text has remained his foundation; "Das Griechische fand nur gelegentlich, zumeist auf Anregung durch die Annot. des Erasmus Berücksichtigung," i.e., the Greek was considered only occasionally, mostly stimulated by Erasmus's annotations, 329. "Hatte Luthers Verdeutschung des Neuen Testaments den griechischen Text zur Grundlage?" *ARG* 38 (1941):300-330.

As Bornkamm indicated, the Vulgate had a powerful influence on Luther, who knew it practically by heart. Other indicators suggest we take a closer look at Luther and the Vulgate. In the first lecture on the Psalms, in 1513-15, Luther expresses his love for the Vulgate by comparing it to the Hebrew. His view of the Vulgate is really from a theological perspective, because he said that the Hebrew text often only expresses the literal sense, while the Vulgate brings out the spiritual sense.[3] Luther once said that he knew the Latin Bible so well that he had become a good *localis* when he was young, i.e., he was competent in locating individual verses.[4] We may rightly conclude from these indicators that Luther's world was the Latin world and that this fact influenced his academic work. In addition, Luther had been working on the improvement of the Vulgate text for academic purposes since 1523.[5] For pastoral purposes, he preferred the German translation.[6] When Luther decided to revise the Vulgate, he did it on the basis of the original biblical languages of Greek and Hebrew. In 1524-25 he revised the Latin text of Deuteronomy on

---

[3]"Item quod translatio hebr. sepius literam tantum exprimit, nostra autem spiritum, sicut patet et Michee 5, Matth. 2 de Bethlehem," WA 3:370,39-41 (on Psalm 64(65)).

[4]"Ego iuvenis me assuefeci ad bibliam; saepius legendo fiebam localis," WA TR 4:432 (no. 4691).

[5]Cf. the introduction to Luther's Latin version of Psalm 119, *Octonarius David* (1527), WA 23:434. John Dantiscus, the ambassador of the Polish King at the court of Charles V, reported in a letter that Luther was translating the books of Moses from Hebrew into Latin in 1523, exactly at the time when he (John Dantiscus) was visiting with Luther in Wittenberg. Cf. Bornkamm, *Luther in Mid-Career*, 292.

[6]" . . . For I hope we will give a better translation to our Germans than the Latins have." WA Br 2:423, 48-53, here 427, 128 (LW 48:363.372).

the basis of the Hebrew Bible.[7] In 1527 he edited a Latin version of Psalm 119.[8] On November 28, 1526, Melanchthon had written Camerarius that he should ask for the privilege of printing the Latin Bible.[9] Further evidence for this enterprise of revising the Vulgate for academic purposes is given by Luther himself, who wrote to the pastor Clemens Ursinus on March 21, 1527, "I am working on the correction of the Bible in truth to Hebrew. Pray for us."[10] The publication came out in 1529, not in complete form, and for academic purposes only, not for public use, as declared in its preface.[11] Ten years later, in 1537, Luther edited the Psalterium in Latin with the explicit intention to differentiate his translation from other contemporary Latin editions.[12]

Latin?

Our question here reckons with the possibility that Luther used the Vulgate for his academic work. This assumption gains a degree of probability when one is aware of Luther's critical attitude toward Erasmus's edition of the New Testament with his controversial Latin translation which accompanied the Greek

---

[7]Cf. WA 14:494 (LW 9:ix).

[8]Cf. n. 5, above.

[9]"Rogavit me Christianus Faber hodie ut ad te scriberem, ut vel in Hispania aula vel Esslingae apud iudicii Imperatoris praetorem Marchiorem a Baden peteres sibi excudenti latina *biblia*, ut scis, privilegium, ne cui liceret recudere intra annos aliquot, quare te rogo, ut primum Esslingiae ea de re agas, indeque rescribas, quid effeceris." CR 1:833 (no. 420).

[10]"Sum in opera Biblia corrigendi ad veritatem Ebraicam, ora pro nobis" WA Br 4:177, 23-24 (no. 1089).

[11]Cf. WA DB 5:1,30-2,1.

[12]Cf. WA DB 10II:185,9-14

text.[13] Since Luther used the Erasmus edition of 1519 for his translation into German, one may assume that he did so for his other work as well. By 1527, the year of his course on 1 John, there had appeared two new editions of Erasmus's New Testament, one in 1522 and the other in 1527. Whether Luther made use of the one of 1522 is not known. However, it is clear that he possessed the edition of 1527; this personal copy is extant with marginal notes, edited in 1980.[14] According to the editor, Luther received this latest copy probably in the spring of 1528, although it had appeared on the book market in the spring of 1527. This means that Luther probably still used the edition of 1519 when lecturing in 1527.

How can one find out which text Luther used in his academic lectures? The best way is to compare the biblical quotations of the most precise source, R, with the Vulgate, with Erasmus's edition, Luther's revised Vulgate and Luther's German translations. We will begin this comparison by looking at 1 John 5:18, which includes the key word *generatio Dei*.

With the Vulgate version in mind and memory, with Erasmus's edition at hand, including the humanist's "fresh translation"[15] into Latin, with the experience of having translated the New Testament into German, Luther must have used as his starting

[13]Cf. H. Bluhm "The Sources . . . ", 144-171; Waltraut Ingeborg Sauer, art. Bibelübersetzungen III, 1, *TRE* 6:239-244, here 241; C. A. L. Jarrott, "Erasmus' In principio erat sermo: A Controversial Translation," *Studies in Philology* 61 (1964):35-40; still very informative is August Bludau, *Die beiden ersten Erasmus-Ausgaben des Neuen Testaments und ihre Gegner*, Biblische Studien 7 (Freiburg: Herder, 1902), 424-569.
[14]Cf. WA 60:192-228.
[15]R. H. Bainton, *Eramus of Christendom* (New York: Crossroad, 1982), 133.

point the term *"generatio"* from the Vulgate, followed by the interpretation of it as indicated by the
"i.e." abbreviation in R. An alternative reconstruc-
tion would be this: Luther used his German translation, which includes the noun *gepurt* (birth) as the
September Testament of 1522 reads; either Luther or
Rörer translated it immediately into the Latin, *generatio*, which alone shows up in R.[16] The Greek original of 1 John 5:18, according to Erasmus, has, instead of the noun, the aorist participle passive of the
verb γεννάω (to give birth, to produce): "the one who is
born."[17] The Vulgate version uses the noun form of
generatio,[18] while Erasmus converted the Greek verbal form into a Latin verbal form which shows up in
R.[19]

---

[16]"Conclusio et Epiphonema et brevis recapitulatio. Sententia, de qua
loquimur, summa summarum eorum, quae diximus: 'Omnis qui.' Supra c. 5. in principio: nasci ex deo. 'Generatio' i.e. qui generatus ex deo
est (ut supra), non potest peccare." WA 20:798, 12-15. Cf. P-version,
lines 26-27.

[17]ὁ γεννηθείς. I used the Microfilm copy of Marquette Library (Erasmus's edition of 1519).

[18]I used the marginals to Erasmus' *Opera Omnia*, vol. 7 (Leiden edition
of 1706, reprint 1962 by Georg Olms, Hildesheim). The Vulgate text
appears on the margin of the *Paraphrases in N. Testamentum*, which
is identical with the Latin version of 1 John as given in *Novum
Testamentum Graece et Latine*, ed. Erwin Nestle and Kurt Aland
(Stuttgart: Württembergische Bibelanstalt, 1963 — 25th edition).

[19]Here follows the survey of all versions which are to be compared:

Erasmus' Greek	:	ἀλλ᾽ ὁ γεννηθείς ἐκ τοῦ θεοῦ τηρεῖ αὐτόν.
Erasmus' Latin	:	sed qui genitus est ex deo, servat seipsum.
Vulgate	:	sed generatio Dei conservat eum.
German 1522	:	sondern die gepurt von got, helt yhn.
R notes 1527	:	'generatio' i.e. qui generatus ex deo est.
P notes 1527	:	sed generatio Dei conservat eum.
Luther's Vulgate 1529	:	sed genitus ex Deo custodit se.
German 1546	:	sondern, wer von Gott geboren ist, der be- waret sich.

We see that R uses the Vulgate's *generatio* and interprets this term with the expression *i.e. qui generatus ex deo est* (. . . who is born of God). This interpretative sentence is a variation of Erasmus's translation from the Greek into Latin because it reads *generatus* instead of *genitus*. Luther's Vulgate revision reads the same as the Erasmus text, *genitus*, but the rest of this verse differs from it. It is interesting to note that Luther's German version of 1522 sticks to the noun form of the Vulgate, so that *generatio* corresponds to *gepurt*,[20] while in 1546 Luther liberated himself from this noun form of the Vulgate and used the verb form as the Greek original does. But this was not yet the case during the lectures on 1 John. Luther used Erasmus's Greek and Latin to understand the Vulgate's expression *generatio Dei*. In other words, the starting point is the Vulgate, which is interpreted with the help of Erasmus's edition. At this time Luther had not yet worked on the Vulgate revision of 1 John. The lectures on 1 John of 1527 are the bridge between Luther's use of the noun form (*generatio* and *gepurt*) of the early 1520s and his use of the verb form (*genitus*) in his Vulgate version of 1529 and in the German version of 1546 (*geboren ist*), for during his lectures on 1 John the noun form of the Vulgate was explained with the verb form of Erasmus's edition.

A sentence-by-sentence comparison of R with the Vulgate verses of 1 John indicates, as a general rule,

---

[20]This observation corroborates the thesis that Luther's text basis for this German translation of the New Testament in 1521-22 was the Vulgate, because the German noun version corresponds exactly with the Vulgate's version. In the final German version of 1546, he followed the usage of the Greek original.

the use of the Vulgate (which Luther had memorized in his earlier days). This use of the Vulgate is particularly evident when it comes to the *Comma Johanneum* (1 John 5:7). According to R, Luther quoted the Vulgate and commented in regard to the Greek text. "The Greek codices do not have this verse," Luther continued, "therefore, we leave this text out."[21] When lecturing about an omission from a certain text, he was referring to a text from which something can be left out: the Vulgate. Thus, the thesis is confirmed that Luther used the Vulgate as his starting point when lecturing on 1 John; he proceeded, then, with the text given by Erasmus. From the investigation on the *Comma Johanneum* we may conclude that Luther used, in 1527, the Erasmian edition of 1519, and not of 1522, because the edition of 1519 had excluded verse seven, while the following edition of 1522 included it again, under pressure from colleagues.[22] When Luther referred to "leaving out" this verse, he could have meant only the text which had excluded it, i.e., Erasmus's edition of 1519. Thus, Luther used the same New Testament edition which had served him already for his German translation.

There is one final indicator which points to Luther's use of Erasmus's edition of the New Testament of 1519. It is found in the lecture on 1 John 2:15-17 on September 11, 1527, where Luther mentions Erasmus for the first time by name. Taking up the observation during the first lecture on the *oratio infantilis*, Luther said that John speaks here like a little child

---

[21] WA 20:780,21 and 780, 25-781,1.
[22] Cf. H. J. deJonge, "Erasmus and the Comma Johanneum," *Ephemerides theologiae lovanienses*, 56 (1980):381-89.

so that Erasmus feels offended.[23] At the end of the lecture, Luther picked up his criticism of Erasmus without mentioning his name, but he clearly was referring to the opinion of Erasmus when, in his preface to 1 John, Luther said, "When John speaks about the world, it is supposed to be loquacious."[24] The decisive word is "loquacious," which Luther rendered in German as *leichtfertig*. The Latin equivalent is *loquax*, which is found in Erasmus's 1519 edition. In the 1522 edition Erasmus omitted the expression; instead we read "less brief, and more elaborate."[25] This argument, together with the other observations, virtually assures us that Luther used the edition of 1519, which is the same one he used for his German translation at the Wartburg.

In his treatment of 1 John 3:1, Luther likewise followed Erasmus and translated "you" (*vos*) and not "us" (*nos*), as the Vulgate has it.[26] This same dependency upon Erasmus's Latin version is true for 1 John 3:21, where we read, according to R, the Erasmian expression *erga deum* instead of the Vulgate's *ad deum*.[27]

---

[23]"Hic vides Iohannem simpliciter loqui, ut infantulus, ut Erasmus infensus." WA 20:661,1-2.

[24]"Quando Iohannes de mundo redt, sol leichtfertig sein." WA 20:666, 20-667,1.

[25]"Quoties hic iterat mundus? Postremo, est in toto huius sermone quiddam minus astrictum, ac fusius, quam in sermone reliquorom apostolorum" (1522).

"Quantum his est mundorum? Postremo, est in toto huius sermone quiddam, ut ita dicam loquacius, quam in sermone reliquorum apostolorum" (1519).

[26]WA 20:694,14. Erasmus's *Annotationes* of 1522, 615.

[27]WA 20:721,16. Luther returns to the original Vulgate in his own Latin edition of the Bible of 1529.

A comparison of R with Erasmus also reveals many differences, which makes it impossible to declare that Luther used Erasmus's edition of the Greek and Latin New Testament as the exclusive basis for his lectures. In fact, one must reject such a thought and remain with the thesis that the Vulgate played an important role during the lectures at least as a starting point for his comments. This is borne out in the following verses 1:8; 2:3,5,11,16,18,20; 3:7,9,13. These verses show a difference between the Latin of R and of Erasmus. When quoting 1 John 4:3, Luther, according to R, used *qui solvit Iesum*, and continued by commenting that the Greek version differs.[28] He first referred to the Vulgate, then to Erasmus.

A remarkable difference appears in 1 John 4:18. Here Erasmus's Latin obviously differs from Luther's. The original Greek, κόλασις (punishment) is translated in the Vulgate with *poena*, which is etymologically close to the German *peyn* in Luther's German translation of 1522. Luther rejected Erasmus's suggestion to use *cruciatum* and retained, in his revised Vulgate of 1529, the original Vulgate's *poena*.[29] Why? Because the original Greek word does not carry the connotation of cross and crucifixion. This verse should not carry any allusion to Christ's cross. Because of his theology of the cross, Luther remained with the Vulgate and rejected Erasmus.

---

[28]"Solvit in Graeco aliter." WA 20·725,7-8.

[29]WA DB 7:336 German; the respective Latin term *poena* is used by R: WA 20:761,18, where *poena* is used with quotation marks in order to indicate that we deal with a Bible quotation. Cf. Luther's Vulgate WA DB 5:780,40.

Thus we see that Luther evaluated the texts critically, not only from a linguistic, but also from a theological perspective.

This latter presumption of theological influence on Luther's choice of words shines through also in his choice in 1 John 3:20. The original verb there is κατα-γινώσκω (to find against, to sentence). Luther, leaning on Erasmus's edition of 1519, translated this verb into German as *verdampt*.[30] Erasmus, in his Latin version, used the word "condemn" (*condemnet*).[31] In 1527, according to R, Luther used *reprehendit*,[32] which is closer in meaning to the original Greek and not as strong as "to condemn." *Reprehendit* is the expression used in the original Vulgate. When Luther, in 1527, returned to the original Vulgate, by rejecting implicitly Erasmus's *condemnet* and by departing from his German *verdampt*, he probably did so because of the theological reason that he did not want to give the human heart the power of condemnation, only of reprehension. Thus, the Vulgate here remains the starting point for Luther. Linguistic and theological considerations lead to his critical use of Erasmus's editions of the Greek and Latin New Testament. In his Latin Bible of 1529 Luther followed the original Vulgate version.[33]

This is also the case with the Johannine *Logos*. Erasmus replaced the Vulgate's *verbum* with *sermo*. Melanchthon in his commentary on John in 1523[34]

---

[30] WA DB 7:334 (NT 1522).
[31] Through all his editions since 1516.
[32] WA 20:717,2.
[33] "si reprehenderit nos cor nostrum"; WA DB 5:780,4.
[34] CR 14:1051-62.

did not follow Erasmus in this, nor did Luther. 1 John 2:5 is translated with *verbum*, not with *sermo*.[35]

It is clear that Luther worked with the Vulgate, so one may suspect that he used a rough draft of his own revision of the Vulgate while lecturing on 1 John in 1527 (which he did not). The changes which Luther did make in his revision are all minor in comparison to the Erasmian translation into Latin. The comparison of R with Luther's revised Vulgate indicates that Luther did not anticipate using his own revised Vulgate version in his lectures on 1 John in 1527. The changes which he made in the final draft of 1529 do not appear in 1527. This is evident in 2:6, where R reads *ille* and the revision has *ipse*; in 2:28, where Luther returned from R's *confundemur* to the original Vulgate's *confundamur* in 1529, and in contrast to Erasmus's *pudefiamus*; in 3:4, where Luther said in his lecture that this verse was obscure to him,[36] and did not offer a solution. However, in 1529 he solved the problem by translating the Vulgate's *iniquitas* with *praevaricatio*; 3:24 indicates that Luther did not yet have ready his revised version, which in this case is influenced by Erasmus.[37] Luther's use of *propiciator* in 4:10 in his revised Vulgate is not anticipated in the lectures, where he used the traditional *propitiatio*, found both in the Vulgate and in the Latin text of Erasmus. The improvement

---

[35] WA 20:644,5.

[36] " 'Iniquitas' iste locus est obscurus." WA 20:699,17.

[37] R: "Et in hoc scimus, quoniam de spiritu manet in nobis." WA 20:722,7-8. Luther's Vulgate revision of 1529 reads, "Et per hoc scimus, quod manet in nobis per spiritum quem dedit nobis." Erasmus has it slightly different: "Et per hoc scimus, quod manet in nobis de spiritu, quem nobis dedit."

in 4:10 is simply an adjustment to the immediate context which speaks of the Son who is sent as *propitiatio*, which Luther gives in the personal form of *propiciator*. Not yet apparent either is the change in 5:7 from *unum* (1527) to *simul* (1529). The original Vulgate has *unum*. Also, in regard to *generatio* (5:18), Luther had only later (in 1529) used the verbal form of *genitus ex Deo*, while R still gives *generatio*, as in the Vulgate. Our thesis remains intact, namely that Luther used the Vulgate, but not the *Vulgata recognita* of 1529, nor any rough draft of it. He also used the Erasmian New Testament, but with critical judgment in the light of the old Vulgate. Altogether, Luther is very conservative when it comes to deviations from the Vulgate, especially when compared with Erasmus and his attempts to modernize the Latin version.

At one point, in 1 John 5:16, Luther remains with the old Latin even in his revised Vulgate, although during the lectures of 1527 he made a change in agreement with the Greek original and with Erasmus.[38]

Greek?

The highest ambition of the intellectual elite of the Renaissance time was to be able to read the Scrip-

---

[38]Greek: δώσει

Erasmus: *dabit*

Luther according to R: *dabit* — with the addition of "scilicet Christus vel deus": WA 20:796,23-24. Luther's revised Vulgate = old Vulgate: *dabitur ei vita*. Luther, furthermore, did not accept Erasmus' changes in 2:11 from *scandalum* to *opprobrium*, and in 2:18 from *novissima hora* to *novissimum tempus*. Luther remained with the Vulgate, as he did by using *verbum* instead of *sermo* for *logos*.

tures in the original Greek and Hebrew.[39] Luther belonged to the elite of his day. He used the Greek-Latin edition of the New Testament. Proof of his use of Greek comes only from actual transliterations of Greek terms as they occur in R. When Luther does use the Greek, his use of Hebrew is not far away, because he regularly interprets Greek notions from their Hebrew background. There is a note on the margin in R's manuscript, at 1 John 2:14, where the Hebrew equivalent of the Latin *iuvenes* (youth) is "transliterated" as Bachurim,[40] which is either R's error or the WA-editor's, because the original Hebrew of Psalm 127:4 to which the passage may refer, lists *neurim* (boys, children). If it is not an error by R, then Luther's use of *Bachurim* was intended to mean youth, as the "first born," or to refer to the village of Bachurim as the "village of the young" (2 Sa 3:16), but not to Psalm 127:4 as the editor suggests.

On September 17, 1527, when lecturing on 1 John 2:20, Luther used the Christological title *Messias*, according to R.[41] In this passage Luther made use of his Hebrew knowledge and lectured in a macaronic way, if not exclusively in German. Rörer then translated it into Latin. R even preserved Luther's apology for being unable to translate the original with better understanding:

---

[39]Cf. Hubert Jedin, "The Bible-epoch of Renaissance," *A History of the Council of Trent*, trans. E. Graf (New York: Thomas Nelson and Sons, 1957), vol. 1, 157-8.

[40]WA 20:660, n. to line 5. On verse 2:12, we find transliterations: " 'Tekna' filii, 'paes' filius, sed proprie qui in die schul ghen." WA 20:657, 20-21; cf. "paedia" 658,1 and 659,6. P does not preserve any Greek here, but W does, WA 20:657,25 and 658,20. — *Tekna* is either a mistake by the editor or by R, because the correct transliteration is *teknia*.

[41]The Hebrew word is not preserved in the sources. WA 20:676,12.

In Hebrew, unction is a clear term. It does not
sound as though one anoints some matter, but
properly as though to anoint a priest and a
king, and [thus, it is] a sacerdotal and regal
term. This the Latin, Greek and German do
not carry [meaning, the Hebrew original], but
another word, I imagine the oil of the barber.
In Hebrew it properly means how one has
anointed the priests and the kings, those who
are priestly and levitically consecrated. . . .
Thus one is called a Christian, when he has
the unction, that which the Messiah also is
anointed with. This unction, *salben* [in Ger-
man], is nothing but that of the Holy Spirit. . . .
I am sorry that we cannot translate it into
other languages.[42]

R does not give the Hebrew terms which Luther
must have mentioned in order to point out that the
Hebrew has two words for unctioning/anointing,
one for sacred and the other for secular use. The
secular use is the one handled by the barber or beau-
tician as *oleum rasoris*, which might be the regular
olive oil, in Hebrew ריח, and the verb to be bright, to
shine, in Hebrew זהה. The sacred use of oil for anointing prophets and kings is the one from which "Mes-

---

[42]"In Ebreo est hell vox unctio, non sonat wie man aliquas res salbt,
sed proprie ein priester und khonig salben et sacertodale et regale
nomen. Hoc latinum grecum teutonicum bringt nicht mit, sed anders
verbum, imaginor oleum rasoris. In Ebreo proprei heist, wie man die
priester und khonig hat gesalbt, die priesterlich et levitice sind ge-
weihet. . . . Christianus dicitur inde, quod unctionem habet, quod
unctus est et Messias. Haec unctio salben nihil est nisi spiritus sanctus. . . .es ist mir leyt, das wirs nicht geben konnen in aliis linguis." WA
20:676,5-17.

siah" is derived, namely, jan. R does not give the Hebrew expressions here, which Luther carefully must have unfolded, as the commentary on 1 John 2:20 leads us to assume. We see here the limits of R's capacity, who had to handle, in this situation, Greek, Hebrew and German languages, and to transfer them into his Latin shorthand system in order to preserve as much as possible. Because of this weakness, it remains to be guessed what Hebrew terms Luther spoke of when interpreting John's Greek expression, χρῖσμα (*chrisma*) (2:20), which is understood by the Vulgate as *unctio*, for which Luther used the verb form *salben* in German (to anoint). This involvement in the various languages is a good illustration of Luther's *bon mot* that the languages are the sheath in which this sword of the Spirit is contained.[43]

Luther observed Hebraisms in the text of 1 John 2:21, namely, "from the truth does not come any lie"[44]; also, in 1 John 3:15, where R has a marginal note on a Hebraism seen in the expression *vitam manentem*.[45] Again, when interpreting 1 John 3:17, Luther said, "Yet he closes his heart to his brother," and he commented, " '*Viscera*,' i.e., to close up mercy, a Hebraism."[46] Luther viewed St. John as a Hebrew who used Hebraisms in his Greek. Another Hebrew word which Luther interspersed besides *messiah* is *abba*.[47] All these observations are to be taken as signs that Luther went cautiously beyond the Vulgate to the original sources.

---

[43]WA 15:38,7-9 (LW 45:360).

[44]"Hebraismus 'Ex veritate nullum venit mendacium,' " WA 20:680,10.

[45]See note to line 15 of WA 20:710,15.

[46]WA 20:714,5.

[47]WA 20:637,11.

The lectures of October 2-14, 1527, contain several problems in terms of languages and the question of the biblical basis in Greek or Latin; there is also a Christologically relevant passage, 1 John 4:14, Christ as the Savior of the world, to be considered within the context of the passage (vs. 1-15). It was mentioned above that, among other things, R is superior to P because of the better text on 1 John 4:2-3.

Luther said that the sense of the Greek text is different from the Vulgate translation. The original Greek says μὴ ὁμολογεῖ, which Erasmus translated with "who does not confess."[48] When Luther interpreted verse 4:2, he used the Christological title *servator mundi*,[49] and when he arrived at 4:14 he spoke of *redemptor mundi*.[50] Neither expression is found in the Vulgate, which uses *salvator mundi* for the Greek original σωτήρ. Even though Luther used the Vulgate as a starting point, and then the Erasmian New Testament, in this instance Luther joins Erasmus in using the Erasmian version of this title, namely, *servator mundi*. This is no orthographical mistake, but a deliberate change from 1516, where the original Vulgate's *salvator* is used, to the edition of 1519, where *servator* is preferred. Why did R write *redemptor mundi*, while Erasmus suggested *servator mundi* (and kept it from 1519 on)? Luther, in 1529, used in his revised Vulgate the title *salvator mundi* as the original Vulgate has it, and as Erasmus had it in 1516. To be sure, there is no substantial change in

---

[48]Erasmus has replaced the Vulgate's *solvit* (he severs) with *non confitetur* in his edition.

[49]WA 20:726,5.

[50]WA 20:751,13. While the following lines 18-19 read *salvator* again and also later WA 20:753,23 and 754,22.

the meaning. All variations express what the Greek σωτήρ means. But why the switch in R from *servator* in 4:2 to *redemptor* in 4:14? I offer the following explanation.

Luther wanted to avoid, in any case, the impression that the final word on this title should be Erasmus's unusual translation *servator*. Although he initially used it, he replaced it with either *redemptor* or *salvator*. Luther might have originally quoted the Greek σωτήρ (or the German equivalent *Heyland*), which R noted as *redemptor*, a legitimate translation. Or Luther, quoting the Greek, translated it himself with *redemptor*. By quoting from Erasmus, Luther meant at the same time to criticize him for this translation. Then he mentioned the alternative expression *redemptor*. For Luther, the title *servator* did not bring out the effectiveness of Christ's coming into the flesh. Therefore, he emphasized it three times by alluding to a Greek word, *energian adventus*[51] (i.e., *efficaciam adventus*).[52] Those who do not confess Christ as the one who is efficacious for us are the ones who *sever* Christ. Ultimately, they negate that Christ is the incarnate Son of God, who was sent to save the world by giving his flesh for the world. Thus Luther objected to Erasmus because of his lack of theological insight: "To Erasmus we must respond. . . . He translated the New Testament and does not sense this."[53] This central issue will be taken up in Part Three. Here we were concerned with the textual side of the Christological title, which the conser-

---

[51]WA 20:726,10.16-17.
[52]WA 20:726,20.
[53]WA 20:728,4-6

vative Luther used in his Latin Bible edition of 1529 — *salvator mundi*, as the Vulgate has it.

Our textual criticism has shown that Luther consulted the Greek in reviewing Erasmus's Latin version. Still, the professor kept his close ties to the Vulgate version. The only question that remains is whether Luther used his German Bible.

German?

In the direct biblical quotations extant in R, there is none in German. They are all in Latin. Only at one point is there a direct reference to the German meaning of 1 John 4:10. He worked on this verse several times and finally decided to use *propiciator* in the 1529 edition of the Wittenberg Vulgate. He worked on this verse also in German during the lectures.[54] The Greek original has ἱλασμός; in the Vulgate it is *propitiatio*, which Erasmus kept also. Luther interpreted it in German with *versunung*. This is most interesting because the etymological root of it might be the old Germanic *sun* (English: son), which makes *ver-sun-ung* mean "son-making." Thus, reconciliation becomes "son-making," as done by the Son, who was sent by the Father to make all men his sons. The verse in which *versunung* occurs is, " . . . and he sent his Son for the *ver-sun-ung* (offering, reconciliation) for our sins" (4:10). As modern German has it in the form of *Versühnung/Versöhnung*, it carries the connotation of the juridicial terms, conciliation, atonement, expiation. Whatever the connotation was in Luther's mind and time, he used the German in his interpretation in 1527.

---

[54]"Nonne deusch geredt, quid est ein versunung." WA 20:743,20-21. —Jacob Grimm and Wilhelm Grimm, *Deutsches Wörterbuch*, s.v. "versöhnen."

Perhaps Luther also used German thought patterns in regard to 1 John 3:23: The Greek original has τῷ ὀνόματι; in the Vulgate it is *in nomine*, while Erasmus took (as in the Greek) the dative form *nomini*. Luther, in his Vulgate revision, kept *in nomine*, and in his German translation he remained close to the Vulgate, *das wir glewben an den namen* (that we believe in the name), which departs somewhat from the Greek or the Erasmian Latin with the dative form. In the lectures Luther is reported to have used *credere in nomen* (accusative case, but with the preposition *in*),[55] which is closer to German, than to Greek and Erasmus's Latin. In German the verb *glauben an* takes the accusative case. Therefore we may conclude that Luther used German here in the lectures when he followed neither the Vulgate's ablative form *in nomine* nor Erasmus's version, but the German idiom.

Finally, there is the matter of 1 John 5:20. The original Greek διάνοια is translated in the Vulgate with *sensus*. Erasmus was not satisfied with that and retranslated it with *mens* in his editions from 1516 on. In his annotations, the humanist explained that the meaning in Latin is *mens* or *cogitatio*.[56] What did Luther make of it? In his 1522 German translation of the Bible Luther translated literally from the Vulgate's *sensus* into German *synn* (*Sinn*). In 1527, during the lectures, according to R, he relied upon the Vulgate version.[57] Luther was aware of the problem which was raised by Erasmus and drew

---

[55]WA 20:721,22, and 722,2.

[56]"Dedit nobis sensum, id est, Mentem, sive cogitationem" (both in 1516 and in 1522, on 618).

[57]WA 20:800,4-5.

help from the German by lecturing, "Final repeti-
tions . . . and his coming gave us the *sensum, titel.*"
He understood *sensus* as *titel*. After offering his
German version, Luther continued by saying, "It is a
fine thing that he [Erasmus] says, *de mente* . . . ,"
that he suggested to read *mens*, and not "of the Holy
Spirit."[58] Over *de mente* is written *sensu* in R,[59]
which points to his understanding of *sensus* as
mens, as Erasmus had it. Then Luther reflected on it
theologically,[60] that when we have this sense/mind,
that Jesus is God's Son, who is sent for us, and that
his words are God's words, then we have the mind of
the Holy Spirit, and Christ's spirit is in us, because
we have him in our mind, take him into our mouth,
carry him with our hands, all of which are Christ's.
Therefore Christ reigns in us. After these considerations, Luther concluded, "Therefore, I like to see here
sensum quasi spiritum (sense as spirit), *verstand.*"
He took *sensus* as *spiritus* in Latin, and as *verstand*
(mind, understanding) in German. He qualified the
latter word by the addition, "which I call *fantasiam,
imaginari sublimia.*[61] This phrase must be taken in

---

[58]"Repetitiones finales: hoc est quod docuimus omnia, quod sumus ex
deo. Quomodo? Sic: ex deo sumus, quod filius dei venit in carnem et ille
veniens dedit nobis sensum, *titel*, ut cognoscamus deum verum, fein
ist, dicit de mente non spiritu sancto." WA 20:800,2-5.

[59]Cf. Note to line 5 of WA 20:800,5.

[60]WA 20:800, 6-9.

[61]"Ergo libenter video hic sensum quasi spiritum, verstand, quae dico
fantasiam, imaginari sublimia." WA 20:800,9-10. This sentence makes
sense only if one takes into consideration that Luther spoke here as a
rhetorician, who used the term *fantasia* as *imaginatio*. See on this
issue Klaus Dockhorn, "Luthers Glaubensbegriff und die Rhetorik. Zu
Gerhard Ebelings Buch 'Einführung in die theologische Sprachlehre' "; *Linguistica Biblica* 21-22 (1973):29.

its rhetorical meaning of "mental picture, appearance, imagination." That is why Luther added to *fantasia* the synonym *imaginari sublimia*, to clarify *fantasia* as "to imagine sublime things." Thus, the Greek διάνοια of 5:20 is the "human mind," not the Holy Spirit. The human mind is given to us so that with it we recognize the true God (5:20).

Conclusion

We have investigated the available sources of Luther's lectures on 1 John according to the historical critical method of textual criticism and have found Rörer's notes to be the most precise, as they are generally recognized in Luther research today. We found the so-called *scholia* in WA 48 not to be the alleged preparatory notes of the professor, but suspect them to be an anonymous Saxon student's notes in fragmentary form. We also tried to find an answer to the neglected question of which Bible the professor utilized. We did find some, though very little, evidence of his German translation's influence on the interpretation of 1 John in 1527. We found more evidence of reference to Erasmus's edition of 1519, and we could establish the thesis that Luther's starting point was primarily the Vulgate, which he knew virtually by heart. It was shown that Luther's Vulgate revision of 1 John did not have any effect on the lectures, because at that time he was working on the Vulgate revision of the Old Testament in the light of the Hebrew Bible. We saw that Luther also identified Hebraisms in the Johannine text. Luther's use of Greek, however, was minimal in these lectures.

Whether Luther was aware of it or not, he heeded Erasmus's warning, which he expressed in his *methodus*, that there are three languages — Greek, Latin and Hebrew — without which it would be stupid, even impious, to deal with the mysteries of theology, because it would mean to touch the Holy with unclean hands.[62] Luther knew his own limitations in Greek. Toward the end of his life, he said at table, "If I were young, I would want to study perfectly the Greek language, and I would enter other annotations."[63] Apparently, it was the older Luther's wish to supersede Erasmus and his annotations to the biblical text. He also wanted to replace his own expositions of previous years where he had depended upon Erasmus. Luther's aversion to Erasmus increased considerably in mid-career, after the controversy over the freedom and bondage of the will. In another table talk of 1533 he said, "Erasmus sticks to his own affairs, that is, to heathen business. He doesn't care about ours, that is, theological affairs."[64] The reason for this animosity must be sought in Erasmus's textual criticism, his linguistic contributions and translation which are always an involvement in theological issues; and it is Erasmus's theology which Luther did not share. It is apparent, then, that any translation is also an interpretation, an insight, which must not be taken lightly.

---

[62]Cf. A. Bludau, *Die beiden ersten Erasmus-Ausgaben des Neues Testaments und ihre Gegner*, 408.

[63]"Wenn ich jung were, so wolt ich Graecam Linguam perfecte studirn, so dass ichs kundte, und wolte andere annotationes drein machen." WA TR 5:310,18-20 (no. 5670) — Said in 1544.

[64]WA TR 1:206,16-17 (no. 466), (LW 54:77).

It was in Luther's mid-career when he came to the conclusion that the languages are decisive for the preservation of the gospel: "And let us be sure of this: We will not long preserve the gospel without the languages. The languages are the sheath in which this sword of the Spirit (Eph. 6:17) is contained."[65]

---

[65]"Und last uns das gesagt seyn, Das wyr das Euangelion nicht wol werden erhallten on die sprachen. Die sprachen sind die scheyden, darynn dis messer des geysts stickt. Sie sind der schreyn, darynnen man dis kleinod tregt." (To the Councilmen of Germany 1524). WA 15:38, 7-9 (LW 45:360). See Bornkamm, *Luther in Mid-Career*, 140.

PART TWO

THE HISTORICAL CONTEXT
OF LUTHER'S LECTURES

INTRODUCTION TO PART TWO

What is the *Sitz im Leben* of our most reliable source, R? As it was said in the beginning, entering Luther's work is like entering an "ocean." This observation also holds true for the context of Reformation history, including the mental world of Luther the professor. So again, limits must be set in order to keep us from getting lost. In this second part, we will concentrate on how the Johannine lectures relate to Luther's academic life in mid-career; then, on how they relate to his personal life and his relationship to contemporary events in the world and in the church of 1527. At one point, however, we will find it helpful to dip into the wider historical context to recall Luther's relationship to Bernard of Clairvaux, insofar as it had an effect on Luther's lectures on the First Epistle of John.

CHAPTER 3

THE PLACE OF LUTHER'S JOHANNINE LECTURES WITHIN HIS ACADEMIC WORK IN MID-CAREER

Between Easter 1521 and spring 1524 Luther did not lecture at all.[1] An array of other immediate concerns prevented him from resuming his normal university duties after his return from the Wartburg.[2] From February 1522 to the beginning of the year 1524, still a friar, he conducted a private course on Deuteronomy in his friary. The Wittenberg pastor, Bugenhagen, was a participant.[3] On March 23, 1524, Luther wrote to his employer, the Elector Frederick, that he was hesitant to resume lecturing, because the Bible translation demanded his primary attention. Besides that, he felt that in his absence Melanchthon's lectures on the Bible had replaced him adequately.[4]

---

[1]Cf. Heinrich Boehmer, *Martin Luther: Road to Reformation*, 118.

[2]Cf. Heinrich Bornkamm, *Luther in Mid-Career*, 229.

[3]Cf. ibid. 241, the *Annotationes* on Deuteronomy were published in 1524: WA 14:489-753.

[4]Cf. WA Br 3:258,10; see H. Bornkamm, *Luther in Mid-Career*, 87, n. 67 (LW 49:74-76). Melanchthon had lectured on 2 Cor in 1522, on John in 1523, cf. R. Stupperich, *Melanchthon*, 173, trans. Robert H. Fischer (Philadelphia: Westminister Press, 1966).

Apparently, Luther was ready to give up his position as professor of the Bible in favor of assuming the work of a free-lance writer and translator of the Bible. He recognized his colleague Melanchthon's potential as professor of Greek at the University. But Melanchthon refused to lecture in theology. Thus Luther was compelled to resume his biblical courses. When Luther officially returned to his chair in May 1524, he gave lectures on the Minor Prophets until early in 1526.[5] In 1527, he published a German commentary on Zechariah, and also his sermons on Genesis.[6] In the summer and autumn of 1526 he gave a course on Ecclesiastes Salomonis, which was printed from Rörer's superb notes in 1532.[7] Afterwards Luther had intended to continue his exposition on the prophets, for that was where his translation into German stood at the time.

On May 4, 1527, Luther announced to Wenceslaus Link his plan to lecture on Isaiah.[8] The university had been temporarily relocated to Jena in August 1527 because of the plague in Wittenberg, so Luther postponed the course on Isaiah until May 1528.[9] The postponement was made because the Prophet's text was so large that Luther did not foresee a possibility

---

[5]Cf. S. Raeder, "Luther als Ausleger und Übersetzer der Heiligen Schrift," *Festgabe 1983*, 253ff.

[6]Cf. H. Bornkamm, *Luther in Mid-Career*, 250, 237, n. 42.

[7]Cf. ibid. 564-5.

[8]"Lecturus simul Jesaiam ne otiosus sim," WA Br 4:198,9, where the misleading note is found that Luther had broken off the started lectures on Isaiah. Here, or with the editor's introduction (WA 20:592), must lie the source of J. Pelikan's mistaken statement that Luther "had to interrupt his lectures after an outbreak of the plague," LW 30:xi.

[9]Cf. H. Bornkamm, *Luther in Mid-Career*, 575.

of finishing it during a time when he was so severely ill, as his biographer explains, adding that the plague-induced departure of most of the students for Jena induced him to select a "less inclusive book,"[10] the First Letter of John, for his remaining faithful students. We note that the course on 1 John was another private lecture series (like the one on Deuteronomy) given in the Augustinian friary, which remained Luther's home after he left the Order and married Katherine.[11] This was the first New Testament text within a decade which Luther treated in an academic course. The last one had been on Hebrews in 1517-18. Now, in the summer of 1527, he selected John instead of a short Pauline letter or some other text from the Old Testament. It was the only course by Luther ever taught on a Johannine text. The specific lecture plan can be reconstructed from R's dating, as follows:[12]

Week 1:

19 Aug.: 1:1. 20 Aug.: 1:2-4. 21 Aug.: 1:5-7

Week 2:

26 Aug.: 1:8-9

Week 3:

2 Sept.: 1:10-2:1. 3 Sept.: 2:1-2. 4 Sept.: 2:3-6

---

[10]Cf. ibid. 567.

[11]Cf. ibid. 256.

[12]Cf. G. Koffmane's Introduction, WA 20:592 (LW 30:x-xi); however, Luther did not lecture 28, but 29 times between August 19 and November 7, 1527, altogether, eleven weeks. He regularly lectured on Mondays, Tuesdays, and Wednesdays. There are four exceptions. In the second week he only lectured on Monday, August 26; the sixth week, September 25-27, he spent at Torgau; in the ninth week, he missed Tuesday, October 15; the last week shows a complete change, when he lectured from Tuesday to Thursday, because of the funeral of Rörer's wife, who had died on November 2.

Week 4:
9 Sept.: 2:7-11. 10 Sept.: 2:11-14. 11 Sept.: 2:15-17
Week 5:
16 Sept.: 2:18-19. 17 Sept.: 2:20-23. 18 Sept.: 2:23-27
Week 6:
23 Sept.: 2:28-3:3. 24 Sept.: 3:3-9
Week 7:
30 Sept.: 3:10-17. 1 Oct.: 3:18-23. 2 Oct.: 4:1-2
Week 8:
7 Oct.*: 4:3-6. 8 Oct.: 4:7-10. 9 Oct.: 4:10-12
Week 9:
14 Oct.: 4:13-16. 16 Oct.: 4:17-21
Week 10:**
28 Oct.: 5:1-3. 29 Oct.: 5:4-6. 30 Oct.: 5:6-8
Week 11:
5 Nov.: 5:9-12. 6 Nov.: 5:13-15. 7 Nov.: 5:16-21

Some years later Luther will preach sermons on
1 John which will be published in 1533.[13] For the
following years of the 1520s, the controversy over the
Eucharist will be the major issue with its climax at
the Marburg Colloquy where Luther and Zwingli
could not reach an agreement on this sacrament.

---

*conjecture, cf. WA 20:730, n. 1.

**there were no lectures given in the week of October 21.

[13]Cf. Etliche schöne Predigten aus der ersten Epistel S. Johannis von
der Liebe. WA 36:416-477 (R and printed version).

CHAPTER 4

MID-LIFE CRISIS IN THE TENTH YEAR OF THE REFORMATION

An analysis of Luther's personal situation would have to include his mental world as well, which could fill volumes. Obviously, this cannot be provided here.[1] We will concentrate, therefore, on the immediate personal situation in 1527, the year of the Johannine lectures, but not by using these lectures as a "backdrop"[2] for the anxious months of 1527, as H. Bornkamm suggests. Rather, we will consider these months of illness, of spiritual temptations, and of aggravations by the enthusiasts and other "heretics" as the *Sitz im Leben* of these lectures.

Luther chose 1 John not only because it is shorter than the text of Isaiah, which he had planned to interpret originally, but also because Luther was impressed by the Christological essence of this epistle. John directed his readers to Christ in the flesh as opposed to Antichrist. Its radiating consolation and strength was needed in times of crises, both personal and world-political.

---

[1] Cf. H. Bornkamm, *Luther's World of Thought*, trans. M. H. Bertram (St. Louis: Concordia Publishing House, 1958).

[2] H. Bornkamm, *Luther in Mid-Career*, 568.

It is my intention, in this chapter, to demonstrate the personal situation in which Luther and his friends found themselves, and to show how 1 John could have been and was of great help at that time when temptations and troubles of conscience were most severe.[3] In the letter of January 13, 1527, Luther wrote to Spalatin that he had a sudden problem with his blood circulation.[4] He also suffered from kidney stones. On April 22 he had to interrupt his sermon because of dizziness and faintness. On July 6 he fell unconscious; this attack left him desperate.[5] He called for his pastor, Bugenhagen, for final confession and absolution, because he expected to die. On August 2 he wrote to Melanchthon, "I have been thrown more than a whole week into death and tossed back and forth in hell." Luther felt his whole body afflicted and all limbs shaking. "I have lost Christ totally and have been shaken by the floods and storms of desperation and of blasphemy against God."[6] Shortly thereafter he began his lectures on

---

[3]Cf. R. H. Bainton, *Here I Stand*, 359-62.

G. Wendelborn speaks of *Angina pectoris* and says that the second half of the year 1527 was the climax of Luther's corporal-spiritual sufferings, cf. *Martin Luther*, 265. The consolation and strength which Luther apparently found in 1 John is of significance and will be taken up again in the section on Luther's "orational approach" in Chapter 8.

[4]"Nuper me subito sanguinis coagulo circum precordia angustiatum, peneque exanimatum fuisse." WA Br 4:160,18-19. (". . . that recently I have been anguished by a blood clot around the chest, and that I almost died.")

[5]"Ego quoque nudius tercius repentina syncope ita corripiebar, ut desperans prorsus arbitrarer me exstinctum iri inter manus uxoris & amicorum, ita viribus destituebar omnibus subito." In the same letter Luther mentions rumors of pestilence: "Pestem apud nos esse rumor est." Letter to Spalatin of July 10, 1527. WA Br 4:221,8-10.

[6]Cf. W. von Loewenich, *Martin Luther*, 359; WA Br 4:226,9-11

1 John. In this situation Luther found in 1 John
medicine for himself and others. It is no surprise,
then, that he applied medical language in his exposition of the text. Elsewhere, he thought of another
Johannine text (3:16) as "best prescription."[7]

August 19, 1527, the day Luther began his course
on 1 John, he wrote to Spalatin and asked that he
would pray for his recovery, if it be the Redeemer's
will.[8] Luther reported in this letter that the university was closed because of the pestilence and that it
had been moved to Jena. Then the professor told
about those who remained with him in the midst of
this monster of Satan, this pestilence. Those who are
known by name are Pastor Bugenhagen (Pomeranus) and the chaplains, Rörer and Johannes Mantel.[9] Rörer definitely was among his students, as we
know; another course participant could have been
Johannes Mantel. Interestingly, this letter, written
on the day of the first lecture, expresses the same
idea as the introduction to the course: "Christ is with
us."[10] Luther also told Spalatin that he had not yet
read the writings of the enthusiasts, nor those of
Zwingli.[11]

Besides Luther's personal problems, he had theological difficulties with Zwingli and Oecolampadius.

---

[7]"Mein bests recept ist geschriben Johannis 3.: Sic Deus dilexit mundum etc. Das ist das best, das ich hab." WA TR 1:111,27-28 (no. 266).

[8]"Ora, queso, pro me, ut & ego plane revalescem, si est voluntas Dei
salvatoris." WA Br 4:232,2-3.

[9]Cf. ibid. 232,9-15, line 25: "Itaque Pomeranus & ego hic soli sumus
cum Capellanis." cf. n. 19 on 233.

[10]"Christus autem adest, ne soli simus"; ibid. lines 25-6. In the lecture
notes (R) we find: "quod adsit dominus"; WA 20:599,12. Luther does
not mention in this letter that on this given day he started his course.

[11]Cf. WA Br 4:233,31-2.

In the letter of August 20, 1527, the second day of his course, Luther wrote that he was waiting for the text by the Sacramentarians (Zwingli, et al.).[12] One might even go so far as to say that Luther selected these lectures on 1 John, furthermore, because of his struggles with the sects.[13] This could very well be because Luther saw how the controversy over the sacrament of the Lord's Supper was intimately connected to Christology. Belief in Christ's real presence in the Supper is a consequence of faith in the incarnation, the test question in 1 John 4:2. Luther's Christology stands in the tradition of classical Christology. Zwingli, in contrast, stressed the separation of the two natures.[14]

In a letter of August 21 to Agricola, Luther again mentioned the Sacramentarians as being "furies."[15] This fighting mood is reflected in the lectures when Luther felt he was a second Job attacked by Satan.[16] His letter continued:

> My hope is that my own battle is of service to many, although there is no evil that my sins have not deserved. Yet my life consists in this, that I know and boast that I have taught the Word of Christ purely and to the salvation of many. This burns up Satan, so that he would

[12]Cf., WA Br 4:234.

[13]Cf. Christof Windhorst, "Luther and the 'Enthusiasts.' Theological Judgments in his Lecture on the First Epistle of St. John (1527)"; trans. Dorothea Woydaek, *The Journal of Religious History* (Sydney) 9 (1977):339-348, here 341.

[14]Cf. G. Wendelborn, *Martin Luther*, 302.

[15]"furias", WA Br 4:235,7.

[16]Ibid. lines 9-10: "posuitque me Dominus illi, velut alterum Hiob ...";
WA 20:599,2-8.

> kill and destroy me along with the Word. That
> is why I have not suffered at the hands of the
> tyrants of this world, while others have been
> killed and burned for Christ and have per-
> ished; I am buffeted all the more in the spirit
> by the prince of this world.[17]

Luther spoke of the martyrdom of evangelical Christians here. He had heard about such casualties at
Halle, where the congregation lost its preacher Georg
Winkler, who was murdered on April 23, 1527.[18] Luther was ready to write them a letter of consolation,
but he said that first he had to recover his health.[19]

Also in August, when Luther reflected on the fact
that he himself had not been burned, one of his
former students at Wittenberg, Leonhard Keiser of
Bavaria, was burned for his evangelical conviction.[20]

After Luther had written to the people at Halle[21] on
September 17, he also wrote an overdue answer to the
pastors of Breslau. Earlier, in 1525, pestilence had
erupted at Breslau, and the question was posed to
Luther, whether it was permitted to flee from im-
pending death. Luther had been unable to answer,
but now during the time of pestilence at Wittenberg
he forced himself to answer them, apologizing for the

---

[17]WA Br 4:235,12-14 (no. 1132).

[18]Cf. n. 2. in WA Br 4:239.

[19]"Ich bin ja freilich willens, wo mir Gott Gnade verleihet, dass ich zu
Kräften komme." WA Br 4:238,1-2.

[20]Cf. G. Wendelborn, *Martin Luther*, 266. When Keiser was impris-
oned, March 7, 1527, Luther sent him a letter of consolation, dated May
20. WA 23:473-74.

[21]Cf. WA Br 4:256 (no. 1151).

delay. Luther's pastoral conclusion was that to flee from dying and death in order to save one's life is naturally implanted by God and thus not forbidden. But not everybody is allowed to run away from an epidemic. Preachers, official persons, such as a mayor, a judge, a physician, a policeman, are not allowed to flee, nor are neighbors to sick persons who otherwise would not have any help.[22] This same issue is treated in his September 30 lecture.[23]

Besides being a pastor to pastors, Luther was very much concerned about the religious situation of the people, especially at Wittenberg and the surrounding region, where official visitations of the parishes were taking place during these days. Luther must have been very much disappointed with the Wittenberg people. When he lectured on September 4 on 1 John 2:3, he felt compelled to relate this text to the local situation: "As it happened in the apostle's time, so we see today many preachers who teach excellently, but who are avaricious and seek glory, and Satan seems to reign more powerful than before, when people were nurtured with the nausea of the monks. But now the devil is at work again with double efforts, so we want to despair. Satan is the reason that so few people in this city have accepted the gospel; but, if in this city there were two who seriously accept the gospel, we did not teach in vain."[24] Luther's disappointment

[22]Cf. WA 23:323-373.

[23]Cf. WA 20:712f.

[24]"tempore apostoli fuit, videmus hodie multos praedictores. . . . Prius nausea monachorum alita. . . . tum desperare volumus. . . . Si in ista civitate duo sunt, qui serio suscipiunt Euangelium, non frustra docuimus, qui pii nos etc." WA 20:642,10-19 — Let us be reminded that the Wittenberg chaplain and, perhaps, his colleague Mantel, were Luther's listeners.

reached the climax in 1530 when he refused to preach to them at all any longer.[25] The parish visitations revealed not much of a better situation elsewhere. But as Luther reported in November to Nikolaus Hausmann, the visitations will be continued.[26]

Luther's personal problems did not prevent him from being pastorally concerned. His pastoral correspondence included a letter to the monk Severinus Austriacus. On October 6, 1527, Luther wrote to him and counseled him about leaving the monastery. Luther recommended that he leave the monastery.[27] Two days later, during the lecture of October 8, Luther declared, "A monk who is converted by the gospel cannot be kept in the papacy, and such a person says, 'they [monasteries] are mere manure.' "[28]

Three months after his great spiritual attack, Luther wrote a letter on October 8 to Michael Stiefel stating that he had been ill bodily and spiritually for three months. That means that Luther still felt this attack.[29] That he had not yet recovered he indicated

---

[25]Cf. H. Junghans, "Luther in Wittenberg," *Festgabe 1983*, 21. Luther was also disappointed that not a single son of Wittenberg was among his students. Cf. H. Junghans, "Wittenberg und Luther — Luther und Wittenberg," *Freiburger Zeitschrift für Philosophie und Theologie*, 25 (1978):104-119.

[26]Cf. letter of 7 November, WA Br 4:277 (no. 1166). The visitations revealed chaos in the land, as states Ch. Windhorst, "Luther and the Enthusiasts." — The visitations took priority over the course on 1 John; therefore Luther went to the respective conference at Torgau on September 25, 1527 and did not lecture. See Luther's lecture plan in Chapter 3. On Torgau, see H. Bornkamm, *Luther in Mid-career*, 493-95.

[27]Cf. WA Br 4:259-263 (no. 1155).

[28]"mera stercora," WA 20:742,16-17. Cf. Monasteries are called "myths" with the words of 2 Peter 1:16, "merae," WA 20:744,13-14.

[29]"Nam ferme tres menses langui non tam corpore quam animo, ita ut nihil aut parum scripserim; sic me Satan cribravit" (cf. Luke 22:31) WA Br 4:263,8-10.

to Jonas on the 19th of October.[30] On October 27 he sent a letter to Melanchthon who was with the University at Jena and said that he was troubled with "sadness of the spirit."[31] In the same letter he spoke about Zwingli and said that this Swiss reformer was most worthy of a holy hatred, a topic Luther dealt with also in his lecture.[32]

Luther still felt ill in late November, several weeks after he had finished the lectures on 1 John. On November 29 he wrote to Brisger that he was still sick and he asked that he pray for him, because he felt tossed back and forth between Christ and Satan.[33] In December, he still did not feel free from anxiety and temptations, but he did not want to be liberated from them if having them was to the glory of God. Luther thought he had so much trouble because he wrote so many books which offended the devil, and therefore Satan was so mad at him.[34] On December 30, 1527, Luther wrote to Jonas that he still suffered from temptations, but the pestilence was gone now from Wittenberg.[35]

But on the last day of the year 1527 Luther reported to J. Propst in Bremen that he was healthy in body, while he remained tempted from the outside world and inside from the devil.[36] He added that he

[30]Cf. WA Br 4:269,11ff (no. 1160).

[31]"tristitiae spiritu bene vexato," WA Br 4:272,27 (n. 1162).

[32]"Zwinglium credo sancto dignissimum odio," WA Br 4:272, 38 (no. 1162); cf. WA 20:621,8 (on original sin), and WA 20:797,7.

[33]"infirmus sum," WA Br 4:288-89,11 (no. 1175).

[34]"Ego quidem tentatione mea nondum sum liberatus . . . "; WA Br 4:299,13-14 (no. 1183).

[35]Cf. WA Br 4:312,3-9 (no. 1191).

[36]"Qui corpore sanus, forisa toto mundo, intus a diabolo patitur"; WA Br 4:313,11 (no. 1193).

would write for the first time against the Anabaptists, but that it was the last time he would write against the Sacramentarians.[37] We observe again how closely related the religious problems are with his personal well-being. On New Year's Day 1528 Luther let G. Wiskamp know that the temptation he suffered through was by far the strongest one since his youth, but Christ so far had triumphed.[38] In the new year, 1528, Luther does not mention any spiritual challenges in his letters any more.

During the months of "depression," as his personal situation is also called,[39] which housed the strongest temptations he had ever experienced, many problems arose which demanded answers. One of them must have been about the "reformation" after ten years of work. I single out this issue here because it gives me the opportunity to illuminate the "backdrop" of Luther's Johannine lectures, which came to an end around the time of all Saints Day 1527. The "backdrop" certainly includes Luther's mid-life crisis as we described it. Apparently Luther was close to desperation at times over the reformation movement. This conclusion comes as no surprise when we consider that Luther had become an outlaw, was being attacked from all sides, and found

---

[37]Cf. ibid. lines 12-15.

[38]"Verum est hanc tentationem esse multo grauissimam et mihi etiam ab adolescentia non incognitam." WA Br 4:319,5-6 (no. 1197). One may ask whether the disappearance of the temptations had to do with the completion of the challenging lectures on 1 John. An answer is probably impossible to give, but combined with the controversy over the Eucharist, it could very well be.

[39]Cf. H. A. Oberman, *Martin Luther: Mensch zwischen Gott und Teufel*, 336.

himself involved in controversies with Zwingli, Karlstadt, Müntzer, Erasmus and countless other leaders of his day. He preached only once during the time when he lectured on 1 John.[40] An indication of his wanting to retire from it all is the fact that he said, "If I stay alive I'll become a gardener," once in July and again in December.[41]

Ten years after the publication of the theses on indulgences there was a gathering in Luther's home, the former monastery. Luther described this private party in a letter dated All Saints Day 1527 to his friend Amsdorf in Magdeburg. At the end of this letter he wrote, "We needed each other's consolation," and, "We drank." Apparently, they were well aware of the tenth anniversary of what they called the "crushing of the indulgences": "we drank in memory of them in this hour and consoled one another."[42] In the same letter to his friend Luther mentioned the desolate religious situation. "If I," Luther wrote, "were at the moment stronger spiritually, I would be able to give an answer to the enemies of the sacrament,"[43] by which he alluded to the controversy over the Lord's Supper with Zwingli. In the same letter, he described his living quarters as having become a hospital.[44]

---

[40]It was the sermon of October 13 on Leviticus 19. WA 25:427-29.

[41]Cf. H. Bornkamm, *Luther in Mid-Career*, 412-13, n. 57.

[42]"Wittenbergae die Omnium Sanctorum, anno decimo Indulgentiarum conculcatarum, quarum memoria hac hora bibimus utrique consolati, 1527." WA Br 4:275,25-27 (no. 1164); cf. WA TR 2:467. See also H. A. Oberman, "Martin Luther: Vorläufer der Reformation," *Verifikationen, Festschrift Gerhard Ebeling*, 114.

[43]"Cupio respondere Sacramentariis, sed nisi fortior fiam animo, nihil possum." WA Br 4:275,9-10.

[44]"In domo mea coepi esse hospitale"; ibid., line 12.

In addition to his own temptations, his weakened body and mind, his need to join the debate over various issues, he found that the pestilence had entered his house. Moreover, his wife would soon give birth to their second child (Elizabeth, born December 10, 1527).[45] His little Hans was teething at the time."[46] Rörer's wife (the Rörers at that time were living with the Luthers, as were also the Bugenhagens)[47] was dying of the plague. The next day, November 2, she passed away, and shortly before this time she had given birth to a dead child.[48] This tragedy in his trusted assistant's life affected the professor at least as much as, if not more than, it did Georg Rörer himself. Luther wrote that this death almost caused his own. "I almost died on Saturday, when chaplain Georg's wife passed away."[49] The mourning period must have continued through Monday, because the lectures were rescheduled for Tuesday to Thursday, instead of the regular Monday to Wednesday.[50]

On the last lecture day Luther wrote to N. Hausmann about the circumstances at home and that he

---

[45]Cf. ibid., n. 10.

[46]"dicitur esse violentia dentium"; ibid., line 16. Not long before, Luther also had had problems with his teeth or gums — which might have been the reason why he did not lecture in the following week. WA Br 4:269,14-15. "Accessit ante duos dies satis vehemens dolor gingivarum [gums]."

[47]Cf. WA Br 4:276,9-28 (no. 1165), where the city pastor's sickness is reported also in order to illustrate that the house had become a hospital: "hodie cacator purgandus factus" (line 28), the pastor had taken a purgative.

[48]Cf. ibid., nn. 12 and 13.

[49]"Paene fui perditus die Sabbathi, cum abortiret uxor Georgii Capellani" (Letter of 4 November 1527 to Jonas). WA 4:176,3-4 (no. 1165).

[50]See above, Chapter 3.

should pray for him, because he was despairing over his son's illness, the pregnancy of his wife — his own *temptatio*. He was in anguish for many months because of these tempests, and in spirit he had grown faint-hearted. But it was Christ's will.[51]

Without his overwhelming strong faith in the saving God, Luther could not have survived his extraordinary mid-life crisis. Luther's Christocentric piety best characterizes his mental state; it was the test and the application of his theological principle, "Christ alone." He not only applied it to his own life, but also to the practice of public piety which had led to the "crushing of the indulgences" ten years before. For Luther the battle between Christ and Antichrist was a real battle, as he indicated in his letters. Luther saw this struggle also at work in the world political arena of 1527, to which we will now turn our attention.

---

[51]"Ego tempestate & pusillanimitate spiritus nunc multis mensibus angor, Christo sic volente." WA Br 4:277,11-12 (no. 1165).

CHAPTER 5

CRISIS IN WORLD POLITICS

The German *Landsknechte* invested the pope with the face and attributes of a war-like Antichrist, living in the Roman Babel. The imperial soldiers began to recognize the pope as the emperor's bitterest enemy. The Emperor Charles's move against the pope in 1527 coincided with Luther's anti-papalism. "Imperial loyalty, Spanish pride, Protestant passion, hunger and want, . . . all these contradictory emotions blazed up together into a frenzied hatred for the rich and vicious city of Rome."[1] Among the imperial soldiers, it seems, were Lutheran lansquenets, led by Frunsberg, who occupied the Vatican. Some recently uncovered graffiti from that time include the name "Luther."[2]

For Melanchthon, the humanist, this Sack of Rome was shocking: "Nothing new, except for rumors about the capture of Rome," he wrote in a letter. "I would wish them false for many reasons, but primarily out of fear for the libraries, which have no equal anywhere in the world."[3]

---

[1]Karl Brandi, *The Emperor Charles V. The Growth and Destiny of a Man and of a World-Empire*, trans. C. V. Wedgwood, 2d printing (Oxford: Allen Press, 1949), 270.

[2]Cf. André Chastel, *The Sack of Rome, 1527* (Princeton University Press, 1983), 92.

[3]"Novi nihil habemus praeter rumores de capta Roma, quos optarim vanos esse cum ob alias multas causas, tum quia, metuo bibliothecis, quae nullo in loco totius orbis terrarum locupletiores sunt quam ibi."

Luther, the theologian, also reacted to the Sack of Rome. In his letter of July 13, 1527, to Nicolaus Hausmann, he wrote, "Rome is devastated miserably together with the pope."[4]

The destruction of the papal Rome must have been an eschatologically decisive event for Luther, for he spoke of it during his lectures on 1 John, which refers to the Antichrist. Remarkably, the immediate context of the passage (1 John 4:3,4) is of an eschatological nature. Luther, in expounding this passage, saw the spirit of the Antichrist embodied in the pope; this spirit has obtained its reign under the pope:

> The pope's laws are more carefully observed than God's. Priests like to get involved with whores. They are arrogant. Nobody punishes a priest for these sins. Only for the haircut [*rasura*] as such he is praised; this is that the pope is feared more than God. . . . The Antichrist's reign is supposed to have something to do with religion, because "it is exalted" or "it is venerated" [2 Thess 2:4]. Is it not true that he grabs all goods? Is not the pope the true cult? The cult of Christ is to believe, to love the neighbor, to carry the cross, (but) he is far above that. . . . [5]

And Luther added,

> It is not allowed to teach the pure faith unless by the pope's explicit authority. Therefore the

---

CR 1:869 (no. 445). This letter to Reiffenstein is dated "Die Jovis post Exaudi" (6 June 1527).

[4]"Roma vastata est cum papa miserabiliter . . . "; WA Br 4:222,9 (LW 49:167-69).

[5]WA 20:731,12-20.

> Antichrist deals with the cult and with reli-
> gion, so that he comes out as the superior. And
> when he comes to ruling, he is right there! Now
> I hope that they are destroyed, etc.[6]

With this last remark on "destruction," Luther was
referring to the Sack of Rome.

It is important to realize that for Luther the question of eschatology was not simply a question of time
in terms of dating the end-time, but a question of the
"quality of doctrine," as he explained in his September 16 exposition of 1 John 2:18.[7] Thus, when
dealing with the destruction of the papal Rome in the
eschatological context of 1 John 4:4, Luther dealt
with the sects that had risen. On the same September
16 Melanchthon wrote to Luther and Bugenhagen
from Jena that he had received news about the "new
Manichees and Arians in Austria."[8] Also on that
day, when lecturing on 2:18, Luther spoke of the last
hour and of the sects. During this same lecture on
2:18, Luther for the first time mentioned the Arians
as opponents of the divinity, and the Manichees as
opponents of the humanity (of Christ). Likewise,
"our own" (sectarians) are against the "flesh of
Christ," which they consider useless, and also
against the spoken word; these are partisans of the

---

[6]"Non licet puram fidem docere nisi concessa autoritate a papa. Ergo
Antichristus ghet cum cultu et religione umb, ita ut superet. Et quando
venit in regnum so ist er vorhanden. Iam spero eos in destructione
etc.," WA 20:732,3-5.

[7]"Sed appellatur novissima hora non a brevitate temporis sed a quali-
tate doctrinae," WA 20:668,4-5.

[8]"nouos in Austria Manicheos, nouos Arrianos," WA Br 4:249,2-3 (no.
1145).

Antichrist.[9] Interestingly, Melanchthon's letter of that same day informs Luther and Bugenhagen that the answers by Zwingli and Oecolampadius had arrived.[10] Here we see Luther correlating in his lectures the latest news with his interpretation of the biblical text. Later, while expounding on 1 John 4:4, Luther again connected the subject of the Antichrist with the sects and heresies, as he had done with reference to 2:18. When John said that the Antichrist already is in this world, Luther applied it to his own day:

> "Already in the world" is of great significance; with this he claims men, heresies, sects: all are included in this word, "world." Yet as much as this spirit is in the world, it cannot hurt you. Your light is the true light. "You have conquered"; you are stronger than they who are so robust. Great words, simply expressed, because in the Christian doctrine the smallest and the least part remains.... it is necessary to console yourselves with these words, because the opposite is apparent, namely, that they appear as victors, we as the conquered.[11]

The apocalyptic-eschatological application of the Johannine text to the contemporary scene represents a strong conviction on the part of Luther. Three

---

[9]"Ariani contra divinitatem, Manichaei contra humanitatem ut nostri contra carnem Christi, quam inutilem et verbum vocale, das sind partiales Antichristi." WA 20:669,6-8.

[10]WA Br 4:250,21 (no. 1145).

[11]WA 20:732,7-19, where Luther adds (lines 22-733,1), "So it was in John's times. And whenever a heresy rises, the greater part belongs to the heretics and not to Christians."

years later (in 1530) and again in 1546 Luther stated in the preface to the book of Revelation that the destruction described in Revelation 18 is underway and such a great splendor falls to the ground. For Rome had to be plundered and to be stormed by her own protector (the emperor) at the beginning of the end-time destruction.[12]

In the preface of a new 1528 edition of an anonymous fifteenth-century Wycliffite-Hussite oriented commentary on the book of Revelation, Luther repeated his polemic against the pope as the Antichrist, and again he referred to the Sack of Rome. He declared that he wrote this preface in order to show everyone that he was not the first one to interpret the papacy in this way.[13] In this preface, written in May 1527 and published in 1528 (H. U. Hofmann), Luther joined the anti-papal tradition of the late middle ages.

News of the *sacco di Roma* spread throughout the world. What now? Was Wittenberg, as "the evangelical Rome," the next target in the war plan of the emperor? This thought might have very well been on the mind of the elector, who had protected the out-

---

[12]"Im XVIII. gehet nu an solche Verstörung, und gehet die herrliche grosse pracht zu boden, und hören auff die Stifftreuber, und Pfründendiebe, die Cortisanen. Denn auch Rom darumb hat müssen geplündert, und durch jren eigen schutzherrn gestürmet werden, zum anfang der endlichen verstörung." WA DB 7:417,18-20 (no. 1546) (LW 35:399-411).

[13]Cf. WA 26:121-24, here lines 1-3 of 124: "ut orbi notum faceremus, nos non esse primos, qui Papatum pro Antichristi regno interpretentur"; lines 14-15 of 124: Papam tamen (sicut est) Antichristum et recte et vere pronunciat. See Hans-Ulrich Hofmann, *Luther und die Johannesapokalypse* (Tübingen, Mohr: 1982), 331-32. See also, WA 20:622,14 on Nicolaus Panormitanus.

lawed Luther in his territory. Already in 1526 he began to surround Wittenberg with a new defense wall.[14] Luther did not think much of this kind of fortification and military strategy. Instead, in these days, Luther composed the famous hymn, *A Mighty Fortress Is Our God!*[15] Luther's Christocentrism permeates this "battle song." It is generally agreed that it was composed in the autumn of 1527,[16] but it is generally forgotten that this is the time when Luther was preparing and delivering his Johannine lectures. In their search for the biblical texts that influenced this composition, scholars seem to have overlooked the most obvious one, the explicit theme of the battle between Christ and Antichrist in 1 John. The essential message of the hymn is the enmity between Christ and the devil with his allies. This theme is visible throughout the Johannine lectures. In fact, the last strophe lists the enemies: hell, devil, rebels, world, flesh, sin and death — the same ones noted at the beginning of Luther's course on 1 John![17]

---

[14]Cf. H. Junghans, "Wittenberg und Luther — Luther und Wittenberg," *Freiburger Zeitschrift für Philosophie und Theologie*, 25 (1978):104-119.

[15]Cf. ibid.

[16]Cf. Martin Brecht, "Zum Verständnis von Luthers Lied 'ein fest Burg,' " *ARG* 70 (1979):106-121, where Brecht refers to Luther's lectures on Isaiah, Zecharia, et al., but not at all to his lectures on 1 John.

[17]Cf. WA 20:599,3.

CHAPTER 6

BERNARD'S INFLUENCE ON LUTHER IN MID-CAREER

In Part Two we have so far dealt with the immediate *Sitz im Leben* of the Johannine lectures. Luther's Christocentrism was the decisive help in this situation; it also helped him to view the pope as Antichrist. The relationship between Luther and the papacy evoked a parallel of a different nature, though, observed in the history of piety. At this point, let us expand the question of the historical context to Luther and the Bernardine tradition.

Bernard of Clairvaux had written a book and had sent it to Pope Eugene III (1145-53), who was Bernard's disciple and also a Cistercian monk. It was the book, *De consideratione*, written in five volumes in the year 1152 or 1153. It included criticisms of the papal administration and utterances about the duties of the pope.[1] In this critical Bernardine tradition one may also see Luther's initially positive attitude toward Pope Leo X, the "pious Leo." Luther said that St. Bernard's book should be learned by heart by all the popes.[2] Most remarkably, Luther also sent his

---

[1]Cf. Karl Bihlmeyer and Hermann Tüchle, *Church History*, trans. Victor E. Mills and Francis J. Muller (Westminster, MD.: The Newman Press, 1963), vol. 2:170.

[2]Cf. WA 7:10,30 (LW 31:342).

book on "Christian Liberty" to the pope.[3] Another historical parallel is both theologians' aversion to reason as a final court of appeal in theology. Bernard fought Abelard, Luther fought the scholastic-philosophical tradition in theology. With Bernard, Luther was convinced that "it is better to drink directly from the source than to drink from the stream that comes from it."[4] A theologian should rely on the fresh water of the Bible alone as the one spring made by God.[5] The Cistercians of Bernard had a distinct way of reading the Bible. Erudition stems from reading the Bible; "ruminating" the Scripture was typical for them[6] as it was for Luther.[7] In the Bernardine tradition exegetical work and preaching has the purpose of giving consolation in times of temptation.[8] Luther made the same use of the text in his course on 1 John. The Augustinian tradition to which Luther and Erasmus belonged had been passed on to them by Ber-

[3]Cf. W. von Loewenich, *Martin Luther*, 172-3. See also Hans-Günter Leder, *Ausgleich mit dem Papst? Luthers Haltung in den Verhandlungen mit Miltitz 1520*. Arbeiten zur Theologie 1, 38 (Stuttgart: Calwer Verlag, 1969).

[4]WA 50:520,3 (1539).

[5]Cf. WA 50:657,1-30. Here also the argument with the spring water is extended to the German translation of the Bible, so that people can also drink this water.

[6]Cf. G. R. Evans, *The Mind of St. Bernard of Clairvaux* (Oxford: Clarendon Press, 1983), 44-49.

[7]"Nothing is more needed than ruminating the word," *ruminandi verbum*, WA 20:600,13. — See also Darrell R. Reinke, "Martin Luther: Language and Devotional Consciousness," *The Spirituality of Western Chrisendom*, ed. E. R. Elder, Cistercian Studies Series 30 (Kalamazoo: Cistercian Publications, Inc., 1976), 152-168.

[8]Cf. Evans, *The Mind of St. Bernard*, 101.

nard.[9] Some refer to it as the art of "affective meditation."[10]

We will limit our observations primarily to Luther's view of Bernard as found in his lectures on 1
John.[11] When Luther expounded 1 John 2:1, he told
his students that it is salutary to learn to understand
oneself, thus following the Bernardine theological
principle of the knowledge (*cognitio*) of God and of
self.[12] A key word for Luther was Bernard's conclusion about himself and his life, "I wasted my time."
Luther quoted this sentence in his lecture on 1 John
2:7. Luther understood it as a rejection of the monastic road. For Luther, the only road is the "middle
road," that you [God] alone are the just one. Bernard:

---

[9]"Natürlich sorgen die Traditionen der Augustiner . . . für die Weiter-
gabe der Theologie ihres Ordensheiligen. Vieles ist über Bernard wei-
tergegeben", U. Asendorf, *Gekreuzigt und Auferstanden, Luthers Her-
ausforderung an die moderne Christologie*, Arbeiten zur Geschichte
und Theologie des Luthertums 25 (Hamburg: Lutherisches Verlagshaus, 1971), 364. — Not only Luther, but also Erasmus was an Augustinian, see R. H. Bainton, *Erasmus of Christendom* (New York: Crossroad, 1982),12.

[10]Cf. D. R. Reinke, "Martin Luther: Language and Devotional Consciousness", 155 and 156. — "Affective meditation" is A. Zumkeller's
term.

[11] Cf. WA 20:624; 637-8; 730; 744; 753; 755-6; 793.

[12]"ut discamus nos intellegere. Illa cogitatio/cognitio est valde saluta-
ris", WA 20:633,9. — At this point one may very well question the
transcript of the abbreviation *cog* as given by the editor (*cogitatio*); I
suspect that Luther meant and said *cognitio* in alluding to Bernard's
principle of *cognitio Dei et sui*. On Bernard, see E. Kleineidam, "Ursprung und Gegenstand der Theologie bei Bernhard von Clairvaux
und Martin Luther," *Dienst der Vermittlung. Festschrift zum 25-jäh-
rigen Bestehen des philosophisch-theologischen Studiums im Priesterseminar Erfurt*, ed. Wilhelm Ernst et al (Leipzig: St. Benno Verlag,
1977), 225. The editor of WA 20:636, 14-15, correctly uses *cognitio dei*
(and not *cogitatio*). On the problem of abbreviations, see above Part
One. Bernard's principle is used again by Luther in WA 40[II]:327,11-
328,3.

'I wasted my time.' "[13] From the Bernard legend we have the following quote:

> For the rest, my Lord has won heaven by a twofold right, namely by inheritance from his Father, and by the merit of His passion; whereof He is content with the one, and gives me the other. Therefore, by His gift, I claim heaven as my right, and shall not be confounded![14]

Because Bernard believed in the abundance of Christ and not in Pharisaic justice, he was saved, Luther declared in his course on 1 John 4:10.[15] But the following day, on October 9, 1527, Luther criticized the monastic tradition of which Bernard was part. He referred to Wycliffe's word that the fathers of the church are damned if they did not do penance, because they are masters of error; pure teachers are very rare in the church; pure is Scripture alone. Gregory and Bernard established monasteries, "and therefore, I must speak up against them," he said, because "either Christ lies or they do."[16] In this context, Luther again returned to Bernard's, "I wasted my time":

> . . . therefore Wycliffe's article is most true. Bernard called it wasted life and time. I myself have paid attention to no holier monk than Bernard, I place him over Gregory, Bene-

---

[13]"Bernardus: tempus meum perdidi," WA 20:624, 3-Migne PL 185,491. Cf. the source S in WA 48:319,25. Cf. also WA 8:601,20-24; WA 45:265,8; WA 46:580,24-32.

[14]Quoted after J. K. Siggins, *Martin Luther's Doctrine*, 187, n. 71.

[15]Cf. WA 20:744,15-19.

[16]"vel Christus mentitur vel ipsi", WA 20:745,9.

dict . . . . : 'My life is wasted and does not record
any achievement.' There is no better phrase in
all of Bernard; another one [is found] in the
sermon on the Annunication. . . . [17]

In this quotation, we observe Luther's appreciation
of Bernard most clearly. It also contains the reference to the Bernard legend, as well as a precious
thought about Christ's merit by suffering, to which
we will turn in Part Three, and the idea of the "gift of
Christ," alluding to the *dulce commercium*,[18] a motif
known in Luther's Christology as "the joyous exchange," to which we also will return later as well.

Bernard's and Luther's experiential theology is
congenial. When he taught Christ as the Savior and
when he felt him in his heart, then, says Luther,
Bernard's spirit did not err.[19] From this study of
Luther's Johannine lectures, one must agree with U.
Köpf's conclusion (who did not, however, take into
consideration these lectures) that Bernard's affective theology influenced Luther's use of the category
of experience.[20] No wonder, then, that already for the

---

[17]WA 20:746,12-19. Luther praisingly referred here in 1527 to Bernard's
sermon on the *Annunciatio* a decade after his reformation breakthrough. Luther had found expressed in this same sermon the key to his
own new understanding of the Christian gospel. This is pointed out by
C. Stange, *Bernard von Clairvaux* (Berlin: Alfred Töpelmann, 1954), 5-6.

[18]"Das Grundmotiv des Wechsels verbindet Bernhard und Luther auf
eine besondere Weise." U. Asendorf, *Gekreuzigt und Auferstanden*,
377. Bernard's and Luther's theology of the cross are closely related,
mediated by Staupitz, who directed Luther to the wounds of Christ.

[19]"Sic Bernardus spiritu non erravit, scivit Christum salvatorem et
sensit corde." WA 20:753,22-23.

[20]"Ich zweifle nicht daran, dass Luthers neuer Rückgriff auf die Kate-
gorie der Erfahrung durch seine Beschäftigung mit dem von ihm hoch
geschätzten Bernhard von Clairvaux beeinflusst ist." Ulrich Köpf,
Religiöse Erfahrung in der Theologie Bernhards von Clairvaux, Beiträge zur Historischen Theologie, 61 (Tübingen: 1980), 235-6.

young Luther the Cistercian monk was the spirit-filled *divus Bernardus*.[21] Both Luther and Bernard were concerned with faith as experience. Both intended to talk according to the Scriptures without philosophical interferences. The formula of "alien righteousness" is already found in Bernard, and this seems to be the reason why, in Luther's view, Bernard is more excellent than Augustine[22] and stands on a plane far above Jerome. Bernard talked at least twice, although briefly, about faith, Luther observed, while Jerome never did; and if Augustine would not have had the Pelagians to write against, there would be nothing about faith either.[23] Clearly, in Luther's view Bernard is to be valued more highly than the other patristic authorities.

A final error, however, was committed by Bernard in regard to Mariology, as Luther saw it. In his lecture on 1 John 2:2, the professor noted that Bernard sought the mother as *paracleta* and, as such, was one of the elect who fell into error.[24] It is again because of Luther's Christology that he criticized Bernard. Luther said the same of Anselm, whom he in his lectures called the "chancellor of the virgin."[25] The Roman

---

[21]WA 2:15,18; WA 56:369,28-370,1: "plenus eodem spiritu."

[22]Migne PL 182,1065 for Bernard; ibid. 183,383-84 which corresponds with WA 56:369,28-370,5; cf. E. Kleineidam, *Ursprung und Gegenstand*. On Bernard excelling Augustine, see WA TR 3:95,6-8 (no. 3370): "Bernhardus in suis praedicationibus excellit omnes alios doctores vel ipsum etiam Augustinum."

[23]"Pauci ex antiquis de fide. Si Augustinus non habuisset Pelagium, nihil de fide. In Hieronymo nihil fidei. In Bernardo bis et perfunctorie." WA 20:775,26-776,1.

[24]"Matrem paracletam ut et Bernardus"; WA 20:637,23.

[25]"Sic et Anselmus, qui dicitur Cancellarius Virginis. Et Bernardum mellifluum propter praedicationes eius de Virgine." WA 20:637,24-

tradition had made Christ a judge, and Mary a *pa-racleta*. Luther saw Bernard and Anselm as part of this tradition, and he referred to Bernard as Dr. "Honeysweet" (*Dr. mellifluus*) for the sweetness of his Marian sermons; Luther admitted that he also had sought Mary as *paracleta* when he wore the cowl. Then the virgin was *mediatrix*, and satisfaction came from good works, but now . . .

> They call us banned monks. We are forced to leave, because they do not want to hear us preaching in this way. I am forced, then, to defect from the pope. Therefore, we are found in this status, that we do not have an abbot, bishop, pope as the Christ. These people damned me in their status, and the pope removed it from me. We are expelled because our prelates will not hear that Christ is the consolation. Christ does not demand a reconciliation, but he himself is the reconcilation.[26]

As we can see, Luther's Christology, his "Christ alone," caused the ecclesiastical difficulties and his departure from Bernardine Mariology. Luther expressed his aversion to the pictorial presentation of Mary and Bernard in the *Lactatio Bernardi*; Luther commented on this image in his exposition of John (1537-38).

> And one has painted St. Bernard in this way, that he adores the Virgin Mary, who leads her

638,2. Originally Bernard was called *Doctor Egregius* by Pope Innocent III. Cf. Henri Daniel-Rops, *Bernard of Clairvaux* (New York and London: Hawthorn Books, Inc., 1964), 15.

[26]WA 20:638,3-9.

breasts to her son, Christ, who sucked on them; Oh! How did we give kisses to Mary, but I do not like Mary's breasts nor her milk, because she did not redeem me nor did she make me blessed.[27]

The criticism is directed not so much against Bernard as against the artistic representation. This kind of image as well as the *Schutzmantelmadonna* (the madonna with the protective cloak) Luther called idolatry,[28] because Mary is not the protector; Christ is the "mother hen."[29] Hans Düfel commented that Luther criticized Bernard for his Mariology, although otherwise he praised him most highly.[30] In one of the professor's last sermons we find another mild criticism: "Bernardus has exaggerated the gospel '*Missus est Angelus*.' "[31] Luther's image of Mary is primarily the result of his application of Christology to Mary. In the first lecture on 1 John, Luther mentioned the name of Mary in the context of John's incarnational theology against the heretical Cerinth, who taught that "Christ was nothing before Mary."[32] In contrast to this position, on the basis of John's text, Luther taught Christ's pre-existence. "Christ did not begin from Mary, but he was from the beginning of the world."[33]

---

[27] " . . . ach was haben wir der Marien küsse gegeben"; WA 46:663,32-36.
[28] Cf. Josef Lieball, *Martin Luthers Madonnenbild* (Stein am Rhein: Christiana-Verlag, 1981).
[29] On this Christological title, see Siggins, *Martin Luther's Doctrine*, 251.
[30] Cf. *Luthers Stellung zur Marienverehrung* (Göttingen: Vandenhoeck & Ruprecht, 1968), 219.
[31] WA 51:218,10 (January 17, 1546).
[32] WA 20:601,17.
[33] Cf. WA 20:602,1-3.

In his lecture on 1 John 2:1 Luther's opposition to the non-Christocentric imagery of Mary becomes apparent: "We made Christ a judge even before the last day, therefore we fear and hate him, and we flee to the Blessed Virgin. We think of her as being without sting, wrath, gall, and so the whole world puts faith in her."[34] He continued by saying that we have "a good God," and that "there is no such Christ as we have invented, whom we would please with masses or by sending to him the mother; he is the breasts and the lap."[35] Whoever, then, would imagine him as being something else, creates a "new monster," an invention of men. Luther repeated, "Christ is ten times, a hundred times, a thousand times, earlier than the Blessed Virgin. It is Christ who shed the blood for us (Romans 8), not against us, as we imagine. This was a false imagination about Christ."[36] Because Christ is the *immaculatus*,[37] *paracletus*,[38] *mediator*,[39] Mary cannot be in the same way *immaculata, paracleta, mediatrix*. When dealing with 1 John 4:20 on Christ who is sent as reconciliation, Luther led his students to find God's mercy in him alone. In contrast to this Johannine position, Luther pointed to the negative example of the *Sentences*, which posed the question as to whether the Virgin Mary merited becoming Christ's mother.[40] Luther ridiculed this kind of ques-

---

[34] WA 20:635,15-17.
[35] "qui ubera et schos"; WA 20:636,8.
[36] WA 20:636,12-14.
[37] WA 20:636,31.
[38] WA 20:634,18. "consolator"; WA 20:637,9.
[39] WA 20:683,4.
[40] WA 20:743,2-4.

tion and posed his own rhetorical question, "What could Adam have as merit, when he stood there naked, and God had to press the sin out of him."[41]

Luther took up the Bernardine term *humanitas Dei*.[42] It recurs in the Johannine lectures only in the source S, where a reference is made to Luke 1:35,[43] namely, the incarnation of Christ. As such, the term is paradoxical and could be interpreted by the doctrine of the communication of the divine and human attributes in Christ. It is on this ground that we conclude that Luther's liberation from the Occamist Christology,[44] which negated any form of *communicatio idiomatum*, was due to Luther's exposure to the Augustinian and Bernardine tradition. We also realize that Luther interpreted Bernard evangelically and did not follow the Roman-Bernardine mysticism to which also Bonaventure belonged. Luther was quite familiar with this kind of mysticism when he declared in a table talk that he once had been on the same ladder as the Roman mysticists — "but I broke a leg on it."[45]

---

[41]WA 20:743,4-5.

[42]This expression is pointed out as being Bernardine by Winfried Zeller, "Zum Christusverständnis im Mittelalter," *Jesus Christus. Das Christusverständnis im Wandel der Zeiten: Eine Ringvorlesung der Theologischen Fakultät der Universität Marburg*, ed. Hans Grass and Werner Georg Kümmel (Marburg: N. G. Elwert Verlag, 1963), 29-40, here 33, n. 34.

[43]I found it in Luther's works in the Source S: referring to Luke 1:35: "Vocabitur humanitas Dei." WA 48:315,11.20. Again, in 1542, Luther in his commentary on Genesis found praise for both Bernard and Bonaventure, because he found their Christology of the incarnation and their theology of the cross to be congenial. WA 43:581,11-12.

[44]This departure from Occamism is pointed out by Reinhard Schwarz, "Gott ist Mensch. Zur Lehre von der Person Christi bei den Ockhamisten und bei Luther", *ZThK* 63 (1966):350.

[45]WA 23:732,8-9. See K-H. zur Mühlen, "Mystik des Wortes. Über die Bedeutung mystischen Denkens für Luthers Lehre von der Rechtfertigung des Sünders," *Zeitwende* 52 (1981):206-225.

In regard to the idea of a threefold *adventus* of Christ, there is great similarity between Bernard and Luther. For Bernard, there is the dwelling of Christ among men in the Incarnation and his coming at the time of the Parousia, as traditional theology has it. Bernard added as another *adventus* Christ's coming by grace to dwell in the soul of the Christian believer.[46]

This idea of a third *adventus* as described by Bernard is also found in Luther's lectures on 1 John in terms of spiritual incarnation or spiritual nativity.[47] Of course, the first advent in the Incarnation and the second advent in the Parousia are essential thoughts of Christian theology, and as such, also of Luther's thinking. What is striking here is the fact that Luther employed the terminology of *adventus* for the Parousia[48] and that he connected with the idea of Christ's coming into the Christian soul, the Christological title *purgator*[49] of the heart, as Bernard had connected his idea of the third advent in the soul with a purification process. However, for Bernard the Christian apparently prepares himself by purification, while for Luther it is Christ as resident in the heart who is performing this task. Furthermore, Christ's "energy" in his advent, his efficacy, is the decisive factor for Luther.[50]

---

[46]Cf. Jean Leclercq, *Bernard of Clairvaux and the Cistercian Spirit*, trans. Claire Lavoie (Kalamazoo: Cistercian Publications, 1976), 25.

[47]See the Chapter 10.

[48]Cf. WA 20:690,1.

[49]Cf. WA 20:706,5.

[50]Cf. Luther's repeated talk of *energian adventus*. See Chapter 1.

Next to the Bernardine matrix of the threefold *adventus Christi*, there are images of Christ which are found both in Bernard and in Luther's lectures on 1 John. Bernard and Luther use not only the Augustinian Christ-title of "physician," but also the metaphor of "sun of justice."[51] With these parallels in Bernard's and Luther's understanding of Christ, it is rather clear that Luther's exposition of 1 John is situated in the medieval tradition.

Conclusion

We have concerned ourselves with Luther's relationship to the Bernardine tradition and have observed his evaluation of this tradition in Christocentric terms along evangelical lines. Besides the theological context, we have dealt with the historical *Sitz im Leben* of the Johannine lectures focusing especially on the "toast" by Luther and his friends to the tenth anniversary of the crushing of the indulgences. We have also considered the world political scene, the Sack of Rome and the fortification of Wittenberg, which possibly gave impetus to the composition of the famous hymn, "A Mighty Fortress Is Our God" (thus precluding the need for human military efforts). We also have reviewed the academic context of Luther's Johannine lectures.

---

[51]In regard to Bernard's Christology, see J. M. Déchanet, "La Christologie de Saint Bernard", *Bernhard von Clairvaux: Mönch und Mystiker. Internationaler Bernhardkongress Mainz, 1953*, ed. Joseph Lortz (Wiesbaden: Franz Steiner Verlag, 1955), 65, where it is pointed out about Bernard: "Il met donc l'accent sur le rôle de 'mediateur' joué par le Christ, lumière d'un monde plonge dans les ténèbres de la mort, docteur d'un peuple ignorant, médecin des âmes, voie des égarés modèle et exemplaire de tous. . . . Il est venu 'Fils unique de Dieu, Soleil de Justice . . . "

On the basis of the evaluated sources, and with an awareness of the historical context, we will now interpret the text of the Johannine lectures as they contain Luther's doctrine of Christ.

We should also recall that there was a time when Erasmus pointed out that Luther's detractors were condemning doctrines of his which had been judged entirely orthodox when voiced by St. Augustine or St. Bernard.[52] Let us also remember that it was Augustine who guided Luther to John.[53] And so, we too are about to venture into the doctrine of Christ's person and work according to Luther's mid-career Johannine lectures.

---

[52]Cf. B. M. G. Reardon, *Religious Thought in the Reformation*, 38.

[53]"Augustin hat ihn (Luther) zu Johannes geführt." Carl Stange, *Bernhard von Clairvaux* (Berlin: Alfred Töpelmann, 1954), 6, where Stange refers to his other work on *The Johannine Character of Luther's Doctrine of Salvation* (1949).

PART THREE

LUTHER'S JOHANNINE CHRISTOLOGY
IN MID-CAREER — 1527

INTRODUCTION TO PART THREE

The heading of Part Three does not imply that Luther's doctrine of Christ (Christology) in mid-career was essentially different from that of the young or the old Luther. Rather, the Johannine lectures serve as a fitting text to demonstrate that Luther's Christology is Johannine always and everywhere, also in mid-career. Karl Barth claimed that Luther's Christology is more closely linked to St. John's Gospel while Calvin's teaching is related more to the synoptic Gospels.[1] Luther's preference for the Fourth Gospel is reflected in his Johannine Christology. Paul Althaus notes that the terminology of Luther's Christology is characteristically Johannine[2]. Another systematician observes that Luther impressively combines Pauline and Johannine relationships.[3] In Lienhard's biography of Luther, it is not surprising to read, "The incarnation is at the heart of Luther's religious steps."[4]

---

[1] Cf. *Church Dogmatics*, trans. G. T. Thomon and Harold Knight (New York: Charles Scribner's Sons, 1956) 1II:24.

[2] *The Theology of Martin Luther*, 182.

[3] U. Asendorf, *Gekreuzigt und Auferstanden*, 335.

[4] M. Lienhard, *Martin Luther. Un temps, une vie, un message*, 447-48.

CHAPTER 7

LUTHER'S PREFERENCE FOR THE JOHANNINE TRADITION

Luther's appreciation of John is apparent, even from his early writings. In his first lectures on the Psalms, Luther identified the Johannine Christology of Christ as God with Isaiah's title, the Lord Almighty.[1] In March 1518 Luther applied the Johannine "I am" sayings to his doctrine of *iustitia*.[2] In a letter of May 9, 1518, he wrote to Jodokus Trutfetter in Erfurt and recalled that Trutfetter had taught him that the primary teachers are Augustine, Paul and John.[3] We may generalize and say that the young Luther recognized John, Paul and Augustine as the most significant theologians.

In 1521, when Luther was at the Wartburg, he considered himself in the same position as John on the island of Patmos.[4] He observed that John also

[1]"Quod Isaie 6 'dominum Exercituum vidi' Iohannes Apostolus etiam de Christo dicit accipi, quia ibi viderit gloriam dei, i.e. Christum deum." WA 3:552,29.

[2]Sermo de duplici iustitia, WA 2:145-152.

[3]" ... ut B. Augustinus, imo Paulus et Johannes praecipiunt," WA Br 1:169-171 (no. 74), here line 74.

[4]Cf. the concluding lines: "geben ynn meyner Pathmos. Prima Junii, 1521." WA 8:140,6 (LW 48:246-47); cf. "Ex insula pathmos," WA Br 2:355,37-8. — See H. Bornkamm, *Luther in Mid-Career*, 3, n. 8, 17 and 51.

had written an apocalypse there on Patmos,[5] John's "awful book against the papacy."[6] Luther would have had no problem seeing himself in the angel and messenger of Revelation 14:6.[7]

John and Paul Are the Leaders

In 1522, when Luther's mid-career began and his New Testament translation was finished, he wrote the famous preface to Paul's Letter to the Romans, which later decisively influenced John Wesley. In this foreword, Luther used Johannine terminology in order to explain central doctrines such as sin and faith. Christ has singled out unbelief and has called it sin. According to John 16, the Spirit will convince the world of sin because they do not believe.[8] Again in this preface Luther referred to John 1. Faith is something which God effects in us. It changes us and we are born anew of God.[9] In the same preface to this important Pauline letter Luther made use of John's terminology in regard to the topic of flesh and spirit. One must not understand flesh only in terms of morality, and spirit only as state of the heart. Flesh, according to both Paul and John, means everything

---

[5]" . . . und yn meyner Pathmos nit mussig sey, hab ich mir auch eyn Apocalypsin geschrieben." WA 8:139,22-23 (LW 48:246).

[6]Cf. R. H. Bainton, *Here I Stand*, 326.

[7]Cf. W. von Loewenich, *Martin Luther*, 14. The comparison with Rev. 14:6 was first made by Luther's pastor, Bugenhagen, in his oration at Luther's funeral. See Wilhelm Pauck, *The Heritage of the Reformation* (Glencoe, IL: The Free Press, 1961), 19.

[8]"Da her Christus alleyne den unglauben sund nennet, da er spricht Johan. 16 der geyst wirt die welt straffen umb die sund, das sie nicht glewben an mich." WA DB 7:8,3-4 (LW 35:369).

[9]"Aber glawb ist eyn gotlich werck ynn uns, das uns wandelt und new gepirt aus Gott, Johan.1." WA DB 7:10,6-7 (LW 35:370).

that is born of the flesh, as John 3 says.[10] This preface makes it difficult to call Luther a "Paulinist,"[11] as though he were a subjective and selective hearer of the biblical word.[12]

In the same German Bible edition of 1522, Luther called John's Gospel the unique, tender, true, chief Gospel; it is the kernel and marrow, together with Peter's First Epistle and Paul's Letters to the Romans, Galatians and Ephesians, but in contrast to the synoptics. Also in 1522, Luther realized that John is a very special biblical author; however, "he is not a Platonist, but an Evangelist."[13] Luther coined this phrase because he departed from the prevailing philosophical interpretation of the Johannine texts in the traditional exegesis.[14]

During the following winter of 1523, Melanchthon lectured on John's Gospel, although he was never a member of the theological faculty.[15] Luther liked this

---

[10] "Sondern Fleisch heisset Paulus, wie Christus, Johan. iij, alles was aus Fleisch geboren ist." WA 7:13,7-8 (LW 35:371).

[11] Kierkegaard is reported to have held this view, cf. G. Ebeling, *Evangelische Evangelienauslegung, Eine Untersuchung zu Luthers Hermeneutik. Forschungen zur Geschichte und Lehre des Protestantismus 10, 1* (Munich: Kaiser Verlag, 1942; reprint Darmstadt: Wissenschaftiche Buchgesellschaft, 1962). 11.

[12] Cf. J. Lortz, *The Reformation in Germany*, vol. 1:184.

[13] WA DB 6:10,25-26 (LW 35:362). See Bornkamm, *Luther in Mid-Career*, 81. "Johannes eyn Euangelist, nitt eyn Platonist," WA 10^I:227,18 (Church Postil). Erasmus displayed tendencies to Platonize the New Testament, especially St. John's texts. See R. H. Bainton, *Erasmus of Christendom*, 61-62.

[14] Cf. W. von Loewenich, "Die Eigenart von Luthers Auslegung des Johannes-Prologes," *Bayerische Akademie der Wissenschaften, Philosophisch-Historische Klasse, Sitzungsberichte* (1960, Heft 9), (Munich: Verlag der Bayerischen Akademie der Wissenschaften, 1960), 52.

[15] Cf. Bernhard Lohse, "Philipp Melanchthon in seinen Beziehungen zu Luther," *Festgabe 1983*, 403ff.

work so much that he sent the manuscript with a cover letter to Nicolaus Gerbel for publication.[16] Melanchthon began his work with the distinction of "law and gospel,"[17] which could not have been more to Luther's taste. Melanchthon continued — and we will meet the same thought pattern in Luther's lectures on 1 John in 1527 — that John was forced to write against the new heretics such as Ebion, Marcion and Cerinth, who deny Christ's divinity. It is not enough to learn that Christ is God and man, and how the natures can be joined, but one should rather consider why it is appropriate that he who forgives sins must be God.[18]

Unlike Erasmus, the young Greek professor at Wittenberg, Melanchthon, translated the Johannine Logos with *verbum*, and not as Erasmus did with *sermo*. Therefore the Wittenbergers remained with the traditional Latin version of "in the beginning there was the *verbum*."[19] Melanchthon observed, "The son is called by John the Word, by Paul the Image of God."[20] Melanchthon, like Luther, rejected the Arian interpretation of the Logos[21] and pointed out that man becomes a son of God not by merit, but by faith alone.[22] It is significant, he says, that John speaks of *ex Deo* (of God), and not *a Deo* (by God) because to be born of God (*ex Deo*) means to become a

---

[16]Cf. WA 12:56-57; CR 14:1043-46.

[17]"Legis et Evangelii differentia," CR 14:1047.

[18]Cf. ibid., 1047.

[19]Cf. ibid., 1051-62.

[20]"Filius a Ioanne Verbum dicitur, a Paulo Imago Dei," ibid., 1050.

[21]"Nihil valet Arii commentum", ibid., 1052.

[22]"sed sola fide," ibid., 1060.

a participant of his nature as also 2 Corinthians 3 has it.[23] Luther liked his younger colleague's works and saw no need to lecture on Romans or on John after Melanchthon had offered his commentaries. We may assume that this is the reason why Luther never lectured on Romans again or ever lectured on John's Gospel. In Luther's absence from the university, Melanchthon had lectured on Colossians and Second Corinthians, then on John's Gospel.[24] In 1527 Melanchthon edited and introduced a medieval exegete's work on John, and it is suspected that Melanchthon made Luther aware of this work.[25]

In a sermon during Holy Week of 1524 Luther pointed out to his audience that John writes "differently from other apostles and more apostolicly."[26] In 1525 Luther worked on one of his rare systematic works, namely, against Erasmus's theory of the will. Luther relied heavily on John and Paul to refute Erasmus; Paul and John are the "leaders" in the argumentation.[27] It is reported that in *De servo arbi-*

---

[23]"Iam hoc etiam significantius est, quod ait ex Deo, non a Deo; nam ex Deo nasci est participem fieri naturae eius. cf. 2 Corith III." ibid., 1062.

[24]Cf. Robert Stupperich, *Melanchthon*, 57.

[25]Cf. *Nonni Poetae Panopolitam translatio sancti Euangelii secundum Joannem.* Haganovae 1527, edited by Melanchthon with a preface, as referred to by Gerhard Ebeling, *Evangelische Evangelienauslegung*, 148.

[26]"Johannes aliter scribit quam alii apostoli et magis apostolice." WA 15:505,3. "More apostolicly" must be understood as preaching more about Christ and his resurrection, as Luther said in 1523: "He who does not preach this, is no apostle." WA 12:268,20-21 (LW 30:12).

[27]"Atque a tanto numero exercituum duos proferemus duces cum aliquot suis legionibus, Paulum videlicet et Iohannem Evangelistam." WA 18:757,9-10 (LW 33:241, Paul and John are called "two high commanders.")

trio Luther alluded 122 times to John in theologically relevant passages (while only twice to Mark's Gospel).[28]

Luther in mid-career, at least since his September Testament of 1522, had made it public that John and Paul were the great theologians for the New Testament; this theological insight found artistic expression by a sympathizer of the Reformation, namely, Albrecht Dürer, in his painting of the "Four Apostles" of 1526.[29] The immediate context of this art event must not be forgotten: the controversy over images.[30] Dürer's picture expresses the relationship of John, Paul, Peter and Mark. John and Paul are presented in the foreground, while Mark stands in the background behind Paul, and Peter behind John; one of the four subtitles to the painting is 1 John 4:1-3; the others are taken from 2 Timothy, 2 Peter and Mark.[31]

In 1527 the controversy over the Lord's Supper heightened; besides the debated understanding of "is" or "signifies" in the words of institution of the sacrament, a controversy swirled around the interpretation of John 6.[32] In 1523 Melanchthon had in-

---

[28]Cf. J. Atkinson, "Luthers Einschätzung des Johannesevangeliums. Erwägungen zu Luthers Schriftverständnis"; *Lutherforschung heute*, ed. Vilmos Vajta (Berlin: 1958), 55.

[29]Cf. Hans Preuss, *Die deutsche Frömmigkeit im Spiegel der bildenden Kunst* (Berlin: 1926), 162, as referred to by Elfriede Starke, "Luthers Beziehungen zu Kunst and Künstlern," *Festgabe 1983*, 907, n. 42.

[30]Cf. ibid., 531.

[31]Cf. ibid — "The Four Apostles" were seen by contemporaries as a "Lutheran Manifesto," Francis Russell, *The World of Dürer 1471-1528* (New York: Time, Inc., 1967), 14.

[32]Cf. Helmut Gollwitzer, "Zur Auslegung von Johannes 6 bei Luther und Zwingli," *In Memoriam Ernst Lohmeyer*, ed. W. Schmauch (Stutt-

terpreted the eating of the flesh according to John 6 as faith in the crucified Christ.[33] In the same way, Luther never understood John 6 as a sacramental text.[34] Remarkably, the final biblical quotation in Luther's work, "This is my body" of 1527, is taken from 1 John 4:3 with the comment that truly he is not of God who dissolves, i.e., severs Christ's flesh. The test is this: whoever makes useless, perishable, common flesh of it like beef or veal, he is not of God.[35]

---

gart: 1951), 143ff. See also Hermann Sasse, *This is my Body. Luther's Contention for the Real Presence in the Sacrament of the Altar* (Minneapolis: Augsburg Publishing House, 1959), 143-155.

[33]"Summarium capitis. In hoc capite potissimum observabis, quod sit manducare carnem Christi, scilicet credere in Christum crucifixum"; CR 14:1106, cf. 1104-5.

[34]Cf. Ulrich Gäbler, "Luthers Beziehungen zu den Schweizern und Oberdeutschen von 1526 bis 1530-31," *Festgabe 1983*, 481-96. See also, Horst Weigelt, "Luthers Beziehungen zu Kaspar Schwenckfeld," *Festgabe 1983*, 473-480, where it is also observed that John 6 was the controversial issue between them; Schwenckfeld joined the Swiss party.

[35]"Denn welcher geist Christus fleisch auffloset, der ist nicht von Gott (Spricht S. Johannes) Und sagt dazu Es solle die probe sein. Nu loset ia dieser geist Christus fleisch auff, weil er ein unnutze, vergenglich und aller dinge ein gemein fleisch draus macht, wie rindfleisch und kalbfleisch, wie wir gehort haben. . . "; WA 23:282,12-16 (cf. LW 37:150). Against the Anabaptists, Zwingli and Oecolampadius, Luther employed 1 John 5:16 and maintained also in 1531 in his manuscript on Galatians that his doctrine of Christ is the true one and, therefore, he will not listen to Zwingli and Oecolampadius: " . . . Sicut ego non audio, quia persuasus meam doctrinam de Christo veram." WA 40:323,2-7. The English translation in LW 26:198 is based upon the printed version and does not give the names of Luther's adversaries (Zwingli and Oecolampadius). Here is another example of redactionary influence, which must be uncovered by the historical-critical method.

Simplex forma loquendi in Iohanne[36]

Luther's understanding of John's simplicity[37] is directed against the philosophizing tendencies of the medieval exegesis. Luther also disassociated himself from philosophical speculation in the work of biblical interpretation, and he continued at the same time to welcome John's simple speech.[38] In the lectures on 1 John, Luther's observation of John's simple way of doing theology is always connected with his other observation that the content is, at the same time, incomprehensible, mighty and great. On the first day of his Johannine lectures Luther pointed out to his students that at the beginning of the first epistle of John there is such a simplicity of expression, that this way of talking is apparently infantile, inept and elliptic. He never had encountered a simpler style, and no other apostle had used such simple ways of expression. It was as if an infant stammered, and yet, there is the highest majesty involved in this simple talk. This is nothing but the Holy Spirit at work.

---

[36]WA 20:605,1.

[37]Cf. Gerhard B. Winkler, *Erasmus von Rotterdam und die Einleitungsschriften zum Neuen Testament. Formale Strukturen und theologischer Sinn* (Münster: Aschendorff, 1974), 45.48.53.85-86. Already W. von Loewenich had pointed out (following Hermann Schlingensiepen), that the principle of simplicity is an essential presupposition for the Reformation exegesis. See Hermann Schlingensiepen, "Erasmus als Exeget," *ZKG* 48 (1929):16-57, W. von Loewenich, *Die Eigenart von Luthers Auslegung des Johannes-Prologes*, 29. It seems that Luther accepted this hermeneutical principle without following Erasmus in theological matters.

[38]"Dissen spruch tzihen sie gemeyniglich ynn das hohe speculiern unnd schweren vorstand von dem tzweyerley wessen der creatur, da die platonischen philosophi von berühmet sind . . . denn Johannes redet gar eynfelltig unnd schlecht." WA 10^I:195,14-196,13.

Attention should be drawn to the content of the incarnation more than to the words used, when the Holy Spirit stammers through John.[39] The *rhetoricus* Luther,[40] the *teutscher Cicero*,[41] was well aware of the greatness of the Johannine content and form; in fact, the professor himself regularly employed rhetorical expressions during his lectures.[42] During his first lecture on 1 John, Luther directed his students to the missing *locutio ornata* in 1 John. What Luther was observing there was a *locutio inepta et ecliptica* which is the opposite of the ornate talk.[43] But with these most simple words he expressed the highest content.[44] The professor called John's words "infantile oration,"[45] and yet John is

---

[39]"Audiamus ergo Spiritum sanctum balbutientem et magis ad rem quam ad verba attendamus, i.e. de hoc verbum, quod non est recens notum sed ab initio fuit." WA 20:601,14-16.

[40]"Ich bin ein wescher, bin magis rhetoricus." WA TR 5:204,27-28 (no. 5511). "I'm garrulous and more rhetorical" (LW 54:440).

[41]H. Herrmann, *Martin Luther*, 272 and 392.

[42]Luther's rhetorics is studied in his lectures on the Psalms of 1513-15 by H. Junghans, "Rhetorische Bemerkungen Luthers in seinen 'Dictata super Psalterium,' " *Theologische Versuche* VIII, ed. J. Rogge and G. Schille (Berlin: Ev. Verlagsanstalt, 1977), 97-128. Oberman H. A. " 'Immo,' Luthers reformatorische Entdeckungen im Spiegel der Rhetorik," *Lutheriana*, ed. G. Hammer and K. H. zur Mühlen. Zum 500.Geburstag Martin Luthers von den Mitarbeitern der Weimarer Ausgabe (Archiv der Weimarer Ausgabe vol. 5), Cologne 1984,17-38.

[43]Cf. Heinrich Lausberg, *Handbuch der literarischen Rhetorik: Eine Grundlegung der Literaturwissenschaft* (Munich: M. Hueber Verlag, 1960), 516 on *Eclipsis* as a rhetorical mistake, see ibid. 269, 346-47. See also R. Breymayer, "Bibliographie zum Thema Luther und die Rhetorik," *Lingusitica Biblica*, 21-22 (February 1973):39-44.

[44]"Simplicissimis verbis exponit maxima." WA 20:602,3-4.

[45]"Alioqui oratio est infantilis." WA 20:601,10. I question the German translation of *oratio infantilis* as "speech easy to understand by children," as given by Hartmut Günther, *D. Martin Luther's Epistel-Auslegung*, ed. Hartmut Günther and Ernst Volk (Göttingen: Vandenhoeck & Ruprecht, 1983), vol. 5:261 (*kinderleicht*).

able to make his listeners pay attention.[46] Luther approached this letter in terms of speech, rhetorics! The idea that John uses elliptic expressions in his letter in 1 John 1:1 may very well have come to Luther's mind while he was watching his baby, John, who was at the time of the lectures about one year of age.[47] In this case, Luther related the personal experience of baby talk to his academic exposition of the Johannine text. And, creative speaker as he was, he climaxed his lecture by calling upon his students to "listen to the Holy Spirit stammer."[48]

Time and again, Luther admired the paradoxical Johannine style and incomprehensible content. On 1:5 he again commented on this same paradox.[49] Verse 2:2 is expressed in dry and thin words, but the matter is so great that nobody can understand it.[50] When he arrived at 4:16, he stated that even though these are simple words, they require the greatest faith.[51] These are brief words, but most sublime.[52] Also, during his exposition of the last chapter of 1 John, he felt again compelled to remark on John's style. On 5:11 he said that these are simple spoken words, but inestimable ones.[53] On 1 John 5:16 he

---

[46]"Vides, quomodo attentos reddat suos auditores." WA 20:607.5

[47]Cf. H. Bornkamm, *Luther in Mid-Career*, 563 (little Johannes, born June 7, 1526). Is the baby named after the evangelist John?

[48]"Audiamus ergo spiritum sanctum balbutientem." WA 20:601,14-15.

[49]"Et licet simplicibus verbis, tamen res incomprehensibiles." WA 20:612,5.

[50]"Tam exilia et tenuia verba, tamen magnas res loquitur ut nemo possit, etc." WA 20:637,15-16.

[51]"Audivimus, quam haec sunt simplicia verba, sed quae requirant maximam fidem." WA 20:757,5-6.

[52]"Brevia verba sed sublissima." WA 20:755,21.

[53]Simpliciter loquitur sed inestimabilibus verbis." WA 20:786,9-10.

commented that these are simple, but very grand words.[54] At one point, on 1:10, Luther observed a variation of the paradoxical Johannine style when the simple speaker John used "horrible" words instead of grand ones.[55] Obviously, this Johannine style of simplicity was so impressive to Luther that he derived a principle from it in regard to academic Christological disputations. In 1540 he demanded that one must speak about Christ "most simply" (thesis 52).[56] Also in 1540, Luther returned to the thought he expressed in 1527 on 1 John about the Holy Spirit, who is speaking in simple ways; Luther then declared, "The Holy Spirit has his own grammar."[57] Ultimately, Luther's principle as observed in John's *simplex forma loquendi* is grounded in Christ's example, because the style of simplicity was also Christ's own style in preaching.[58]

During the lecture on 1 John 2:15-17 Luther mentioned Erasmus for the first time by name. In that context, Luther spoke of simple speech again as something which he saw at work in John, and Luther used this as argument against Erasmus's preface to 1 John, where some derogatory remarks on John's "world"

---

[54]"Ista sunt simplicia sed valde grandia." WA 20:797,15.

[55]"Simplex est locutor Sanctus Iohannes, sed horrenda verba loquitur." WA 20:631,16-17.

[56]"In eadem rem variis modis eloqui doctus iubeatur quam potest simplicissime loqui." WA 39II:96,7-8.

[57]"Spiritus sanctus habet suam grammaticam." WA 39II:104,22. See Yves Congar, *Martin Luther, sa foi, sa réforme. Etudes de théologie historique* (Paris: Cerf, 1983),44.

[58]"Einfeldig zu predigen, ist eine grosse kunst. Christus thuts selber." WA TR 4:447,19 (no. 4719).

were to be found. Luther took this inability of Erasmus and the "wise men" to understand the simplicity of John to be proof that they do not understand 1 John 2:15-17. Thus Erasmus and the other learned men must feel offended. If they knew what the "world" means in John, they would hold John's words on the "world" in higher esteem. Since they do not understand it, they are ignorant about the "world."[59] Erasmus's principle of simplicity was accepted and turned against him when he dared to criticize Luther's favorite Evangelist, John. Luther attacked not only Erasmus, but also other "perverse interpreters" like the Franciscans, who also misunderstand the "world."[60] They are all offended by the simplicity of Christianity.[61]

John Is Master and the Highest Authority After Christ

The lectures on 1 John must have had quite some effect on Luther. On August 15, 1528, he preached, not on Mary, but on John 17:3 and again brought up John's simplicity, by which he teaches most potently that Christ is God, because in order to give eternal life he must be divine.[62] Luther was so fascinated by

---

[59]"Si scirent, quid esset mundus, in maiori honore Iohannis verbum haberent." WA 20:661,3-4.

[60]"Ecclesiasten perverse interpretati sunt, Franciscani inde coeperunt contemnere pecuniam, das heissen sie contemnere mundum." WA 20:661,4-6.

[61]"Sapientia debet offendi in simplicitate Christiana." WA 20:661,2-3.

[62]"Sic nullus Euangelista loquitur ut Johannes, einfeltiglich loquitur et tamen potissime concludit Christum essem deum, quia vitam aeternam dare est opus divinitatis aeternae," WA 28:90,4-5.

John 17 that in October 1528 he again preached on this passage; the verse John 17:20 should be "written with golden letters," because of its impact on us.[63]

In 1528 Luther preached on St. John's Day, December 27. He called John an evangelist who makes one's heart laugh; he is a mighty powerful evangelist, who causes an uproar among enthusiasts and devils.[64] The previous day Luther also preached, and pointed out how John taught that Christ was truly God, "a born God."[65] It is said that Luther preached twelve times on John 17 during the year 1528.[66]

In 1529 the Wittenberg Latin Bible, the Vulgate in revised form, was published. In the preface Luther repeated that there is no doubt that John and Paul by far supersede the rest of the books.[67] On Pentecost Monday, 1529, Luther focused on the differences between Paul and John. "John always preaches his gospel in a peculiar manner, a way that differs from Paul and the others. First he leads us to Christ the man and his spoken word, then from Christ to the Spirit and to the Father."[68] The previous day, on Pentecost, Luther gave John the title "Highest Evangelist"[69] and humbly added that he did not feel

---

[63]"Hunc textum mugen wir aureis literis scribere, der ghet uns an." WA 28:178,23-24. — "Hunc textum absconde in cor tuum," ibid. 179,5-6.

[64]" ... der rhumort unter die Schwermer und Teuffel." WA 27:529,8-9.

[65]"geborner got," WA 27:523,4-7.

[66]Vilmos Vajta, "Luther als Beter," *Festgabe 1983*, 279ff.

[67]WA DB 5:478,33-36, "Nam dubium non est, quin Euangelium Joannis et Epistolae Pauli, praesertim ea quae ad Romanos est scripta, longe excellent reliquos libros omnes, meritoque his debet palmarium concedi."

[68]WA 29:373,1-3.

[69]"summus evangelista," WA 29:366,26. See Eduard Ellwein, *Summus Evangelista. Die Botschaft des Johannesevangeliums in der Auslegung Luthers* (Munich: Kaiser Verlag, 1960).

qualified to interpret John. This biographical statement is preserved in German[70] and in Latin.[71] After
having conceded this, in the following years Luther
continued to compare John with Paul and with the
other evangelists.

In 1530, when preaching on the Sermon on the
Mount (Mt 5-7), he spoke of John and Paul, who
inculcate the gospel in a more sublime way than do
the synoptic authors.[72] John is "a master above all
the other evangelists, because he always drives
home this article that Jesus Christ is true man and
true God. These two natures he joins together.[73] The
central verb is the German *treiben*, which is an old
German word and may have been derived from the
sea-farer's language. It may have been related to the
verbs "to drive" and "to propel."[74] Likewise, John is
"a master in the article of justification,"[75] which

---

[70]"Es gehoret wol eyn ander man darczw den ich." WA 29:366,26-27.

[71]"Johannes est Euangelista ad quem exponendum pertinet alius
quam ego." WA 29:366,14-15.

[72]"Denn er [Matthew] sampt den andern zweyen Euangelisten Marco
und Luca treibet sein Euangelion nicht so hoch und viel auff den
hohen artikel von Christo als S. Johannes und Paulus." WA 32:352,35-
37 (cf. LW 21:64).

[73]"Also ist der Euangelist Joannes ein Meister über alle andere Euangelisten, dan ehr jmmerdar diesen Artickel treibt, das Jhesus Christus
sei warhafftiger Mensch undt wharer gott. Diese zwo Naturen verein-
iget ehr zusammen." WA 33:116,25-32 (LW 23:77).

[74]Cf. on this "U.S. Lutheran — Roman Catholic Dialogue: Justification By Faith," *Origins*. NC Documentary Service 13 (6 October
1983):304, n. 214. This verb *treiben* is the key word for Luther's hermeneutics: "whatever inculcates Christ" (*was Christum treibet*). The
genuine sacred books always propel (*treiben*), teach and preach
Christ. WA DB 7:385,27 (LW 35:396).

[75]"Ein meister in dem Artickel der Justification," WA 33:200,15-16 (LW
23:129).

places him in a position of priority.[76] One must interpret the Scriptures according to the article about the Father who sent the Son, and the article which teaches that one is a child of God not by one's own merits.[77] Therefore, John has priority over the other gospels. "We must first give the floor to John."[78]

In a table talk of 1531 Luther superbly characterized John and Paul in regard to Christology: "John the evangelist describes Christ as God *a priori*. Paul, however, *a posteriori* and from the effect."[79] In another table talk it is reported that Luther would not believe Melanchthon's report that Erasmus wished that John's gospel had never been written.[80]

Luther, after having dealt with the Johannine tradition over the years, again in 1533 (as in 1521), identified himself with John when he said that he was not considered worthy to shed his blood for Christ, as many of his fellow confessors of the gospel had done. "Yet this honor was denied to the beloved disciple, John the Evangelist, who wrote a much more condemning book against the papacy than I

[76]WA 33:165,41-166,11; cf. 167,15; 171,41 (LW 23:108).

[77]"Nach diesem Artikel mus man die Schrift deuten," WA 33:165,21-40 (LW 23:108).

[78]"So mus man Joannem lassen furgehen, der do lehret, wie wir zum ewigen leben und zur gerechtigkeit kommen, und das man darnach gute werck thue." WA 33:166,5-9 (LW 23:108).

[79]"Johannes Euangelista Christum Deum esse describit a priori, Paulus autem a posteriori et ab effectu." WA TR 1:584,20-24 (no. 1178). See Gerhard Ebeling, *Disputatio de homine*. Zweiter Teil: Die philosophische Definition des Menschen. Kommentar zur These 1-19. Lutherstudien 2 (Tübingen: Mohr, 1982), 317-18.

[80]"De Erasmo Philippus quidam ait ipsum dixisse, er wolt, das Johannis euangelium nie geschrieben were. Ad quod cum ego: Ey, das ist nicht war! Philippus iurabat verum esse." WA TR 2:384,13-15 (no. 2263a — cf. no. 2263b).

ever could."[81] What Luther had in mind was the Book of Revelation, to which he alluded in this table talk.[82]

In 1534 Luther again attacked Erasmus. In this polemical context Luther attributed "the highest authority among the Christians" to John, ranking him after Christ himself. Luther rejected Erasmus's judgment of John's writings as repulsively "fastidious" and "odious."[83] It seems that the more Luther realized Erasmus's aversion against John, the more he favored the Evangelist.

In 1535 Luther used the terminology of 1 John 5:1 and 13 to express the doctrine of justification: "Justification is the true regeneration into newness, as John says, " ... they who believe in his name are also born of God.' "[84] This Johannine expression is found in thesis 65 of the disputation for Hieronymus Weller and Nikolaus Medler on September 11, 1535, regarding *de fide*.

---

[81]"Sed iste honor negatus fuit dilecto Christi discipulo Ioanni Euangelistae, qui tamen multo peiorem librum scripsit contra papatum, quam ego unquam scribere potui." WA TR 3:83,15-17 (no. 2922b). See also R. H. Bainton, *Here I Stand*, 360-1; H. Bornkamm, *Luther in Mid-Career*, 555; H. A. Oberman, *Luther: Mensch zwischen Gott und Teufel* (Berlin: Severin und Siedler, 1981), 334; Oberman in this regard refers to Luther's correspondence with Bugenhagen.

[82]Cf. Hans Ulrich Hofmann, *Luther und die Johannesapokalypse*, Beiträge zur Geschichte der biblischen Exegese 24 (Tübingen: Mohr, 1982), 332.

[83]"De Joanne Apostolo et Euangelista, qui post Christum summae autoritatis apud Christianos est, quis tam fastidiose et odiose (non dicam hostiliter) loqui ausit" (i.e. Erasmus), letter to Amsdorf on March 11, 1534, WA Br 7:32,129-130 (no. 2093).

[84]"Justificatio est revera regeneratio quaedam in novitatem sicut Joannes dicit: Qui credunt in nomine eius et ex Deo nati sunt." WA 39^{I}: 48,14-15. See Carl Stange, "The Johannine Character of Luther's Doctrine of Salvation," *Lutheran World Revue* 2 (October 1949). 65-77.

The great honor which the Bible-professor Luther attributes to John found its academic expression in the curriculum reform at the University of Wittenberg in 1533-36. In this first "Lutheran University" the new "biblical humanism" championed by Luther and Melanchthon had finally triumphed. Although other books of the Bible were to be studied and interpreted, the statutes of the University provided that special emphasis had to be given to Romans and the Gospel of John from the New Testament and to the Psalms, Genesis and Isaiah from the Old Testament, since they most clearly set forth Christian doctrine. Theological students were required to be graduates from the Liberal Arts College with a major in Latin, Greek and Hebrew. A *Biblicus* had to be conversant with Romans and St. John.[85]

In 1538, several years after the theological curriculum reform, in his exposition of John 14:10 we find Luther again drawing an equation between Paul and John:

> This is the knowledge (*kunst*) in which St. John (an outstanding evangelist in this regard) and St. Paul instruct more than others do. They join and bind Christ and the Father so firmly together that one learns to think of God only in Christ alone.[86]

---

[85]Cf. E. G. Schwiebert, *Luther and His Times. The Reformation From a New Perspective* (St. Louis: Concordia Publishing House, 1950),608-9.

[86]"Dis ist die kunst, davon S. Johannes (als ein ausbündiger Euangelist jnn diesem stück) und S. Paulus fur andern leren, das sie so fest jnn einander binden und hefften Christum und den Vater, auff das man lerne, von Gott nichts zudencken denn jnn Christo." WA 45:519,22-26. His Johannine sermons, edited by Cruciger in 1538-39, were valued

On March 29, 1539, the same year when Luther's historical study of the church appeared, he preached on John and the dogmatic Christology, stating that "John carefully wants to keep the Lord Christ in the two natures."[87] In his 1539 study of conciliar history the professor arrived at the conclusion that the decision of the main councils of the early church in their trinitarian and Christological debates do not contain any article of faith which would go beyond that of what St. John had written. In fact, John is richer and more powerful than the dogmatic articles of these councils.[88]

In what seems to be Luther's last sermon on a Johannine text, the one of August 5, 1545, preached at Halle on John 5:39-43, Luther defined his theology in contrast to the Jews, the Turks and "our popes and cardinals." They do not believe the preaching about Christ and eternal life. They take all that to be tales and stories, even dirt. "We, however, who are Christians," he continued, "see and hear that Christ is not only man, but also God, who gives life. John presses (*treibt*) this issue in particular in his Gospel, where he testifies that Jesus of Nazareth, Son of Mary, is true, natural God and man in one person, to whom all of Scripture points."[89]

---

higher by Luther than his own interpretation of the Sermon on the Mount, cf. H. Junghans, "Luther in Wittenberg," *Festgabe 1983*, 35.

[87]"Johannes diligentissime, ut Christum behalt in den zwo naturen," WA 47:715,27. See above n. 77.

[88]"Denn solche vier Artickel sind gar viel reichlicher und gewaltiger auch allein in S. Johannis Evangelio gestellet." WA 50:605,21-22.

[89]"Eben so sind unser Bepst und Cardinele u. die gleubens auch nicht, haltens fur fabeln und merlin, ja fur lauter kot, was man von Christo und dem ewigen leben prediget. Wir aber, die wir Christen sein, sehen und hoeren hie, das Christus nich allein ein mensch, sondern auch Gott sey, der das leben geb. Welches stueck Joannes auch furnemlich

In summary, the "Word of God" as the message of Christ is most clearly perceived by Paul and John.[90] While in 1516 Luther called Paul the "most profound theologian"[91] and the "divine Paul,"[92] in mid-career he dubbed John the "highest authority among Christians after Christ."

John, in this role, set the stage for what the early councils teach about Christ, namely, that he is both God and man in one person. This is the dogmatic basis on which Luther stood and from which he approached his exegesis of 1 John. In light of this insight, one must confirm the finding of Siggins that St. John's language is so congenial to Luther that his Christology is essentially Johannine. In addition to this, one may have serious doubts whether W. von Loewenich's thesis can be maintained that Paul dominated Luther's exegesis of Johannine texts.[93] With Siggins, one gets the impression that Luther read the Pauline text in light of John.[94] This seems to be the case, especially for Luther's Christology.

Luther's preference for John paralleled preference for the dogmatic tradition of the main councils of the

---

treibt durch aus jnn seinem Euangelio, das et zeuget, das der Jesus von Nazareth, Marien Son, sey warhafftiger, naturlicher Gott und Mensch jnn einer person, auff den die gantze schrifft weise." WA 51:3,26-33.

[90]Cf. Gerhard Bott, Gerhard Ebeling and Bernd Moeller, *Martin Luther: Sein Leben in Bildern und Texten*, 32.

[91]"disputatio profundissimi theologi Pauli Apostoli"; WA 55:36,22-23.

[92]Leif Grane, "Divus Paulus et S. Augustinus, interpres fidellissimus: über Luther's Verhältnis zu Augustin," *Festschrift für Ernst Fuchs*, ed. G. Ebeling et al (Tübingen: Mohr, 1973),133-146.

[93]*Luther und das Johanneische Christentum* (Munich: Kaiser Verlag, 1935),14 and 88.

[94]*Martin Luther's Doctrine*, 145.

early church. At least for Luther, the Johannine doctrine of Christ is identical with the conciliar dogma of Christ as God and man in one person. The simplicity of John's style brings the doctrine out most clearly. In regard to his Christology, Luther is certainly not a *Dr. Exaggerator* at all, but a champion of the orthodox doctrine of Christ's two natures in one person.

CHAPTER 8

THE DOGMATIC FOUNDATION[1] IN THE OPENING LECTURE: CHRIST — ONE PERSON IN TWO NATURES

The most valuable of the macaronic student notes (R) are those of Luther's opening lecture, because they set the tone for the rest of the course, and they are especially productive and rich for our exploration of his Christology.

In correspondence to his general concept that one lives between Christ and the devil, Luther typically began his course with the opening phrase:

"Which was from the beginning." Satan fights against us everywhere, and "God places us

---

[1]One must take into consideration that we are dealing here with the concept of "old ecclesiastical dogma," a notion not available to Luther, which came into existence with the modern historiography of dogma, at the end of the nineteenth century. See Georg Kretschmar, "Luther und das altkirchliche Dogma," *Una Sancta* 37 (1982):293: "Wenn man sich dem Thema 'Luther und das altkirchliche Dogma' stellen will, ist es gut, sich von Anbeginn an klar zu machen, dass 'altkirchliches Dogma' ein fester Terminus erst der modernen Dogmengeschichts-schreibung seit dem Ende des 19. Jahrhunderts ist."

here," 1 Corinthians 5. Here the world, Satan, heart, flesh and enthusiasts fight us, so that we have no peace, nothing good, through which we see that God wants to tempt [try] us.[2]

In this situation of temptation and struggle, God has given his Word to be preached; and it is exactly in these circumstances that we should experience how mighty his holy Word is, and that it is more powerful than sin and death. Luther detailed his personal situation (and that of his students) and summed it up with a comparison from Matthew 10:16. We are living "in the midst of wolves."[3] The spiritual wolves are everywhere, guided by the devil. He endangers us not only in one way; if he does not attack from the left, he does so from the right.[4]

Orational Approach

In this bedeviled situation there is only one refuge: the Word of God. We are to pray about and to meditate on the Word of God. The art of interpreting Scripture has to do with orienting oneself toward Christ by approaching the Word of God not rational-

---

[2]WA 20:599,2-5.

[3]"in medio, inquit, luporum," WA 20:599,7.

[4]Cf. WA 20:599,9 and 601,1-2. — See Erwin Mülhaupt, "Der Begriff 'linker Flügel der Reformation' von Luther her gesehen," Luther 48 (1977):76-80. For Luther, the left wing meant the side of the pope. For instance, the pope's doctrine of the sacraments would be "leftist." The right wing meant the side of the radicals who take away everything from the sacraments; thus, the "enthusiasts" are "rightists." — Luther wants to take the middle road. Furthermore, from Luther's point of view, the peasants' rebellion takes place on the right hand, cf. WA 40:110,20-22.

ly but orationally,[5] or, prayerfully. This is what Luther announced at the beginning of his lectures:

> As we are so attacked by death [there was pestilence in Wittenberg], sin, heretics, I proposed to myself to lecture on this epistle, in order to console each other mutually, and *to pray together* against the bothersome devil, who endangers us not only in one way. I also know that God is with us. "I will not desert you," Epistle to the Hebrews [13:5]. Therefore, I will treat this Epistle in the most simple way possible.... And then we also have the promise "where two or three etc." [Mt 18:20].[6]

Luther here used his "orational" approach to Scripture interpretation. He did that in the awareness of Christ's presence during his lectures. Christ will be there where two or three are gathered in his name. And, indeed, during the plague only a handful of students had remained with Luther at Wittenberg. The professor, fully conscious of his position as expositor, expressed the hope that God would be pres-

---

[5]By preserving the expression "orational" I intend to express a contrast to "rational," as Luther has it in his Preface to the Wittenberg Edition of his German Writings in 1539, WA 50:657-661 (LW 34:279-288). In this preface, Luther reveals his threefold rule of interpreting the Bible: *oratio, meditatio, tentatio* (which he called "David's Rule"). In 1520, in his letter to Pope Leo X, Luther expressed his aversion to ecclesiastical rules in expounding the Bible, because he was afraid that such rules would imprison the Word of God, which teaches all freedom (WA 7:9,27-31). In the preface of 1539 Luther offered a guide to the correct study of theology, and this approach is directly applied here in his lectures on 1 John: to approach the biblical text orationally, meditatively and with reference to life experience (*tentatio*). See below Chapter 10 on Christ The War Lord and Victor.

[6]WA 20:599,7-12 (emphasis added).

ent when he was lecturing, just as he was certain that the devil as well would be there. "So here, we hope, that when I speak in the name of God and you listen, the Lord is present, as Satan is."[7] This idea of Satan's presence has to do with Luther's conviction that the devil was the "first exegete."[8] When one interprets the Bible, Satan is there to disturb him. For Luther it was a rule of life that when the Word of God started to blossom, then "Satan takes no rest, but arouses sects"; therefore, the devil prefers us to be sluggish, and "lets us snore in our works" instead of being alert and fervent.[9] The devil makes us quiet and secure and has our own flesh as his foremost ally.[10] Ideally, students of the Bible are to be alert and fervent. Christians must not be sluggish and think it is enough merely to hear the Word. Rather, Luther says, "it is always necessary to take the Word into serious and careful consideration, because the devil is at work constantly. But it is not just because of the devil that one must be alert and fervent, but because the Word of God itself is fervent, burning, a living word of salvation, which concerns us daily in our predicament of death and sin. It is a word of righteousness. Since we are never without sin and death, so God proposes his word of salvation.[11]

In the continuation of his introductory hermeneutical remarks, Luther observed that the purpose of

[7]"Sic hic speramus, quando ego loquor in nomine dei et vos auditis, quod adsit dominus sicut et Satan." WA 20:599,12-13.

[8]Satan interpreted God's Word first, according to Genesis 3. On this, see G. Ebeling, *Evangelische Evangelienauslegung*, 381.

[9]WA 20:600,4-6.

[10]WA 20:600,7-8.

[11]"Tractatio verbi"; "verbum salutis proponit"; WA 20:601,3-5.

this Epistle by John is to give Christians consolation and strength against the heretics who amputate the Word.[12] Among John's adversaries were Cerinth and others "who negated Christ's divinity," and also the Christians who thought it was enough to listen to the Word, and who therefore had become sluggish; against both kinds of Christians, the heretical and the sluggish ones, John speaks here, so that we may become aware of these heretical positions and active in mutual love, like Christ, who loved us. Luther warned that, although we know all this and that Christ loves us, we must still "ruminate" the Word.[13] This expression evokes the picture of cows chewing grass again and again. In the same way, the Christian must ruminate the Word of God in an "orational" sense.[14] Again, the reason behind this praying over and ruminating, meditating on the Word of God is, that "when man knows it well, he has the devil by the throat."[15]

Luther saw John's situation as being identical with his own. As heretics had broken into John's fold, so also the enthusiasts had invaded Luther's own fold at Wittenberg; and then there is the sluggishness of the Christians. Likewise, the occasion for John's epistle was the presence of heretics and slug-

---

[12]"Heretici verbum amputant." WA 20:600,7 (as Irenaeus had said against Maricon).

[13]"Hoc scimus sed umquam tam bene quam maneant necessitates ruminandi verbum." WA 20:600,12-13. On "ruminating" see Chapter 6 on Luther and the Bernardine tradition. See Evans, *The Mind of St. Bernard*, 48.

[14]Cf. above n. 5.

[15]"Ratio: quia si bene scit homo, habet diabolum in collo." WA 20:600,13.

gish Christians.[16] To encounter this challenge, John had taken up the pen, and correspondingly, the essence of his epistle was "to teach the pure faith against heretics, and the burning love against those who were luke-warm. The genre of the epistle is exhortatory and didactic [doctrinal]."[17] "It is an immeasurably beautiful text with [important] articles and verses."[18] "It is the epistle of John, because it has his fabric and style."[19] It is in this same simple style of John in which Luther himself intended to expound this epistle. "I will treat this epistle in the most simple way possible."[20]

With these announcements Luther in one way followed Erasmus — in regard to the "simplicity" principle of interpretation. In other ways Luther did not follow Erasmus. Luther highly appreciated John's style and content of consolation and maintained John's authorship of both the Gospel and First Epistle.[21]

God's Flesh Is Christ's Flesh

After the prolegomena, the professor began his exposition of 1 John 1:1[22] with a discussion of hermeneutical and doctrinal-dogmatic issues. According to his orational approach to interpretation, he

---

[16]WA 20:600,3-4.

[17]WA 20:601,6-7.

[18]"Es ist ausermassen pulcher text cum articulis, numeris." WA 20:599,14.

[19]"Ioannis haec Epistula habet filum et stylum." WA 20:600,1.

[20]"simplicissime tractabo," WA 20:599,11.

[21]Cf. Chapter 7.

[22]WA 20:601,8.

also ended his first lecture on 1 John 1 with a prayer invitation. "Let us pray for one another that God will be gracious to us, that he will have mercy on us, because we are an opprobrium to the whole world."[23] The clear focus of attention is pure dogmatic faith in Christ's divinity and humanity. It is here that Luther used the unique expression *Dei caro* (God's flesh) as the equivalent of *caro Christi*[24] (Christ's flesh). In *Dei caro*, Luther's term from 1527, we have the young Luther's concept of Christ being the God who is hidden in the flesh.[25]

In the opening lecture on 1 John Luther used this unique expression *Dei caro* in the context of two key references (John 14:9 and Col 2:9), of which R. Prenter has stated that they represent completely Luther's Christology.

> The main point in Luther's Christology may be found in Colossians 2:9, "For in him dwelleth all the fullness of the Godhead bodily," which may be connected with John 14:9, "He that hath seen me hath seen the Father." The Christology of Luther is completely expressed in these two Scripture passages.[26]

Both the Johannine and the Pauline texts refer to the notion of *Dei caro*. The reference to John 14:9

---

[23]WA 20:606,10-11.

[24]WA 20:604,14.

[25]Cf. WA 3:503,2-7 (LW 10:445). Cf. "Et vestigia tua quia in carne absconditus." WA 3:529,20. Cf. "Deus in carne absconditus est." WA 4:7,2.

[26]R. Prenter, *Spiritus Creator*, 267. Cf. M. Lienhard, *Witness to Jesus Christ*, 37.

preceded[27] the one to Colossians 2:9[28] and followed the text on *Dei caro*,[29] which itself is connected to Luther's explicit confession of faith in the word of the Church's dogma:[30]

Nobody can speak better about Christ than he himself speaks about himself. Christ says in John 16 [actually 4:9]: "Philip, who sees me," etc. . . . So Scripture speaks [about Philip not believing]. We believe: Jesus Christ is constituted as one person, of course out of two natures, but one person, and a double nature: whatever is said about Christ's person concerns the whole person. What they say is this: Christ according to his divinity cannot suffer. . . . He [Christ] is not divided from human nature, but I have to take the whole Christ. So he said to Philip, "He who sees," etc. He has seen the humanity, the enthusiasts say. But when Christ says, "You see me," [he saw] not only the humanity, etc. . . . If I believe in Christ's humanity, I believe in the whole person. "My flesh is true food" is not said for nothing, because the humanity would be nothing in itself; but it is God's flesh (*Dei caro*). One should not dispute about dividing Christ, but the contrary. The natures are distinct, but there is only one person. I say this so you understand John's simple way of speaking. . . . They saw the Son of God, because they touched the liv-

[27]WA 20:603,5-10.
[28]WA 20:605,11-12.
[29]WA 20:604,14.
[30]WA 20:603,10-12

ing person that is constituted of God and
man. . . . Note Philip's word! . . . This is significant in the holy Scriptures. I myself know of
no other God other than in this humanity. If
you would have walked away from this person, who is born of Mary, to seek him elsewhere, then the devil is leading you. Consequently, you could say, "I do not know of any
other God except of him." In Christ the total
fullness lives [Colossians 2:9]. The others [are]
speculations of majesty and they terrify us.
Let us be more like chicks, and let us remain
under the wings of the hen.[31]

This is the confessional and dogmatic statement
which contains the traditional orthodox Chalcedo-
nian dogma of Jesus Christ as one person: *esse unam
personam constitutam.*[32] Always connected with the
formula of one person is the other statement about
the two natures: *ex duabus naturis* and *duplicem
naturam.*[33] In 1543 Luther spoke, instead of *"ex,"*
about *"in" duabus naturis,*[34] while in 1540 he had
used the expression *Christi persona constat duabus
naturis unitis,*[35] with a simple ablative. Leo and
Chalcedon held the unity *in,* not out of (*ex*), two

---

[31] WA 20:603,5; 605,13.

[32] WA 20:603,10-11. Cf. the disputation of 1540: "Humanitas et divinitas in Christo constituunt unam personam." WA 39^{II}:100,18 (LW
34:145), or with the preposition *"in"* in the same disputation: "Est res
incomprehensibilis . . . quod duae naturae in una persona unitae sunt
. . . duae naturae unitae in una persona," WA 39^{II}:98,18-19.

[33] WA 20:603,11-12.

[34] WA 54:89,35-36.

[35] WA 39^{II}:114,17-18 (de divinitate et humanitate Christi 1540).

natures.[36] Apparently Luther varied the expressions because he felt there was no essential difference. Luther also speaks of "composition" in place of "constitution," as he did in his *Commentary on Galatians* in 1535.[37]

Besides the one person and the two natures, Luther taught that "whatever is said about the person of Christ concerns the total person," *ghet die gantze person an.*[38] This dogmatic confession is the basis for the professor's interpretation of 1 John. Luther contrasted his dogmatic-biblical-confessional statement with Zwingli's unorthodox position.

Implicit in this confessional formula is the doctrine of the *communicatio idiomatum*, which comes up later during this same lecture.

"What they [Zwingli and the enthusiasts] say is this: Christ, according to his *divinity* cannot *suffer*. If they do not return to their senses, they will negate Christ as God."[39]

Luther continued to affirm against their position,

> Those two natures are one person: whatever therefore concerns one part of the person is said to happen to the whole [person]. In brief

---

[36]Cf. Y. Congar: " . . . alors que S. Léon et Chalcédoine tenaient a affirmer l'unité *in*, non *ex*, *duabus naturis*"; Congar, *Martin Luther, Sa foi, sa réforme*, 112.

[37]"Et tamen Scriptura loquitur aliquando de Christo ut Deo, aliquando ut de composito et incarnato." WA 40^I:415-10-13 (LW 26:264).

[38]WA 20:603,12. See Chapter 9.

[39]WA 20:603,13-14. Cf. S in WA 48:315,7, where it is stated that Christ as God as much as Christ as man had suffered. Luther probably had Zwingli in mind, who held the position that Christ's humanity alone can suffer: "cum sola humanitas pati possit," CR 90:776-785, as referred to by Gollwitzer, "Zur Auslegung von Johannes 6 bei Luther und Zwingli," 155.

> form, he says: The Jews crucified the Son of
> God, not Christ's humanity, for the humanity
> is delivered up, but it is his Son begotten for
> us.[40]

This means that the *unigenitus* Son is delivered for
us, and the *communicatio idiomatum* is at work here
so that one cannot separate the divinity and humanity in Christ. Thus, the objection that Luther's doctrine of Christ would exclusively emphasize God's
Alleinwirksamkeit (God's effectiveness alone) in
Christ is invalid,[41] because there is no room for mo-
nophysitism in Luther's Christology of the two natures. Luther found also 1 Corinthians 2:8 a reference
to the whole person as the God-man. He supported
this reference to Paul with the one from Luke 1:35,
and concluded as follows:

> So, what is attributed to the one part of the
> person is attributed to the whole of the person.
> When somebody is hurt in the leg, one says:
> the dog bit Peter. The whole person is in-
> volved. Hans beat him: For what happens to
> one part of the body is referred to the whole
> person. Therefore, do not let yourselves be
> drawn into this scholarly distinction. Indeed,

---

[40]WA 20:603,14-17.

[41]Cf. E. Vogelsang, *Die Anfänge von Luthers Christologie*, 55, 180-181.
Cf. Y. Congar, "Regards et réflexions sur la christologie de Luther,"
Das Konzil von Chalcedon. Geschichte und Gegenwart, ed. Aloys
Grillmeier and Heinrich Bacht (Würzburg: Echterverlag, 1954), 457-
86. Congar departed from this position more than a quarter of a century later in his Nouveaux Regards, *Martin Luther, Sa foi, sa réforme*
(Paris: Cerf, 1983), 105-133. Now Congar correctly understands Luther's Christology, according to which both natures have their functions in the salvation (and *not* exclusively Christ's divinity alone).

one says of those who crucified the humanity of Christ, that they crucified the "Lord of glory."[42]

This *distinctio scientifica* in the cited passage is Zwingli's separation of Christ's two natures. The Swiss reformer placed more emphasis on the separation of the two natures than on the unity. For Luther these "scientific" distinctions could not hold water, because the "for us" is decisive, as the next sentence indicates: "The Son is given for us, that he be the inestimable price for the removal of eternal death. It needs to be an eternal price. 'He who . . . his own' etc. Romans 8."[43] The practical-soteriological side of Christology is decisive for Luther, and this he found in Paul, Romans 8:32. Attached to this statement is the other one, which, if isolated, would give a wrong impression. It reads as follows: "I do not believe in the humanity of Christ born, crucified."[44]

We must keep in mind that we are working from fragmentary lecture notes by a student. The immediate context is important here, since otherwise one would suspect Luther of negating the incarnation and the crucifixion. This phrase must be understood as an explication of the immediately preceeding sentence about the eternal price for eternal death. For Luther, the humanity of Christ alone could not constitute this eternal price, therefore, he said he does not, in regard to salvation, trust in the humanity of Christ "alone." The "humanity of Christ" is the

[42]WA 20:603,19; 604,2.
[43]WA 20:604,2-4.
[44]WA 20:604,4-5.

"humanity of God" in the Bernardine tradition and as Luther said according to the source S.[45] What the professor of theology rejected was an interpretation of the doctrine of the two natures without the communication of the attributes, which would result in the separation of the two natures in Christ. Therefore, Luther continued, "These people call it 'idiomata' and separate."[46] Although the phrase *communicatio idiomatum* as such is not used, the doctrine certainly is meant here.[47] Luther continued by saying that "in substance it is true, because as such the natures are distinct, but when Christ is placed objectively before me and is offered to me, he is not divided from the human nature. I have to take the whole Christ. So he said to Philip, 'Who sees me,' " etc.[48] With this reference he returned to the key quotation from John 14:9.

At this point Luther identified those "others" as the "enthusiasts," who interpret John 14:9 as referring to having seen the humanity alone. "He (Philip) has seen the humanity, the *Schwermeri* say."[49] Against this position Luther quoted Christ's reply to Philip, "You see me . . . , " and commented that he saw "not only the humanity." "To everyone the humanity was visible, but still [the humanity] is

---

[45]Cf. WA 48:315,11 and 17-20.

[46]WA 20:604,5, where the edited text mistakenly has idiom*o*ta rather than idiom*a*ta.

[47]The printed version (P) rightly complemented the original at this point with the complete phrase "communicatio idiomatum."

[48]WA 20:604,5-9.

[49]"Sic ad Philippum: qui videt, etc. Vidit dicent humanitatem Schwermeri." WA 20:604,8-9.

connected with the divinity."[50] For Luther it is not possible to separate the two natures and to interpret each one separately. Therefore, modern Luther interpreters are wrong when they stress the distinction of the two natures rather than their unity and base their understanding of Luther's "wonderful exchange" on this separation.[51] On this point, Luther explicitly confessed, "If I believe in Christ's humanity, I believe in the whole person,"[52] i.e., the God-man, Christ. This unity in Christ was expressed by Luther elsewhere as *Durchgötterung des Leibes Christi*, divinifying of the body of Christ.[53] Luther used the illustration of permeation. As water is sweetened by sugar (*durchzuckert*, permeated by sugar), so is Christ's flesh *durchgöttert* (permeated with divinity). This comparison must be read within the context of Luther's anti-sectarian polemics.

In this same context, Luther drew assistance from another Johannine passage, which became the occasion for much debate — John 6:55-63.[54] Luther

---

[50]WA 20:604,9-11.

[51]Cf. T. Beer, *Der fröhliche Wechsel und Streit*. One must agree with Raymund Schwager's criticism of T. Beer's position. Schwager rightly objects to Beer's tendency to interpret Luther's Christology in the sense of separation, which leads to contradictory positions. Cf. R. Schwager, "Der fröhliche Wechsel und Streit. Zur Erlösungs- und Rechtfertigungslehre Martin Luthers," *Zeitschrift für katholische Theologie*, 106 (1984):27-66.

[52]WA 20:604,12-13.

[53]" . . . sondern es ist ein leib und blut, der vol Gottes ist oder das durchgöttert ist wie ein wasser, das durchzuckert ist, daran schmecket man kein tröpflin wassers, sondern süssen, lieblichen Zuckerschmack und krafft. So auch, wer seinen Leib ergreiffet, der hat nicht allein ein schlecht Fleisch und Blut CHRISTI, sondern ein durchgöttert fleisch und blut," WA 33:224,3-12 (LW 23:143).

[54]Cf. H. Gollwitzer, "Zur Auslegung von Johannes 6 bei Luther und Zwingli" — Cf. Melanchthon in 1523 on John 6, CR 14:1103-06.

referred to this text, "my flesh is true food," and commented that this was not said for nothing, because the humanity is nothing in itself. It is God's flesh, *dei caro*.[55] At first one might think of the controversy over the Eucharist, which, of course, forms the backdrop for the discussion. But one must keep in mind that Luther always rejected the use of John 6 for the debate on the sacrament of the altar;[56] rather, it must be taken as a Christological statement, which is admittedly the basis for the sacramental understanding.[57] The term "Christ's humanity" as "whole person" and "God's flesh" are identical in meaning for Luther. But if one tries to separate the humanity from the divinity, then the humanity becomes meaningless in itself, as Luther emphasized in his course on Titus.[58] Against the interpretation of Christ's humanity in isolation from his divinity Luther said, "But it is God's

---

[55]WA 20:604,13-14.

[56]Cf. H. Gollwitzer (See n. 54) and H. Bornkamm who both point out that Luther's position against Zwingli is that John 6 can in no way, positively or negatively, be applied to the Lord's Supper. Bornkamm, *Luther in Mid-Career*, 509 with n. 37, Cf. 225.

[57]After Luther's interpretation of *dei caro* in this first lecture, he indicates the connection between Christology and the doctrine of the Eucharist: "So, in the sacrament of the altar, I feel bread and wine. The heart [says]: I feel Christ himself and the body (*corpus*) and blood of Christ." WA 20:606,8-9. It is evident from the choice of the term *corpus* (body) that Luther was referring to the words of institution, "This is my body" (*hoc est corpus meum*), while in the Christological passage above, he chose the notion of "Christ's flesh" (*caro Christi, dei caro*). There is a clear distinction between Christological and sacramental terminology. At the same time, it is also obvious that for Luther both are closely related.

[58]"Humanitas Christi si esset sine verbo, esset res vana." WA 25:64,15-16 (LW 29:82).

flesh!"[59] Immediately afterwards the professor repeated that one should not dispute about the divided Christ, but on the contrary, talk about the Christ united in two natures. The natures are distinct, but united in one person.[60]

In regard to the unity of the one person, which should not be discussed in terms of separation, Luther used the expression *dei caro* and concluded, "I say this, that you might understand the simple form of talking in John, because he says that he has seen the Word of Life."[61] For Luther this simple Johannine modus of speaking is identical with the dogmatic formula of the God-man, Jesus Christ. Again, he continued:

> John and the apostles have seen Christ not according to the humanity which, of course, is the object for the eyes, but here there is the divinity. Having seen Christ on earth, they saw the Word of life, which was from the beginning, i.e., they saw the Son of God, because they touched the living person constituted of God and man. The person is seen, is kissed: everything takes place in the person and not in one nature alone. Note Philip's word![62]

---

[59]WA 20:604,14. Also, in 1527, Luther, when writing on the Eucharist in German, wrote, "Ein Gotts fleisch, Ein geistfleisch," WA 23:242,36 (LW 37:124, n. 209). The English version reads: "It is God's flesh, the Spirit's flesh."

[60]Cf. WA 20:604,14-605,1.

[61]"Hoc dico, ut intelligatis simplicem formam loquendi in Iohanne, quod dicit se vidisse verbum vitae, quod etc.", WA 20:605,1-2.

[62]"Non secundum humanitatem, quae quidem est obiecta oculis sed tamen ibi est divinitas. Videntes Christum in terra viderunt verbum vitae, quod fuit ab initio i.e. filium dei, quia tetigerunt vivam personam

Luther interpreted what Philip saw:

> His eyes were unable to see the one who stood
> by him. Beware — do you not see the Father in
> me? Because it is the Son of God with whom
> you are talking. This is significant in the Holy
> Scriptures. I myself know of no other God ex-
> cept in this humanity.[63]

This is typical of Luther's Christology.[64]

Luther did not believe in Christ's humanity in
isolation from the divinity. Therefore, he said he
"did not believe in Christ born and crucified," and in
the same breath added that he does not believe in
any other God except the incarnate and crucified
God-man, Jesus Christ. When he spoke of Christ's
humanity, he always meant the Christ in the sense
of the one person in two natures, human and divine.
Therefore, Luther confirmed, "If you walk away
from this person who is born of Mary, and you seek
elsewhere, then the devil is leading you. Consequently, you can say, 'I do not know of any other
God than this person. In Christ the total full-

---

constitutam ex deo et homine. Persona videtur, osculatur: omnia in
personam et non in solam naturam. Nota verbum Philippi.... "; WA
20:605,2-7.

[63]"Oculi ipsius mochten des nicht, qui astabat: cave, patrem non vides
in me? quia ille est dei filius, quo cum loqueris. Hoc est insigne in sacris
literis. Ego de nullo deo scio quam in hac humanitate", WA 20:605,7-9.
"This humanity" is the humanity of the God-man, Jesus Christ, the
incarnate Son of God.

[64]"Es ist kein ander Gott on disen Christum, der uns ein liecht unnd
sunne worden ist." WA 31^I:63,21-22 ("There is no other God without
this Christ, who has become to us a light and sun.") Also see WA
40^I:77,1-2 (on Galatians, 1531): "prorsus nullum deum scito extra is-
tum hominem et haere in ista humanitate."

ness lives.' ''[65] With this last sentence Luther arrived at the second key quotation of which R. Prenter speaks. Rörer did not indicate the origin of this sentence about the *tota plenitudo*, which lives in Christ. The printed version (P) does note the full quotation and indicates Colossians 2 as its origin.[66] Undoubtedly, and correctly, later editors recognized Colossians 2:9 as the source.[67] Here, in this Johannine lecture, Luther uses the key Pauline quotation simply to finish his exposition, and he says in reference to it, "The others are speculations about the Majesty, and they terrify us."[68]

Later in the course, when the professor expounded on 1 John 4:2, he again turned to Colossians 2:9 in order to express "that Christ is everything: the way, the justice, the redemption, because 'in him dwells . . . , " etc.[69]

Luther's Christological considerations were directed against "speculations," which terrified him. He took refuge in the biblical words of John 14:9 and Colossians 2:9. With the assistance of the Holy Spirit, he and his students listened to the Holy Spirit and paid attention to the great content rather than to the simple form. Luther pointed out that if the majesty of Christ is expressed in such simplicity, then it must

---

[65]"Si aberraveris ab ista persona, quae nata ex Maria, et quaeris alibi so furt dich der teufel. Ut dicere possis: Nescio de alio deo quam de illo. In Christo habitat tota plenitudo." WA 20:605,9-12.

[66]WA 20:605,34-35.

[67]Cf. the marginal reference, WA 20:605,11.

[68]"Die andern speculationes sunt maiestatis et terrent nos." WA 20:605,12.

[69]" . . . ut Christus sit omnia: via, iustitia, redemptio, quia 'in ipso habitat,' etc., quando hoc felt, etc." WA 20:728,20-21.

originate from the Holy Spirit.[70] What does Luther hear? In his lecture he said that one is dealing here

> with the Word, which has not been born recently, but which was from the beginning. With the first saying he killed Cerinth,[71] who taught that Christ was nothing before Mary. It is against him that he also wrote the gospel. I myself speak about Christ, however, as follows: that he did not begin from Mary, but that he has been from the beginning of the world. When the world was instituted, he was there. What was? The Word was.[72]

The "Word" was there, and Christ was the Word. The question-and-answer period continued: "What kind [of word]?" Answer: "[the word] of life, the fountain of life." Then Luther added,

> With the simplest words, he interprets the greatest [things]. He was born, of course with humanity, but certainly he was from the beginning. He does not say "before the beginning," but "from the beginning" and "in the beginning," as Moses says [Genesis 1:1]. In other words, he does not describe him as having been formed when everything else was

---

[70]WA 20:601,8-15. See Chapter 7 on John's style of simplicity.

[71]WA 20:601,17. The stronger expression, "killing Cerinth," appears in a different version (WA 48:314,7), *prima dictione ferit Cerinthum*. This expression is identical with the word *percutit* as used in the lecture notes of R and P.

[72]WA 20:601,16; 602,3. "Quid? Erat verbum."

formed. And this Word was of such a kind that it had to be clothed with flesh.[73]

God's Flesh Under Physical Examination

Luther states that the Word was with God from the beginning and, as such, dwelt in majesty. But as such it could not be recognized by men, and because "this Word was so much of this divine kind," it had to be clothed with flesh in order to be understood. Luther interpreted Christ, the Word of God, according to Genesis 1:1, as the *creative* Word of God. Luther unfolded his exposition of 1 John 1:1 as follows:

He described the true and eternal God now as true and temporal man, because the divinity cannot be heard or seen. But what is seen is the man. We have clearly seen, i.e., we have contemplated, what first simply came into view. But it could happen that someone is deceived by his vision and [may think] it is a phantom. But we diligently kept a close eye [on him], and we are not deceived. Christ according to his humanity was not a phantom, but we truly saw his body parts, the person, every familiar activity which is common to man.[74]

[73]"Quid? Erat verbum. Quale? Vitae fons vitae. Simplicissimis verbis exponit maxima. Natus quidem cum humanitate sed certe ab initio erat. Non dicit ante initium, sed ab initio et 'in principio' ut Mose. Id est, illum non formatum significat, cum omnia formarentur. Et hoc verbum tantum fuit tale, ut esset indutum carne." WA 20:602,3-7.

[74]"Descripsit verum et aeternum deum, iam verum et temporalem hominem ... perspeximus i.e. contemplati sumus, primum est simplex visio sed posset aliquis falli visione et esse phantasma. . . . sed vere vidimus eius membra, personam, omnem familiaritatem, quam homo solet facere." WA 20:602,8-14.

In the given quotation, "We have clearly seen" is to be understood as "We have contemplated."[75] Luther declared that all the senses and forces were involved when the apostle encountered Christ, including the eyes with which he closely looked at Christ in order to make sure that he was not a *phantasma*. He affirmed, "We have seen his *membra*, the person," etc. A decade later, in his strong German, Luther expressed the same thing: Christ did not flit like a phantom, but lives as a real human being among others.[76]

Luther reenforced his statement about the real humanity of Christ with an affirmation from 2 Peter 1:16, "We did not follow any myths."[77] Thus, for Luther, John and Peter as eyewitnesses confirm the humanity of Christ. The idea that someone might think of Christ as a ghost might have risen from the thought of his virgin birth. To this Luther said elsewhere, "Although the mother was a virgin, he still was not a phantom."[78] Luther, in his lecture on 1 John 1:1, made his plea with John's words: "Listen to us, because what we say, we say with certainty, for we

---

[75]These terms *perspicere* and *contemplare* are to be understood as expressions of Luther's hermeneutics and with his rhetorical background. *Perspicuitas* means the clearness of expression. Interestingly, the P-notes call 1:1 an amplification with the rhetorical term *auxesis* (WA 20:602,33 (LW 30:221)), which functions like a proof. See H. Lausberg, *Handbuch*, 145-46. Rörer does not have the reference of *auxesis*. The term *contemplare* is of a mystical nature and, at the same time, used hermeneutically as an equivalent to meditation in Luther's "orational" approach to Scripture.

[76]WA 46:634,14: " . . . hat nicht gefladdert als ein gespenst, sondern gewonet unter den Leuten."

[77]WA 20:602,15. P attributes the reference to 1 Peter 1:8.

[78]WA 27:485,6. "Quamquam mater virgo, tamen non erat ein gespenst."

heard and clearly have seen (*perspeximus*) God."
Luther then talked about the sense of touch:

> Furthermore, we examined [*palpavimus*] him,
> so that there should be no doubt about our
> sermon. . . . Here is a worthwhile observation
> for our age, that he says of the Word of Life
> that he has seen, clearly seen [*visum, perspec-
> tum*], and touched him with eyes and hands.[79]

In S we read, "He touched, i.e., he certainly examined
him."[80]

Just as the sense of hearing and seeing had been
used to verify that Christ was a true man, the sense
of touch also was at work.[81] The word *contractaver-
unt* (touched) is the Vulgate's expression in 1 John
1:1. But Luther goes beyond this and uses the expression, "We palpated him."[82] The original Latin verb
palpare means "to examine by touching like a physician." It is *terminus technicus* of medieval medicine.[83] In other words, a medical examination would
prove that Jesus was a true human being. Luther,
later in his lectures, returns to the use of medical
language. He probably experienced personally the
physician's *palpare* during his own illnesses, especially in 1527. Luther deliberately chose to interpret
the Vulgate's *contrectare* in this intimate way. Lu-

---

[79]WA 20:602,15-19.

[80]"Contrectavit, id est certo exploravit." WA 48:314,10; 395,1.

[81]"contrectatum oculis et manibus", WA 20:602,19.

[82]"palpavimus," WA 20:602,17.

[83]An illustration of *palpare* is given in *The Middle Ages* (published by
the National Geographic Society, 1977), 292-93, where a drawing is
shown from the museum of Chantilly (Musée Condé).

ther applied this kind of language in order to coun-
terbalance his other expression, which is just as
thought-provoking, namely, that Christ as *dei caro*,
as the Word of life, was born of Mary.

All these terminological efforts by Luther had the
purpose of counterbalancing the contemporary heretics, "who begin to swarm with new errors and glory
themselves in their discovery of the right way."[84]
Luther followed John in this, who had to select his
words carefully against Cerinth and other heretics.
In Rörer's manuscript, above *incipiunt disputare*
(they begin to dispute) is written the dogmatic formula, *de idiomatibus naturarum*. This means that Luther lectured on the heretics who began to dispute the
Christological dogma of the *communicatio* of the
two natures in one person. This same expression
occurs in the printed version.[85] In S we read, "He
says that he has palpated not the humanity of God,
but the 'Word of Life,' which was from the beginning,"[86] and that "he has touched the 'Word,' heard
and seen it"; but now "they begin to swarm and to
break in with their errors by saying, his qualities
are to be attributed to whatever nature one wants

[84]"Nostri heretici incipiunt disputare, quomodo sit humanitas a divinitate seperanda: Divinitas non potest audiri sed humanitas. Sic incipiunt desipere novis erroribus et gloriantur se invenisse modum." WA
20:602,19 - 603,2

[85]WA 20:603,24. Twelve years later, Luther gave his translation of this
dogmatic expression when he studied the history of the councils:
"Denn Idioma griechisch, proprium, latine; ist ein ding, Lasts uns
dieweil ein eigenschaft heissen" (i.e., in German).

[86]"Quemadmodum Iohannes hic dicit se palpitasse non humanitatem
Dei, sed 'verbum vitae,' quod fuit ab initio." WA 48:315,19-20.

to attribute them."[87] Luther, toward the end of his first lecture, returned to "our theologians, who do not know" what John teaches. "Therefore, John [wrote] that he saw, clearly saw, and touched the eternal Word. But only the skin? [No] — I have touched the person himself, who is the Word of Life."[88] Thus, John wrote also for Luther's contemporaries who doubted the Johannine Christology as Luther expounded it.

He Who Is Now on the Mercy Seat

With the notion of *dei caro* Luther expressed the divinity incarnate in Christ. But in the incarnation Christ did not lose his divine majesty. Luther pointed out this aspect, because he wanted to avoid the wrong interpretation of the "mercy seat." He had stated, according to Colossians 2:9, that the divine fullness was in Christ, and that any other ideas are speculations about the majesty which terrify him. He continued by saying: Let us be more like little chicks and remain under the wings of the hen, because if we flee from the hen, then one shall see similar things happening as in the Old Testament.[89] Luther understood the Old Testament saying that God is "above the Cherubim." Christologically

---

[87]"Contrectasse se dicit 'verbum,' audisse et vidisse, quomodo haec conveniunt? Sic iam incipiunt desipere et irrumpere erroribus suis, dicentes cuilibet naturae reddendas suas prorietates." WA 48:315,1-3.

[88]"Hoc nesciunt nostri theologi et floriantur. Ergo Iohannes se vidisse perspexisse tractasse verbum aeternum. Tamen solum cutem? Ipsam personam palpavi, quae est verbum vitae." WA 20:606,2-4.

[89]The notes do not give us any further details. I suspect Luther is referring to Exodus 25:22.

speaking, "So it is with Christ. Be it in the land of the Jews or outside of it, they worshiped at the mercy seat."[90]

Luther, who spoke of God's flesh earlier, continued on 1 John 1:1 by saying that one should not segregate the person from Christ's humanity.[91] Through the incarnation, the mercy seat is connected with Christ's humanity.

> What the Jews saw as the mercy seat was not faith, but this is faith: to see God, because by the Word alone he has sent himself to be here. So touch (*tangere*) Christ's flesh. . . . But the heart of the apostle said: You, eyes, see; you, hands, touch the divine person and the Son of God.[92]

Here Luther interprets the mercy seat of the Old Testament according to Colossians 2:9-10. In Christ we have the mercy seat. From this insight, the passage in Luther's lecture (which is otherwise most difficult to understand) becomes clearer. The WA editor overlooked not only the reference to Exodus 25:22, but also the connection to Colossians 2:9. Instead, he only refers us to Colossians 1:9, having

---

[90]"Sic cum Christo. Sive Iudei in terra sive extra, adorabant ad propiciatorium." WA 20:605,16-17.

[91]"Sic non segreganda persona humanitatis Christi." WA 20:605,21-22.

[92]WA 20:606,5-8: "Quod Iudei videbant propiciatorium, non erat fides sed deum videre haec est fides, quia solo verbo hic se alligavit." It is noteworthy that Rörer originally had written above *deum videre* (to see God): *parentem in propiciatorio*, which is to be understood as to see God in Christ, who is obedient in the work of reconciliation on the mercy seat.

been misled by the printed version.[93] Luther lectured as follows in the context of his reference to the "mercy seat":

> Someone could say, Let us not separate the mercy seat from the divinity. As the psalm verse says, "God of truth,"[94] and "our God makes us safe."[95] Is he, then, so small?[96] He fights for us and he does everything — he who is now on the mercy seat. So we should not segregate the person from Christ's humanity. The same applies to Thomas's, "We cannot know the way."[97] How could we? "I am the way, look at me, I am the truth," [Jesus says].[98]

In a later lecture on 1 John, Luther also identified the mercy seat with "satisfaction."[99] E. Wolf also addressed Luther's Christocentric interpretation of this passage, that nobody can come to God except through him who is the carrier of our sins and the mercy seat.[100] Andres Nygren pointed out that "mer-

---

[93]WA 20:606,29-30 (P). R gives us only the allusion to Paul, *ad Coloss* (606,2), but with the clear catchword attached to it: *quod quidque quaerit proprium caput* of Colossians 2:10. Therefore, I believe Luther wanted to refer to 2:9-11 and not to 1:19, as the WA editor suggests. The reference to 1:19 is possible from line 606, 1, but in light of the mentioned catchword, Luther had in mind the immediate context of 2:9.

[94]"deus veritatis" (Ps. 31:6).

[95]Cf. Psalm 68:7,21.

[96]Original in German: "ist er denn so klein," WA 20:605,20.

[97]Cf. John 14:6.

[98]WA 20:605,18-23. Lines 20 and 21 are decisive: "pugnat pro nobis et omnia facit qui iam in propiciatorio."

[99]"propiciatorium i.e. satisfactio," WA 20:638,19 (on 1 John 2:2).

[100]E. Wolf, "Die Christusverkündigung bei Luther," *Peregrinatio*, 68; "Und niemand zu Gott komen sol denn durch diesen, der da ist unser Sündentreger un Gnadenstuel." WA 21:435,14-15 (Cruciger's summer postil, 1544).

cy seat" in medieval art and theology represents the crucified Christ.[101] Luther reflects this tradition when he says, "Christ fights for us . . . and he is on the mercy seat."

Exodus 25:22 describes the mercy seat, between the two cherubim, and provides the matrix for Luther's thought (which the WA editor did not point out).[102] Together with this Old Testament background, and the verses Romans 3:25[103] and Hebrews 9:5[104], Luther's New Testament understanding of mercy seat becomes obvious.

Because Christ as *dei caro* (in the sense of Colossians 2:9) is the residence of the fullness of God, he is also the seat of mercy, and the head of all (Colossians 2:10). Luther summed it all up toward the end of his first lecture on 1 John 1:

> A wonderful saying: humanity is seen and yet it is the Son of God and the Life. If you seek the Way, etc., elsewhere, it is all over, because "it pleased God to make all fullness reside in him" [Col 2:9, cf. 1:19]; therefore, Paul is quite concerned when everybody seeks to be his own head among the Colossians, because Christ alone is the head of every principality and power (Col 2:10).[105]

---

[101]A. Nygren, "Christus, der Gnadenstuhl," *In Memoriam Ernst Lohmeyer*, 89.

[102]Cf. WA 20:605,14-16, neglects to direct the reader to Exodus 25:22. See also Exodus 37:7, WA 10^{III}:26,11 (LW 51:82). See Bornkamm, *Luther in Mid-career*, 70.

[103]Greek: ἱλαστήριον; Vulgate: propitiatio.

[104]Greek: ἱλαστήριον; Vulgate: propitiatorium. From the Vulgate's two differing versions (cf. n. 103), additional complications stem which do not help to clarify Luther's thoughts on Christ as the mercy seat.

[105]WA 20:605,23;606,2.

Indeed, Prenter is right when he understands Luther's Christology as revolving around Colossians 2:9 and John 14:9.

The opening lecture on 1 John brought to light the biblical basis of Luther's high Christology and his understanding of Jesus Christ in terms of the dogmatic tradition of the early church, which proclaimed Jesus Christ as two natures in one person. Luther made it crystal clear that the basis of his faith is Jesus Christ, the God-man, the incarnate God, as God's flesh (*dei caro*). As the humanity is the necessary precondition for Christ's work of reconciliation and redemption, so also the true divinity is a necessary precondition,[106] because Christ, as Word of Life incarnate, is the one who occupies the divine mercy seat.

Luther's Christology is the traditional, orthodox, catholic doctrine of the two natures in one person. In this regard, Luther's Christology of 1527 in mid-career is the same as Luther's doctrine of Christ in his first lectures on the Psalms, 1513-15. Scholars generally agree that up to 1521 Luther held to the teaching that Christ is *Deus incarnatus*.[107] This remains essentially the same in Luther's mid-career lectures on 1 John in 1527: Christ as *dei caro* is the

---

[106]Cf. P. W. Gennrich, *Die Christologie Luthers*, 59-64.

[107]Cf. E. Vogelsang, *Die Anfänge von Luthers Christologie*, 16. Vogelsang spoke of Luther's self-deception in this regard of keeping in line with the orthodox tradition of the Church, *Christusglaube und Christusbekenntnis bei Luther* (1935) as he followed K. Holl's thesis: "und das war eine Täuschung." "Was verstand Luther unter Religion?" *Gesammelte Aufsätze zur Kirchengeschichte*, vol. 1, Luther, 7th ed. (Tübingen: Mohr, 1948), 71. Also, see D. Vorländer, *Deus incarnatus. Die Zweitnaturenchristologie Luthers bis 1521* (Witten: Lutherverlag, 1974).

incarnate God, in the *gantze person* (whole person) both God and man. He who sees the man Jesus, sees the Father (John 14:9), and in this person, Jesus Christ, all the fullness of the Godhead dwells bodily (Colossians 2:9). The *communicatio idiomatum* was the doctrine, which for Luther expressed most concisely what he wanted to say in terms of the person of Christ. It is the same as John teaches on Christ in his form of speech (*forma loquendi*) and in his simple style of writing.

As Ratschow elaborated in regard to the years 1535-40, Luther will continue to treasure this Christological faith of the father's as *fides catholica*.[108] This is the "unfolding" of which Junghans spoke.

Luther clarified in his opening lecture on 1 John that Christ is God's flesh because the Son of God is the one who is *in carne* (in the flesh), who came *in carnem* (into the flesh). Luther alternately used these expressions, "in the flesh" and "into the flesh," without change of meaning.[109] Luther again picked up on the "dogmatic" theme of his opening lecture when dealing with Christ's humanity and divinity toward the end of his course, when he interpreted 1 John 5:11.

---

[108]Cf. H. Ratschow, "Christologie und Rechtfertigung: Luthers Christologie nach seinen Disputationen," *Iustificatio Impii*. Festschrift für Lauri Haikola zum 60.Geburtstag am 9.2. 1977, ed. Jussi Talasniemi (Helsinki: 1977), 204-26. This was earlier pointed out by Wilhelm Maurer, "Die Anfänge von Luthers Theologie," *ThLZ*, 77 (1952):1-12: "Sie (die Rechtfertigungslehre) ist erwachsen aus einem neuen Verständnis der grossen altkirchlichen Dogmen der Trinität und der Christologie... Die Rechtfertigungslehre des jungen Luther bedeutet die Anwendung christologischer Erkenntnisse auf die Anthropologie" (p. 4).

[109]It is hard to determine whether this is Luther's own distinction or whether it is the stenographer's translation. The Vulgate version of 1 John 4:2 has *in carne*. — So far, Chapter 8 has dealt with Luther's exposition of 1 John 1:1.

Christ is before Mary was. He was not born of Joseph, nor simply the son of the carpenter.[110] Christ's flesh is God's flesh. So Christ's flesh is not to be misunderstood as a perfect creature like the Arians believe, but Christ is God by nature because in him is eternal life:

> If, therefore, you want to have eternal life, you need to have the Son. If you want to have him, you need to have the testimony. Therefore, our life is to want to see nothing but God's testimony and to believe in it, etc. This verse [5:11], therefore, argues that Christ is true God, because if there is eternal life in Christ, he naturally needs to be God, because no creature gives itself life. Everything is created out of nothing. If he can give and be eternal life, he must be God, and God by nature.[111]

Christ must be divine, because of us and for our eternal life. Christ is not just a perfect creature, but eternal God, as Luther taught in agreement with the catholic teaching against the Arians:

> The Arians say that Christ is a perfect creature, etc. But how can he give life, who receives it? . . . They used the same words as the catholics, but they had their own sense with which the disciples of the Arians understood Christ as the son, but not as the natural and substantial [Son].[112]

---

[110]Cf. WA 20:764,3.

[111]WA 20:786,18-24 on 1 John 5:11.

[112]"Sic Arriani: perfecta creatura est Christus etc. . . Iisdem verbis utebantur quibus catholici, sed habebant tropos suos, quibus Arrianorum discipuli intelligebant Christum filium sed non naturalem, substantialem." WA 20:786,26; 787,4.

Toward the end of the course on 1 John, Luther said,

> Final repetition: this is all what he [John] taught, that we are [born] of God. How? In this wise: we are of God, because the Son of God came into the flesh and his coming gave us the sense, the title, that we recognize the true God; it is a fine [thing]. . . . The Ebionites pictured God without the Son, for they mixed the Old Testament and the New Testament. Theirs is a God formed by human thinking. . . . The Arians laughed at these manifest verses. Our sects do the same. The Arians say that Christ is true God, but they negate the eternal life substantially; [for them] he is the principle creature; he is far above all the angels created and, therefore, he is a God and a true God, because as a truly made matter he is not a shadow, but he is also not a natural and substantial God.[113]

The sum of our faith is, Luther said by using John 16:3, that we know the Father and the Son. This is "our highest article"; by this one, the rest of the articles are served, which the Son has ordained.[114] For Luther, there is no question that the two natures of Christ guarantee that "Christ was the Son even before the incarnation and before all the ages. He is

[113]"Repetitiones finales: . . . . res facta sed non naturalis et substantialis deus." WA 20:800,2-21.

[114]"Ibi summa nostrae fidei . . . Iste summus articulus noster, isto servato reliqui servantur, quos ordinavit ille filius." WA 20:800,22; 801,2.

God and man."[115] Furthermore, as the humanity of
Christ is the necessary precondition for his work of
reconciliation and redemption, so is his divinity. It is
the soteriological interpretation of the incarnation
which is transparent here in Luther's teaching, and
that is why Luther said: Christ has come into the
flesh in order to justify us.[116] He was sent "so that
you are in righteousness without sin."[117] Those who
negate the Christ as being sent so that we may live
through him, are the ones who commit malediction
of Christ.[118]

The person of Christ in two natures is, so far, one of
the two focal points of Luther's Christology. We have
dealt with the person of Christ, and now the other
focal point, the work of Christ, must be addressed.
We do that by examining the Christological aspects
in Luther's original expressions in German which
are extant in R and P.

---

[115]"Duae naturae. Fuit filius ante incarnationem imo ante secula, i.e.
esse deum et hominem." WA 20:725,14-15.

[116]"Venit in carnem iustificaturus nos." WA 20:735,7. With C. Stange
we concur, that for Luther the incarnation and the work of salvation
are identical: "Beides, die Menschwerdung und das Heilandswerk, ist
ein und dasselbe." "Die Person Jesu Christi in der Theologie Luthers,"
ZST 6 (1928):461.

[117]"Sed scito Christum missum, ut sis in iusticia sine peccato." WA
20:742,23-24.

[118]WA 20:752,7-8.

CHAPTER 9

THE CHRISTOLOGY IN LUTHER'S ORIGINAL GERMAN

When dealing with the German fragments in the Latin lecture notes, we reach the historical Luther, because these German elements are the direct notes of his oral teachings without having been translated into the Latin shorthand. It is therefore, in order, on the text-critical basis of Part One and in light of the historical context of Part Two, to examine now the original words which Luther used. With the Latin elements, we can never be quite certain whether Luther himself used them or whether they are R's or P's immediate translation from German into Latin. With the German, we are touching bedrock and ought to examine the Christological terminology. Since R and P differ in their German notes at times, it is appropriate to combine R's and P's German elements for this purpose. In P we found the tendency to eliminate German sentences, but when they are preserved in spite of this tendency, they deserve recognition. We cannot take all German elements into consideration, but only the Christologically relevant ones.

The Whole Person — He Is the Breasts and Lap

First of all, Luther emphasized that whatever concerns the person of Christ, concerns the whole person,[1] presupposing in this German sentence the doctrine of the communication of the divine and human attributes (although he did not used the theological terminology for it as such). If one does not approach the Christological question in this way, then one follows the devil's leading.[2] 1 John 1:1 is a verse the students should consider wholeheartedly.[3] It refers to the incarnation, which has the soteriological purpose to save man, because man's own righteousness does not effect it. Something else is needed in order to fight with *death*, namely the *Life*, which is Christ. It must be perfectly clear that the incarnate Christ is not a phantom or ghost.[4]

The "advocate" in 1 John 2:1 is interpreted as *ein patron*, a pastor, a bishop, who represents us before God.[5] He, therefore, is the one who speaks for us.[6] He is an intercessor, and the angels are not playing in front of him (presumably for his amusement), but Christ is before God because he has a duty to perform, i.e., he has to be the paraclete, the comforter, and speaker for us who tells the Father, "Father, be gracious to this one, be merciful to him, because I have shed my blood for him.[7] Luther recreated the

---

[1]"ghet die gantze person an. . . . nimbt die gantz person mit"; WA 20:603,12 and 18.

[2]"so furt dich der teufel," WA 20:605,10.

[3]"erwergt euch mit gantzem hertzen drauff," WA 20:609,11-12.

[4]"gehort," WA 20:609,20. " . . . es helt den stich nicht. Cum morte pugnare gehort vita zu quae est Christus"; WA 20:776,7. — "gespenst," WA 20:615,5.

[5]" 'Advocatum.'. . . Paulus Gal. 6. ein patron, ein pfaffen, bischoff, qui est coram deo und vertritt uns"; WA 20:634,12-13.

[6]"Ist ein fursprech," WA 20:634,17.

[7]"Ist ein fursprech, non ludunt coram eo angeli, sed eius officium: esse paracletum, troster und fursprech. Pater, dem genad, sey im barmher-

divine dialogue, letting the Son speak German to the Father. On the next lecture day Luther repeated that Christ is the advocate who speaks the best for us.[8] Not Mary, but Christ, is the intercessor, "the breasts and lap."[9]

Christ, the Smoke-Screen Maker

Beginning with 1 John 1:5, the German becomes more frequent. The symbolism of darkness and light created a wide range of German expressions. The sects, who hate the light, enter and want to divide the light[10] with their reasoning. Reason "has hung its own thought on to God."[11] But the true light says that God is not a phantom.[12] The true proclamation does not hang something around God's neck or smear something onto him. Darkness is what they smear onto God.[13] This means they carry darkness into God. They are bolder (*frecher*) than the sons of light and boast with God's name.[14] P's notes elaborate this by saying they want to smear darkness onto our Lord God. They

zig, quia effudi pro illo sanguinem." WA 20:634,17-19. Remarkable in this macaronic text is the synonymous use of grace and mercy: however, in the verbal form: *dem genad* (be gracious to that one there), *sey barmherzig* (be merciful to him). Apparently, in Luther's German "grace" and "mercy" are synonyms. P: "des neme ich mich an" (line 34).
[8]"der das best fur uns redt," WA 20:635,14-15.

[9]"qui ubera et schos," WA 20:636,8.

[10]"Neben dem liecht tretten viel secten herein . . . et wollen das liecht zertrennen." WA 20:614,16-18.

[11]"Ratio kan hie nicht fur uber. . . . Ita hat sie iren gedancken got an gehengt." WA 20:615,1-3.

[12]"gespenst," ibid., line 5 (a product of *cogitatio*).

[13]"non habs got an den hals gehengt . . . is yhm nicht an geschmirt et in collum ghengt"; WA 20:615,8-9.

[14]"illi sectarii sint frecher quam filii lucis, quia semper plus glorientur et brusten sich mit gots namen quam alii"; WA 20:616,1-2.

smear God on their cowl and glue the divine truth onto lies.[15] Nothing should be added to God's light for it is nothing but Christ's light.[16]

On 2:1 Luther said that Christ's righteousness stands for us, and he cannot be condemned.[17] The just one is the one who is not condemned.[18] Therefore, Christ is the speaker for us, and not a "master with a stick" as he seems to them.[19] P adds here: It is sin which causes troubles of the heart.[20] Rather, Christ is the one who with his justice makes a fog (smoke-screen) before God's eyes so that he is unable to see anybody as a sinner.[21] God is a "right father," a "heavenly father."[22]

When dealing with verse 2:18, Luther took up the fight against the early heresies and the question of the "whole Christ" which is attacked by the Arians and by the pope.[23] But, a "heretic against the person

---

[15]"Sie wollen tenebras schmieren an unsern Herr Gott. Gott schmieren sie an die kappe und kleben die göttliche warheit an die lügen." (P) WA 20:615,36-38.

[16]"dissue et damna umb des leidigen Zusatz, quod dei lux sol heissen, cum alia non sit quam Christi", WA 20:617,19-20. "Unglaub fingit sibi deum", WA 20:643,15. "Sie malen ihren Gott anders ab denn er ist (P), WA 20:643,30.

[17]"Hats recht . . . et non potest verworfen werden"; WA 20:637,7-8.

[18]"Justus: den man nicht verwerffen mag"; WA 20:637,12.

[19]"Sic et hodie illorum est stockmeyster." WA 20:637,20. P preserves at a different place a corresponding German phrase: "Wolte ich es vergessen, war Christus bald da mit der ruthe und sagte: hastu das gethan?" WA 20:704,35-36 (When I wanted to forget it, soon Christ was there with the rod and said: 'did you do that?')

[20]"Die sünde richtet das hertze leid an." WA 20:637,34 (P).

[21]"Quia Christus macht sua iustitia tantam nebulam deo fur augen, ut nullum possit videre peccatorem", WA 20:644,12-13.

[22]"ir habt hun ein rechten vater." WA 20:659,9 (R). "Lieben kindergen, ihr habt auch einen himmlichen Vater." WA 20:659,30 (P).

[23]"Ii, qui hoc caput angreiffen, die sind veri Antichristi. Illi Arriani etc. die greiffen Christum bei eim stuck an, illi totum Christum, das ist regnum Papae." WA 20:669,11-13.

of Christ is not so big as when he would be against the merit of Christ," adds P.[24] R speaks in Latin of a double sin if one does that.[25] P in addition reports Luther's saying about Pelagius: he was the ground and cornerstone of all papists.[26]

Christ Is the Lord of the Queen, the Church

Luther does develop an ecclesiology here. He points out a Christocentrically oriented concept of the church: The church is queen, and she belongs to the Lord of Lords, she belongs to Christ, because of 1 Timothy 6:15.[27] The church is composed of those who carry his name. Those are Christians because of their anointing, which makes them priests and kings.[28] Christ alone dresses us with the name Christian.[29] When proceeding to 2:20, Luther applied his Christology to the Christian anthropology, saying that Christians derive their name from Christ's work, and that Christ puts that name of Christian on us, because a Christian is he who does not insist on works.[30]

The Christian's Lord is Christ, who distributes the same lotion and Holy Spirit, and thus the Christian

---

[24]"Haereticus in personam Christi ist nicht so gross als in meritum Christi." WA 20:669,31-32.

[25]Cf. line 15.

[26]"der war der Grund und Eckstein aller Papisten." WA 20:670,35-36.

[27]"Ecclesia est regina et 'dominus dominantium' sie gehort Christum an, qui est dominus." WA 20:675,9-10.

[28]"Rurt da mit wo her wir Christen heissen. In Ebreo est hell vox unctio, non sonat wie man aliquas res salbt, sed proprie ein priester und khonig salben. . . . " WA 20:676,5-7.

[29]"Nomen hoc zihet uns Christus allein an." WA 20:676,20.

[30]"Christianus ist der nicht auf den wercken stehet." WA 20:676,22.

puts faith in him, and they are baked into one cake, so that he shares in Christ's righteousness. *Ex sola fide,* by faith alone, we become Christians. Through him I put all my misery on him, and he puts all good things on me.[31] Here the motif of the "joyous exchange" is expressed in German with Luther exclaiming: God of heaven, how is this preaching lost![32] Satan smells the roast.[33] We are lacking faith.[34] The Carthusians' cowl does not do it — do not bring this piety forth before God![35] Without Christ, nothing is done well.[36] The wicked press down the Christians. The heretics are seen on the devil's side, who make a fog in front of the truth, but the Son survived so many clouds, he does not care about them; so it is with the gospel which speaks to itself, "I will still remain, the sun will drive away the clouds of the sacramentarians."[37] All this is so, because you know *the* truth in Christ.[38]

---

[31]"Christus ist sein herr, qui teilt im die selben salben et spiritum sanctum mit, et sic trauet er auf yn, et unus kuch. . . . Ergo ex sola fide Christiani fimus, per quam in duo eum et econtra ipse me et per hunc leg ich all mein ungluck auff ynn, econtra omnia bona ipse auff mich." WA 20:677,3-7.

[32]"Hergot vom himel wie sind die predig verloschen." WA 20:677,9.

[33]"was gilt, reucht den braten wol," WA 20:677,11-12.

[34]"Es felt nur dran, quod non credimus." (R) WA 20:677,15. "Aber es fehlt uns am Glauben." (P) ibid., line 38.

[35]"Sic Carthusianus . . . est from, sed er khom fur got da mit nicht." (R) WA 29:678,12-13. "Carthusianus potest dici ein Cleusner, pertector cilicii." (R) WA 20:676,23. "Cartheuser-Kappen geben es nicht." (P) WA 20:677,31.

[36]" . . . sine Christo ist nichts wolgethan", WA 20:679,16-17.

[37]"die rotten gehen altzeit oben un trucken die Christen unter. . . . quia Satan macht ein nebel fur die veritatem . . . die son hat so viel wolcken uberlebt et tamen nubes lassen nicht nach, aber sie fragt nicht darnach. . . . interim Euangelium: noch werd ich bleiben, die Son wird die wolcken der Sacramentirer all weck treiben." WA 20:680,12-20.

[38]"Sciatis *die* veritas in Christo." WA 20:679,23.

The Natural Son of God Does Not Stink in the Tomb

One of the hardest rocks to be dealt with is the following macaronic text about Christ's humanity and divinity:

Ebion makes one cake out of the New and the Old Testament, which the Turk picked up, as the papists [picked up] Pelagius's error and Arius [picked up the error] of Cerinth. Arius was more careful, though. Cerinth was a gross negator of Christ's divinity. Till then the gospel was [proclaimed] orally, but because of him he [John] wrote the gospel and the epistle. He applies the miserable inscription that all [men] are liars, such as we [are] when we say that Christ as the natural son of God must stink and lie [in the grave]. They carry Christ's humanity [to the graveyard] chiefly in order to press the divinity down [into the grave]."[39]

The Jews also gave Christ little honor and rejected the truth. John, however, expounds that Christ

---

[39]"Ebion macht ein kuchen ex novo et vetere testamento, hoc suscepit Turca ut papistae Pelagii errorem, Arrius Cherinti. Arrius ging aber seuberlicher da mit umb, Cherinthus crassus fuit abnegator divinitatis Christi et fuit, quando Euangelium adhuc fuit in voce, propter quem scripsit Euangelium et Epistolam. Applicat miserum elogium, quod omes sunt mendaces. Qui dicimus Christum naturalem dei filium, mus stincken und liegen sein. Illi extulerunt humanitatem Christi maxime, ut divinitatem deprimerent." WA 20:681:8-15. The Latin words used here are *efferre* = to carry out to the graveyard, and *deprimere* = to press down, i.e., within the imagery of the grave. To this imagery the German expressions fit: *mus stincken* = he must stink like a corpse, and *liegen* = to lie (in the grave). In other words, those are not telling the truth who say that Christ must be like a corpse remaining in the grave; if one says this, then one has buried Christ and has pressed the divinity down into the grave together with the humanity.

should be God's and man's son.[40] He uses a "syllo-
gism." This is our consolation. Thus, when the
Arians fail Christ, they fail God.[41] At the end of the
interpretation of John 2, Luther taught the orthodox
catholic position: the Son has the Father's nature, or
kind.[42] The German *art* is synonymous with nature.[43] At this point R has exclusively German elements; in contrast, P translates imprecisely into Latin that Luther supposedly taught that "the Son must
be similar to the Father."[44] This sentence is smoothed
out in the English translation which reads, "For the
Son must be like the Father."[45]

Luther was very much concerned about retaining
the orthodox doctrine of Christ. Corresponding to
this Christology, he stated his implicit ecclesiology
from a Christocentric point of view. Luther's applied Christology, i.e., his theological anthropology,
comes to light when he interpreted the beginning of
John 3. Man is also a son of God, but one must
approach this fact like a "poor cinderella";[46] Christ

---

[40]" ... ut Iudei fecerunt, dant illi ein geringe ehr et auferunt verum. ...
Exponit Iohannes, quod Christus sol sein gots und menschen son."
WA 20:682,1-3.

[41]"Syllogismus, quo probat, Das ist unser trost: ... Sic Arriani wenn
mans Christi felt, hat man gots gefelet." WA 20:682,8-10.

[42]"Oportet filius habeat die art patris." (R) WA 20:692,11-12.

[43]Cf. *Duden, Etymologie, Herkunftswörterbuch der deutschen Sprache*
(Mannheim: Dudenverlag) s.v. "Art".

[44]"Patri enim filius debet esse similis", WA 20:692,31.

[45]LW 30:264. The Latin basis for this English version is the adjective
similis, which in Greek would be *homoios*. But this is exactly what
Luther did not want to say when he said in German that "the son has
the nature of the father." Unfaithful to the text basis P, the translator
brought forth the original meaning better than his source, P. As proof
that Luther is keenly aware of the difference between the words *similis*
and *idem*, check WA 20:698,12: "erimus similes, non idem ...."

[46]"pauper aschenpradel", WA 20:694,18.

is man's brother and the Son of God.[47] One must push through to this truth, because it is concealed by all kinds of contrary scandals.[48]

When Man Is Born of God, Sin Is Grilled on the Spit

The sins are gone, where one is born of God, Luther explained on John 3:9, because sin is grilled (like bratwurst/spanferkel) on a spit. Both R and P preserve German elements.[49] This image implies that all make-believe and false appearance of piety are melted away until the real thing comes forth.[50] God is merciful to the sinner, to the contrite and humble ones, but to those who sin freely, he does not give it (his mercy).[51]

When Luther came to speak of faith and good works, he said, "This faith is stabilized by fruit, by use, by practice. Otherwise faith is very weak."[52] Luther concluded his interpretation of John 3 with references to Isaiah 55:11 and Colossians 3:16, saying that the "word does not go without fruit."[53]

---

[47]Luther addressing Christ directly: "Sed du must mein bruder sein et dei filius." WA 20:695,4-5. P has the additional rhetorical question: "Sollten so viel Heilige gelehrte leute das nicht gewust haben?" (Should so many learned saints not have known this?) WA 20:695,32-33.

[48]"Ego debeo filius dei et frater Christ esse, das ist zugeteckt ab omnibus scandalis contrariis." WA 20:697,13-14. P lists three such covers: the world, the flesh, the devil: "Mundus ist eyn Deckel, Caro der andere, Diabolus der dritte." WA 20:697,37.

[49]"Was sol ich viel sagen? . . . in veru peccatum steckts." (R) WA 20:705,15-19. "Nasci ergo ex Deo est pugnare peccatum, da wird die sünde am brand spiess gesteckt." (P) WA 20:706,25-26.

[50]This sentence is extant in Latin: WA 20:705,16-17.

[51]"Propicius est et multae misericordiae contritis et humilibus, sed qui libere peccant, den schenckt ers nicht." WA 20:713,18 — 714,1. P adds in this context: "das auch Gott ietzt seinen zorn möchte lassen sehen"; WA 20:713,34-35 (that also God would want to let his anger be seen).

[52]" . . . alioqui fides est seer schwach"; WA 20:716,4.

[53]" 'Verbum eius non revertitur' geht nicht an frucht ab." WA 20:722,4-5.

Christ, the Nucleus and the Juice in the Shell,
the Money in the Sack

In the lecture on 1 John 4:2 Luther selected two colorful images to depict Christ. He is the nucleus in the shell and the money in the wallet. In the papacy, Scripture is available but the juice and the nucleus have been sucked out, because the devil took the nucleus from the pope and left him the shell. Those under the papacy do say something about Christ's death; however, Satan always fights against Christ's flesh, suggesting that his flesh is good for nothing.[54] The second image is connected with Rom. 5:1, that we say about the gift that one finds Christ in the sack into which he put himself.

> It is the money in the sack [that counts], [but] they make an empty wallet out of it. And when those spirits are disturbed, it gets worse: they negate Christ's divinity, they let it be said that Christ came into the flesh, but they deny the fruit [of his coming] . . . When this [Col. 2:9] is missing, . . . Satan can tolerate whatever else may be said about Christ, if only the buying power is gone.[55]

Luther contrasted the empty wallet and empty shell, which is the papacy and false teaching, with

---

[54]"Sub Papatu vidit abnegationem Christi crassam hinweg genommen, abstulit nucleum papae et reliquit illi testam. In papatu ghet die schrifft, aber der safft et necleus ist erhaus gesogen, quia dicunt: Christi mors etc. . . . " WA 20:728,10-13.

[55]" . . . Es ist das gelt im sack, ipsi marsupium vacuum machen sie draus. Quando illi spiritus obturbuntur, wirds erger werden, negabunt Christi divinitatem, lassen ghen quod Christus venit in carnem, sed fructum negant . . . , quia 'in ipso habitat' etc., quando hoc felt etc. Satan potest pati, ut dicantur de Christo omnia, sed ut vis absit." WA 20:728,16-22.

the full wallet and the nucleus and juice, which is the doctrine of the incarnation, of Christ's flesh, but which always is to be understood as divine as well, since Col. 2:9 speaks of the fullness of deity residing in Christ in bodily form.

In all these fights with the devil "it is our consolation" that Christ, who came into the flesh, is greater, and if the enemies had four worlds, he is richer yet,[56] Luther commented on 1 John 4:2. Regarding 1 John 4:6 Luther said that the belief in the incarnate Christ justifies us. This requires another spirit than the spirit of the world, which, like the Jews, says that Christ was born of Joseph.[57] He continued by exclaiming, "Nothing but comfort!"[58] Those people who are opposed by 1 John 4:8 cannot be convinced by anybody, because "they stand on their head."[59] 1 John 4:9 "is a beautiful text,"[60] because by the words, "through him we have life," John pushes the pope with all of his foundations into nothingness.[61] The good man says as sinner to God, "Have mercy on me!"[62]

---

[56]"Sed 'qui maior' Christus adveniens in carnem est apud vos. . . . der ists, et si haberent 4 mundos, tamen noster est ditior etc., das ist unser trost." WA 20:733,7-10. P speaks in this regard in German of the small flock: "ein klein häufflein," WA 20:733,31.

[57]"Iudei: natus ex Ioseph. . . . Sed quod venit in carnem iustifcaturus nos, da gehort ein ander geist zu, non spiritus mundi." WA 20:735,6-8.

[58]"Eytel consolationes . . . las unsern herrn frumb sorgen." WA 20:735,12-13.

[59]"Sie sthen auff yhrem kopff." WA 20:740,6.

[60]"ey ein schoner text"; WA 20:741,4.

[61]" 'Per eum' stoest papam cum omnibus suis fundationibus in nihilum." WA 20:741,19-20.

[62]"sey mir nur gnedig"; WA 20:742,18.

Christ Alone the Propitiation

When proceeding to 1 John 4:10, Luther added that this verse does not let any monastery stand.[63] Then, most remarkably, he continued, "Is this not in German, propitiation? If it is not Christ, but your moral works [merit] of congruity, I ask, what, if anything, do they do for propitiation? Is it [not] that which Christ does, who is the Son of God? I wish the devil would have taken away my works a hundred times before I should say this [that they merit anything before God]."[64] This macaronic passage is an example of Luther's protest against the scholastic doctrine of "appropriate merit" based on his Christocentrism, that Christ alone is the *versunung*. But Satan calls on sayings about works.[65] The "perfect love" of verse 4:12 Luther interpreted according to the hermeneutical principle that "Scripture interprets Scripture," with reference to the Psalms and to Paul. "Why then does he say 'perfected'? I think that he speaks of perfect love like the Psalm does, as being *integer*, sound, whole. Paul [speaks of] the right love, although it is not perfected. Their understanding of

---

[63]"die nicht ein Kloster sthen sollen lassen," WA 20:743,18.

[64]"Nonne deusch geredt, quid est ein versunung, si Christus est non tua opera moralia, de congruo, quaero, an illa faciant aliquid ad propiciationem? vel illud, quod Christus facit, qui est filius dei? Ich wolt, ut mea opera der teufl het hundert mal hin weck gefurt, quam ut haec dicerem," WA 20:743,20-24. The scholastic doctrine of *meritum de congruo* was that every sinner could, at some point in his life, at least for a single moment, arrive at a love for God above everything else. This momentarily achieved act of love for God was considered appropriate merit (*meritum de congruo*), and because of it, God would not refuse his grace and would answer to this human act appropriately with his justification of the sinner. See O. H. Pesch, *Hinführung zu Luther*, 160.

[65]"Et Satan nimbt die spruch de operibus zuhilff." WA 20:745,28; 746,1.

love is a beggar's work, but where one is in God and God is in us, there is healthy love, not idle love.... He wants solid love, not the hobbling one. This is miserable love, which they mend in such a way."[66]

On love and fear (4:18), Luther declared that there is a big struggle there, when God is acknowledged as Father. So it was with Jacob and Job, because then Satan grabs a person by the head and throat. And so it was with Christ's flesh before his suffering, when he did not want to take the cup of suffering; but in this spiritual struggle Christ "turns himself around" and says, "Thy will be done."[67] Here the Latin expression *caro Christi* refers to both the human and the divine in the person of Christ who is suffering; but Christ is able to "turn himself around" in the midst of these troubles and to let the Father's will be done. Luther presumes here, without making it explicitly clear, that because of the communication of attributes, Christ achieved this turn. For Luther *caro Christi* and *caro Dei* are identical.

Returning to the beginning of the lectures, Luther took up the theme of the whole Christ, whose wholeness includes his presence in preaching and in the sacramental life of his people, and this presence cannot be cut off.[68] This is so because Christ comes to

---

[66]" ... ut psalmus: Integros, sanos, gantz, Paulus: 'languaentes circa,' sani in fide, i.e. sani in charitate, die rechte lib quamquam non sit perfecta. ... ist ein bettelwerck. ... Ista est languida charitas, vult solidam habere, non die humplerische. ... das ist charitas misera, die sie also flicken." WA 20:749,13-24.

[67]" ... tum Satan greifft im nach dem kopff et gorgl. ... Sic Christi caro renuit calicem et in medio pugnae wirfft er sich herumb et dicit: fiat voluntas." WA 20:761,3-7.

[68]"abschneiden," WA 20:753,10. The Latin context reveals the issue of wholeness. WA 20:752,25; 753,10, especially line 29, "Hoc est ergo totum [Christum] negare."

us through the water of baptism.[69] Christ's blood is taken into the preaching, through which the blood is dispersed.[70] In contrast, the sects, for instance, call baptism a dog's bath.[71]

Reviewing the German fragments, the active verbal expressions are striking: to enter, to divide, to hang upon, to smear, to glue, to condemn, to make a fog (smoke-screen), to attack, to anoint, to put on, to trust, to smell, to press down, to survive, to stink, to drive away, to honor, to fail, to cover, to suck, to push, to turn round. Equally conspicuous is the absence of the Johannine Christological title of "Savior of the World," which in German would be *Erlöser* or *Heiland der Welt*. The only explanation of the absence of the German version of this title is that Luther was so involved in refuting Erasmus's Latin version of *servator*[72] that he used other synonymous Latin titles, such as *redemptor* and *salvator*, and he took the German expressions, which he used profusely elsewhere, for granted.

Luther accepted the dogmatic catholic tradition very seriously when he lectured in German on Christ as the Son of God and Son of Man — emphasizing the virgin birth and refuting the assumption that he was from Joseph. At the same time, Luther refuted Docetism's claim that Christ was a phantom. Lu-

---

[69] " 'Per aquam' so khombt er zu uns." WA 20:777,14.

[70]"i.e., yn die predigt sanguinis Christi wird gefast, per quam spargitur." WA 20:778,6-7.

[71]"Sie heissen es ein hundsbad." (P) WA 20:779,26. R has this expression in Latin: "Nostri spiritus: caninum balneum"; WA 20:780,4; see also S-notes: "caninum balneum vocant"; WA 48:323,23.

[72]"Statt salvator übersetzt Erasmus stets 'servator.' " August Bludau, *Die beiden ersten Erasmus-Ausgaben des Neuen Testaments*, 470.

ther's central idea of "Christ in the flesh" shines through the German fragments and includes both the humanity and the divinity of Christ, the Son of God. For Luther, the flesh of Christ is always also the flesh of God. Luther's Christology is always the Christology of the *communicatio idiomatum* in the whole person. Because of this, Christ as the "natural Son of God" cannot stink in the grave. Anyone who would say that his body began to decay would negate his divinity.

Luther not only defended and upheld the ancient dogmatic tradition of the person of Christ, but he also applied this dogma to the doctrine of salvation. Christ alone is *versunung*. This applied Christology yields the idea of the "joyous exchange." In terms of eschatology, Christ will be the one who is the comforter and the smoke-screen maker on the last day. He is the speaker for us before God, and he is our brother. All insights into this "beautiful text" are lost by the papacy, where the juice and nucleus have been sucked out and only the shells (the empty wallet) remain without the contents, i.e., the work of Christ. Mary is not the *paracleta* and the lap for troubled Christians, but Christ is the *paracletus*, and he is "breasts and lap." These are strong images emphasizing the soteriological Christology in Luther's lectures on 1 John.

Since the formula of Chalcedon is the summary of Luther's doctrine of the person of Christ, then it is understandable that he became quite upset over Zwingli's interpretation of the separation of the two natures and Zwingli's *alloeosis*.[73] At the same time,

---

[73]Cf. J. Koopmans, *Das altkirchliche Dogma in der Reformation.* Beiträge zur evangelischen Theologie 22 (Munich: Kaiser Verlag, 1955), 80.

Luther had to refute the accusation that he would mix the two natures in one *wesen* (existence), and he therefore affirmed: "This is not true, we do not say that divinity is humanity, or divine nature is human nature."[74]

If our observation is correct, that the Athanasian scheme of Christ's humanity and divinity is connected to the question of salvation in the form of the "joyous exchange," then this thought pattern, found in the German fragments, belongs to the historical Luther. It is as well found in his Reformation tract on "Christian Liberty."[75] It is then in this unfolding and application of the classical Christology to soteriology where Luther's contribution lies in the history of the theology. Luther preached exactly this same unfolding of the Christological dogma in terms of soteriology also in a sermon in his mid-career (1525), which I quote here to illustrate the consistency of Luther's doctrine of Christ:

> For Christ is not called Christ because he has two natures. Why should this be of any concern to me? Rather, he bears this glorious and comforting name because of the office and work which he took upon himself. . . . That he is by nature man and God, he has for himself, but that he redirected his office and poured out his love and that he becomes my Savior and Redeemer, this happens for the sake of my

---

[74]"Sie schreyen uber vns das wir die zwo natur ynn ein wesen mengen. Das ist nicht war. Wir sagen nicht das Gottheit sey menscheit odder gottliche natur sey menschliche natur . . . ," WA 26:324,1-3.
[75]"Cf. U. Asendorf, *Gekreuzigt und Auferstanden*, 330.

consolation and my well-being. It concerns me, because he wants to redeem his people from sins.[76]

---

[76]"denn Christus ist nicht darümb Christus genennet, das er zwo Naturen hat, was gehet mich dasselbige an? Sondern er treget diesen herrlichen und tröstlichen Namen von dem Ampt und werck, so er auff sich genomen hat, dasselbige gibt im den Namen. Das er von natur mensch und Gott ist, das hat er für sich, aber das sein Ampt dahin gewendet und seine liebe ausgeschüttet und mein Heiland und Erlöser wird, geschiet mir zu Trost und zu gutt, es gilt mir darümb, das er sein Volck von Sünden los machen wil." WA 16:217,32; 218,17.

CHAPTER 10

THE WORK OF CHRIST EXPLICATION IN THE WAY OF CHRISTOCENTRIC MYSTICISM WITH IMAGES OF THE MEDIEVAL CATHOLIC TRADITION

*Christ as Medicus in the Church
as His Hospital and His Most Potent Medicine*

We have covered one example of Luther's utilization of medical language in his first Johannine lecture. Luther pointed out that when Christ was, so to speak, under physical examination, they palpated, or touched, him. Luther's life situation was such that he was afflicted with illness, as we pointed out in the contextual part of this dissertation. This exposure to illness and medical attnetion could very well have triggered the application of medical language in the interpretation of 1 John. In a letter of November 1, 1527, Luther called his home a hospital,[1] and during the lecture on 1 John 2:12 he spoke of the church as a hospital.

---

[1]"in domo mea coepit esse hospitale." Cf. WA Br 4:275,12.

> So the church is a hospital, where we are transferred from darkness to the place where there is cure from sin. Therefore, [sin] is not yet carried away. Christ says, "Hear me, ask, pray, follow me! I will liberate you."[2]

It is in the church where one finds the cure from sin and comes out of the darkness. But those who do not want the hospital, who, like the monks, want to cure themselves, are insane,[3] Luther says, because sin is remitted not by one's own care, but because of Christ's liberation, apprehended by faith alone. The fasting of the monks does not help either. It only makes the illness all the worse as more sin settles in when they grow proud of their fasting. The heart of these people is not healed through self-help, but rather is inflated all the more.[4]

All this illness amounts to the need for a physician. It is Christ who is the source of grace and mercy, who is "the innocent, the holy, the just, the immaculate, and *medicus*."[5] The enumeration of adjectives causes us to hesitate to translate this term *medicus* with the noun "physician." These adjectives are meant to unfold the verse 2:1, where Christ is called "just" and an "advocate." Whether Luther meant the noun or the adjective "medical" does not

---

[2]"Sic est ecclesia hospitale, quando transferimur de tenebris in locum, ubi est curatio peccati. Ergo nondum ablatum. Christus: audi me, roga, ora, sequere me, liberbo te." WA 20:655,13-15.

[3]"insaniunt"; WA 20:632,1.

[4]"Quia peccatum simpliciter remittitur per fidem, deinde curatur non nostra curatione sed quod gemo, oro. Monachi quanto magis ieiunant, tanto plus insidet peccatum.... Non sanatur per hoc cor, sed inflatur potius." WA 20:655,19-656,4.

[5]Cf. WA 20:637,30-31.

make much difference. Within this enumeration it functions to point out the healing aspect of Christ's ministry. If not here, then certainly elsewhere Luther called Christ "the physician" after the Augustinian and Bernardine tradition. It has been demonstrated in Luther research that Luther imitated Augustine in using medical language to describe the doctrine of justification as a continuing healing process.[6] Luther understood "justifying" as "healing."[7] Man needs Christ the physician in the church as his hospital because man's flesh has been poisoned to death.[8] In the struggle with the flesh one needs a healing remedy: it is faith alone,[9] which exercises itself in prayer.[10] The best remedy against sin is to have the Scriptures copied, read and meditated upon within the heart, because it drives the devil away.[11] The most valuable *medicina* is Christ with his power. Therefore, Physician Christ's medicine is his

---

[6]"Thus the Wisdom of God, setting out to cure men, applied Himself to cure them, being at once the Physician and the Medicine." Augustine, *On Christian Doctrine* (Book 1, XIV), trans. and ed. D. W. Robertson, Jr. (The Bobbs-Merrill Company, Inc., Indianapolis, IN, 1976), 15. Cf. F. Huck, "Die Entwicklung der Christologie," *ThStKr* 102 (1930), 121.

[7]Cf. P. Althaus 238, n. 71. Also, see R. Arbesmann, "Christ the Medicus humilis in St. Augustine," *Augustinus Magister* 2 (Paris: 1954):623-629.

[8]"Peccat quo ad carnem suam, quae adhuc est infecta usque ad mortem." WA 20:635,7.

[9]Cf. WA 20:776,18.

[10]Cf. WA 20:790,18.

[11]"Scriptura semper est scribenda, legenda, meditanda corde. . . . Quando audit Satan verbum dei legere, non manet." WA 20:790,6-7.
—"Remedium praesentissimum contra peccatum est meditari verbum dei, sit in furoribus quibuscunque." WA 20:629,5-6. This prescription may have its origin in the Cistercian tradition. See Chapter 6 on Luther and Bernard.

powerful word, which must be preached. This power is the most potent *medicina* against everything.[12] This latter statement Luther spoke from experience, because only through Christ and faith in him was Luther saved from his temptations and illnesses. This experiential dimension in Luther's lectures is also evident when he cited his common experience with a doctor: When a physician reveals an illness to an infirm person, he does not do it in such a way that the patient will be killed or remain sick, but he raises his spirit with a promise. The patient is relieved and he sighs, but he still is not freed. He is healed to the extent that with a good heart and with faith he adheres to the promising physician's hope and faith.[13]

Christ by Birth and Merit for Me

Luther's Christology has two focal points: the person and the work; the one person in two natures, divine and human, and the work or merit of the cross for the salvation of the world. In the tradition of Bernard's Christology, Luther spoke of Christ's "birth and merit." When expounding on 1 John 2:1 he referred to this concept and again at 4:10.[14] Both times we find the reference only in R. While we have quoted Luther extensively on 4:10, we have not yet done so on 2:1 where Luther called Christ's birth and

[12]"Ideo vis Christi praedicanda, quod valeat tanquam valentissima medicina adversus omnia," WA 20:759,18-19.

[13]" . . . et roget medium. Tum ille suspendit eum promissione. Sic suspirat et gemit et tamen nondum liberatus. Sanus eatenus, quod corde bono et fide heret in spe et fide promittentis medici." WA 20:655,10-12 (on 2:12).

[14]See chapter 6 on Bernard and Luther with the Bernard legend. p 119 WA 20:624,4 and 746,15-17.-WA 47:585,19-20, where Luther indicates that he likes to use this example of St. Bernard very often.

work the foundation on which to remain. It is the
Bernardine foundation.[15] Earlier we looked at it from
the traditional-historical perspective. We now want
to examine Christ's birth and merit with reference to
God's *Alleinwirksamkeit* (God's effectiveness
alone).[16] Here clearly Christ's merit (besides his divine nature by birth) is shown as being essential, i.e.,
both the divine birth and the human merit — never
separated as such, but always considered according
to the *communicatio idiomatum*.

Even the "Christ *for me*" emphasis, which is
generally thought of as typically Lutheran, is found
in Bernard. It occurs in the Johannine lectures several times, especially when Luther speaks of belief in
Jesus "as my Christ,"[17] the God-with-me.[18] The idea
of "Christ with me," or "for me," is connected to the
thought of Christ's advent in the heart of man. In
other words, Christ's first coming, in the flesh, is
continued in his spiritual coming, in the spirit, heart
and soul of the believer.

Christ who is born of God is the central thought
which is applied now to all believers. In 1 John 5:1-2
those who are born of God are distinguished from the
heretics.

---

[15]"nativitatis et meriti, das heist fundamentum manere." WA 20:624,
4-5.

[16]See above, on "God's Flesh is Christ's Flesh." Also see Congar's old
"regards" on Luther's Christology and Beer's position (cf. Introduction).

[17]"ut credam Iesum esse meum Christum"; WA 20:766,17-18.

[18]"Christus est tecum deus." WA 20:768,9. On Bernard's Christology in
this perspective, see J.-M. Déchanet, "La Christologie de Saint Bernard," *Bernhard von Clairvaux: Mönch und Mystiker. Internationaler Bernhardkongress Mainz, 1953*, ed. J. Lortz (Franz Steiner Verlag:
Wiesbaden, 1955), 64.

> Therefore, let us arm ourselves with the scripture,
> that Jesus is the true Christ, and so we are born of
> God, in whom everything is fulfilled . . . in whom
> are all treasures . . . [5:1]. In other words, now, he
> talks about the Son of God, in order to speak
> against the Arians who say, "We love the Father
> and seek God's glory alone." John says, "It is a lie
> . . . , because it is impossible for you to love the
> Father without the Son, whom you persecute, be-
> cause you negate that he is the Christ, . . . who is
> born of God . . . [5:2]. Here he applies this birth of
> God also to other sons. . . . The world hates us
> because we believe that Christ is born of God.[19]

Luther explicitly talks of an application of Christ's
being born of God to the believers, who are then, also,
born of God. Luther uses the term *nativitas dei*, while
the Vulgate uses the expression *generatio dei* in 1
John 5:18, but both are represented in the German
word *Geburt* (birth). It is the "spiritual birth" with its
fruit of love (*charitas*).[20]

The incarnation of Christ, soteriologically understood, is the reason why the believer's spiritual
birth is possible. It has to do with the justification of
the sinner in the Johannine text,[21] and as Bernard

---

[19]Cf. WA 20:765,21-766,14, especially 11-12.

[20]"Quia charitas est testimonium et fructus istius nativitatis spiritualis"; WA 20:738,13-14.

[21]In 1518 Luther expressed this as follows: In the righteousness of
Christ lies the power to become sons of God, and the birth of God
conserves man. Quoting 1 John 3:9: "Iusticia huic contraria similiter
est natalis, essentialis, originalis, aliena, quae est iusticia Christi
Joann: iij. Nisi quis renatus fuerit ex aqua et spiritu. Item Ioan.i.
Quotquot eum receperunt, dedit eis potestatem filios dei fieri. Et.
i.Joan.iij. Qui natus est ex deo, non peccat (est peccator) sed generatio
dei conservat eum." WA 2:44,32-36.

understood Christ's birth and merit. Here also the Bernardine idea of Christ's *adventus* in the soul entered Luther's interpretation together with the Bernardine understanding of Christ's birth and merit for the salvation of man. Bernard talked of "birth and merit," which Luther expressed in terms of "person and work." Both meant the same thing: Christ, the God-man, is born for us and died for us and our salvation.

Spiritual Birth, A Work of God

The young Luther departed from traditional mysticism, which sought a "spiritual union with Christ" as the end of a mystical process in which man played an important role. Luther taught "justification by faith" in terms of God's *Alleinwirksamkeit*. With this understanding, Luther also departed from scholasticism and kept company with Augustine, as E. Vogelsang has pointed out.[22] When Luther talked of God's work of conversion and rebirth, he spoke simply of faith in Christ (*fides Christi*), which justifies us; and he spoke of Christ as reigning in the believer's heart. Righteousness is imputed to us by faith in Christ, as regards both his person and his work of redemption; this is justifying faith.[23]

---

[22]Cf. Erich Vogelsang, *Die Anfänge von Luthers Christologie*, 68-81.

[23]Vogelsang did not take into consideration that the young Luther's use of *generatio* is the Johannine expression of 1 John 5:18 (Vulgate), nor did Vogelsang see any connection to Bernard's threefold *adventus* (see above Chapter 6). In this context of the doctrine of justification, the talk of God's *Alleinwirksamkeit* has its proper place. This is different when the Christology is considered, as is pointed out in the previous section on "Christ by Birth and Merit for Me."

During the lectures on 1 John, the young Luther's concept of *generatio dei* as *incarnatio spiritualis Christi* was expressed as *nativitas spiritualis* in 1 John 4:7[24]

The expression "born of God" (*natus ex deo*) occurs frequently in 1 John. As shown in Part One, Luther took 1 John 5:18, which in the Vulgate version contains the expression *generatio dei*, as a summary of the Johannine letter and interpreted it with Erasmus's annotations as one "who is born of God" (*qui genitus est ex deo*). The one who is born of God is the one who is begotten by him. He is saved and protected. The devil cannot touch him and, therefore, he does not sin. It is a Johannine expression of the doctrine of justification by faith. In Latin, Luther expressed the "birth from God" with both *generatio* and *nativitas* when interpreting 1 John 5:18.[25]

Luther interpreted further that this new birth consists of belief in the incarnation of the Son of God.[26] This sonship, Luther said, applies to the believers, as in 5:2: "the 'God-born ones': here he applies this nativity of God also to other sons."[27] The Christological foundation is evident. All this is done by God, because birth is not possible without seed, which has its origin in God. This is being begotten of God. Luther combined the Bernardine notion of Christ's birth and merit for me, and his concept of the *adventus* of Christ in the heart[28] with the Augus-

---

[24]WA 20:738,14.

[25]WA 20:798,14-799,6.

[26]WA 20:800,3-4.

[27]WA 20:766,11.

[28]See Chapter 6.

tinian understanding of God's seed, the word of God, being planted in the heart of man.

Brought Forth by God's Seed and Defended by Christ's Teeth: Non stant simul peccare et nasci ex deo.

When interpreting 1 John 3:9 Luther drew upon John's division of the world under God and Satan. On the previous verse, Luther had said that Christ and the devil are enemies; whoever is from the devil is not from Christ. Christ destroys the devil's work, and what Christ builds up is torn down by the devil. Christ causes us to produce the fruits of faith; the works, therefore, belong to Christ. Satan tears them down and puts works of the flesh in their place.[29] One is either born of God or of the devil. From the works, each one knows whether he is from the devil or from Christ. So the two princes oppose each other. There is no middle ground. Either we are under Christ or under Satan.[30]

The Johannine concept of birth from God, and not of the flesh, is interpreted by Luther to mean that a Christian cannot be a fictitious creation. John speaks here as he does in his Gospel (1:3). Christianity is not a theory, but a reality. Christians are born of God, so theirs is no make-believe (*fucus*) or superficial piety. If one is born of God, one does not sin, because being born of God cleanses away sin, crucifies and burns sin, so that a man cannot bring sin to completion. Indeed, Luther describes sin as being "grilled on the spit."[31] Clearly, then, to be justified is to be the saint,

[29]WA 20:704,20-705,3.
[30]WA 20:705,7-9.
[31]WA 20:705,18 (R). 706,25-26 (P).

Part Three

who cannot sin. Here Luther, with John, drew a clear line of distinction. Either one is born of God and does not sin and cannot sin, or one is steeped in sinning. Only if one can lose this nativity, then one can sin, because that which is born of God cannot sin.[32]

Luther continues: Christianity is this, that the hatred of sin becomes bigger day by day, as does the love of justice. Therefore, the contrast — if someone sins and brings sin to fruition, he is not of God, because being born of God stands in conflict with sin.[33]

John maintains the essential difference between "remaining in Christ" and "sinning," because wherever Christ is, he takes away sins.[34] In the light that these two positions (that of Christ and that of Satan, who fight each other) are irreconcilable, Luther had to conclude, *"Non stant simul peccare et nasci ex deo"* (They do not stand at the same time: to sin and to be born of God).[35] They fight each other.[36]

Commenting on 1 John 3:8-9, Luther told his students, "These sayings have been neglected by us, because we did not understand them." But now Luther had found the explanation, because "the seed [*semen*] God planted in us does not tolerate any sin within us."[37]

---

[32]"Potest nativitatem ex deo amittere, tum potest peccare." WA 20:706,2-4.

[33]WA 20:706,2-12.

[34]"Quia pugnant illa duo: 'Manere in Christo' et 'peccare.' Ratio: ubi est Christus, tollit peccatum, ergo manet in eo negotio, quod est 'Tollit peccatum.' " WA 20:702,16-18.

[35]WA 20:707,9-10.

[36]"Pugnant enim haec duo, quod aliquis sit natus ex deo et peccet." WA 20:707,7-8.

[37]"Quia repugnant peccatorem esse et natum esse ex deo. Potest nativitatem ex deo amittere, tum potest peccare, sed stante et manente semine in eo non potest. Illae locutiones sunt nobis neglectae, non intelleximus. Est simplicissima sententia: Semen in nobis dei non patitur nobiscum ullum peccatum." WA 20:706,2-6.

The seed is God's word, as stated in 1 Peter 1:23.[38] Augustine also spoke of *semen Dei* as the word of God.[39] Luther interpreted 1 John 3:9 as follows:

> For there is God's *semen*, i.e., the word. You are born of the *semen*, 1 Peter 1. God's word remains, it is eternal *semen*. It stands [firm], it cannot be driven out. Yes, "he cannot even sin."[40] It is now the most simple sentence. . . . because Christ is the purger of sins, he is sitting in the heart by faith, and he says: brother, here you were beginning to be concupiscent, unworthy of honor, your name [Christian] is affected by the disgrace. So he obeys, so that the sin does not reign. The sin, of course, complains, but Christ bites [sin] to death with his teeth.[41]

The seed, the word of God, as Peter and Augustine spoke of it, makes all the difference. It is eternal, as Christ is eternal. Where God's word has taken root, Christ is also present in man's heart and drives out sin. Because Christ is present, sin cannot reign in the heart. Sin realizes this and complains (*murmurat*).

---

[38]"Quare? quoniam semen dei i.e. verbum. Nati estis ex semine 1. Pet. 1. Verbum dei manet, est aeternum semen." WA 20:705,20-706,1. (It is 1 Peter 1:23 and not 1:13 as WA-editor has it WA 20:706,24).

[39]We may assume that Luther follows Augustine at this point, who in his commentary on 1 John says: *Semen Dei, id est verbum Dei,* Migne PL 35,2016.

[40]"Imo non potest peccare." WA 20:705,20-706,1.

[41]" . . . quia Christus est purgator pecctorum, qui sedet in corde per fidem et dicit: frater, ibi concupiscere cepisti honorem indignatus, nomen tuum opprobrio est adfectum. Sic servat, ut peccatum non regnet. Peccatum quidem murmurat, sed Christus dentibus suis mortificat." WA 20:706,5ff.

Therefore Christ again must become active and must make use of his spiritual teeth: Christ bites sin to death with his teeth. This language is already found earlier in the lecture. "The biting is there at once with spiritual teeth";[42] and a little later he said, "Christ is in us."[43]

Earlier, in his first lectures on the Psalms, in 1513-15, Luther had spoken of Christ who reigns in us through faith.[44] What is said in the Johannine lectures is nothing new, but an unfolding of Luther's earlier teaching. Furthermore, Luther's language here, in mid-career, is still mystical, not in a philosophical sense or with respect to any human effort to effect a mystical union, but mystical in Johannine terms. Luther's hermeneutics are at work here. He interprets 1 John with reference to 1 Peter 1 and Romans 7. Luther interprets Scripture with Scripture. He is, therefore, not a subjectivist who refers only to the Bible as he pleases, to make it fit into a personal theory. But he places his *non stant simul peccare et nasci ex deo* side by side with his famous *simul iustus et peccator*, drawn from Romans 7. Luther does this in the lecture on 1 John 2:1-2 when he declares that John himself described the status of Christianity as something which reason cannot grasp and which can be captured alone by faith: "that the same man is a saint and [yet he] sins."[45]

---

[42]"morsus dentium spiritualium statim adest"; WA 20:702,20.

[43]WA 20:723,8.

[44]Cf. E. Vogelsang, *Die Anfänge von Luthers Christologie*, 55 (with the quote found there: "per quam [*fides Christi*] in nobis regnat." For Vogelsang, this is the reformation discovery.

[45]"3. Septemb. Declarat s. Iohannes, qualis sit status Christianitatis. Est admirabilis, qui nulla ratione comprehenditur sed sola fide creditur, quia ratio non capit, quod idem homo sit sanctus et peccet." WA 20:635,3-5.

"Everyone begotten of God, does not commit sin." For these two fight, that someone is born of God and he sins. The apostles solve it: "That we are justified by alien justice, therefore, etc." Elsewhere: "How can we live in sin, when we died to it, etc." [Rom 6:2]. To sin and to be born of God do not stand *simul*. There are relics and feces of sin, but the thing itself is such, that when standing in this birth, sin does not follow.[46]

Sin is reduced to feces and relics because Christ's work of purging him from sin is effective.[47] Or, to remain with Luther's metaphor, "Sin is grilled on the spit." What remains of sin is its sediment (*feces*).

Ten days after the end of the course on 1 John Luther wrote in a letter on November 17, 1527, to Hausmann, that the prince of demons himself had begun to attack him, and that he dealt with Scripture so mightily and expertly that Luther's own knowledge of Scripture would not be sufficient, if he did not adhere to the "alien word."[48] H. A. Oberman inter-

---

[46] 'Omnis qui natus est, peccatum non facit.' Pugnant enim haec duo, quod aliquis sit natus ex deo et peccet. Solvunt Apostoli: 'Quod sumus iustificati aliena iusticia, ergo' etc., alibi: 'Quomodo in peccato vivere, cum eo mortui, etc. Non stant simul peccare et nasci ex deo. Sunt adhuc reliquiae et feces peccati, sed res talis est, quod stante nativitate illa non sequatur peccatum." WA 20:707,6-11.

[47] Also see the section below on "Christ's blood," which, as "God's blood," does not leave any dirt behind.

[48] "Ego sane suspicor non gregarium aliquem, sed principem ipsum daemoniorum in me insurrexisse, tanta est eius potentia et sapientia Scripturis in me armatissima, ut, nisi alieno verbo haeream, mea scientia in Scripturis non sit satis." WA Br 4:282,6-9 (no. 1170).

prets this "alien word" as the gospel,[49] which was not Luther's own invention, but the word of God, which must be believed.

Besides Oberman's explanation of the "alien word," it may be possible to relate this expression concretely to Luther's comment in his Johannine lectures that certain aspects of John's theology had escaped his mind.[50] Thus with the "alien word" he could have been thinking about 1 John 3:9 and the paradox that a Christian is "at the same time saint and sinner," and of the fact that one who is born of God "cannot sin." Reflecting on his struggle with these concepts, Luther could remark to Hausmann, that he was not learned enough in the Scriptures, and that the devil as exegete had attacked him. Apparently, this "word" was as impressive in terms of its being "alien" as a decade or so earlier Romans 1:17 had been alien to his understanding. If Luther's "alien word" was a reference to 1 John 3:9 and the difficulties of interpreting it, then Luther's other comment on John (as being too complicated for him)[51] becomes more understandable.

Luther returned to the same verse at the end of the course, in the last lecture on November 7, 1527, when he summarized his interpretation and when he presented his and John's *Conclusio et Epiphonema et brevis recapitulatio*:

[49]Cf. Oberman, *Luther: Mensch zwischen Gott und Teufel*, 240. Oberman interprets, in general, the problem which Luther had was not so much a difference in theory, but in the experience of the reformation doctrine of justification, and Oberman quotes from another letter by Luther (1 January 1528): Others I have saved, myself I cannot save (Oberman, 240-1; WA Br 4:319,9-10).

[50]Cf. WA 20:706,5. See above.

[51]See Chapter 7 (Luther's comments on John on Pentecost, 1529).

"*Generatio*" [5:18], i.e., he who is born of God is (as said above)[52] someone who cannot sin. Those two fight each other: to sin and to be born of God; but sometimes there is fluctuation, like when someone does not forgive one's enemy. Then he sins like a man, not as having been born of God. As in Romans 7, "I do . . . " etc., the Christian man is twofold: As long as he lives in faith he does not sin, but whenever he is preoccupied with fervor (like when this birth is not in use)[53] the flesh dominates and seduces.[54]

Luther again confronts 1 John 3:9 with Romans 7 to explain the *generatio dei*. Here he introduces, in addition to what he has said so far, the notion of the "two-part [duplex] Christian man." The Christian, insofar as he lives *in fide*, does not sin. But when his new "birth from God" is not in use (*usu*), if he becomes preoccupied with fervor and begins to fluctuate, "the flesh dominates and seduces." He posits, as an example, a man who does not forgive his enemy. The man who is born of God does forgive his adversary, but if he does not forgive then he sins *ut homo, non ut natus ex deo*. Sin seduces and dominates when the birth is not in use. Thus Luther confirmed

[52]Parentheses in the original. Luther meant by "as said above" the interpretation of 1 John 3:9.

[53]Parentheses in the original: "(ut ista nativitas non est in usu)"; WA 20:798,18-19.

[54]" . . . Duplex est homo Christianus: In fide quantum vivit, non peccat, sed quandoque praeoccupatur (ut ista nativitas non est in usu) fervore. Praedominatur caro et seducit, . . . " WA 20:798,17-19.

that sin and "birth of God" cannot "stand" each other (*non stant simul*).

> Inasmuch as he is born [of God], it is impossible for him to sin. He has what conserves him. What [is it]? The birth [of God]. "And the evil one" [5:18], be it Satan or the world, [cannot touch him]. How is that? when a Christian has followed diversely, i.e., when he did not do what he wanted to do; for when he is in the state of his [new] birth, he can be tempted, but he cannot be conquered.... Therefore, let us be eager to remain in the faith and in the birth of God and then we will be without sin, and we are clean and we cannot sin.[55]

Christ as Resident in the Heart

Luther offered an unusual definition of faith: Faith means "to make room."[56] "To cede to sin" means to make room for the devil.[57] "Faith" means to make room for Christ. When Luther expounded on 1 John 5:4, he said that to believe is to be born of

---

[55]" ... sed in quantum natus est, tum impossibile, ut peccet. Habet quod conservet eum. Quid? nativitas. 'Et malignus' sive Satan sive mundus. Quomodo hoc? cum diversum duxit Christianus in mentem, i.e. non facit hoc, quod vellet, quia quod stat in nativitate, potest tentari, vinci non.... Ergo studeamus manere in fide et nativitate dei et tum absque peccato erimus, et sumus muniti et non possumus peccare." WA 20:798,19-799,6.

[56]WA 20:704,5, where the editor preserves a German expression which Luther must have used when talking about faith, hope in Christ, and which R wrote above the Latin word for believe, *credere*. Cf. footnote to line 5: "über *credere* steht raum geben (above *credere* is written "to give room"). — The image is also found in Augustine: Migne PL 37, 1876 (on Ps. 144).

[57]WA 20:704,5-6.

God, and being born of God means that Christ takes up residence in one's heart. Whether the play on words in Latin is intentioned here or not, Luther understood *credere* (to believe) to mean *cedere* (to cede) to Christ, who takes up residence in the heart. In the heart the birth occurs through the Word (*semen*), which is preached to us: Christ the Son of God.[58] Luther applies his Christology to the doctrine of salvation. To be born of God by faith in the Son of God is a gift of God.[59]

Justification, in its Johannine version as presented by Luther, strikes the heart. It is a gift of God, by grace alone. Christ purges the heart. However, there is no work of zeal involved on man's side. Luther says that the heart is cleansed through grace, not through works and zeal.[60] Christ is the grace-giver and the physician.[61] The preaching about Christ as the comforter must be in peoples' hearts, and those, then, die in joy, in whose hearts he dwells.[62] Christ alone must be preached to troubled hearts.[63] Christ lifts up the hearts of everyone. Whoever tries to purge himself with his own efforts is an ignoramus, who

---

[58]"Nasci ex deo est credere verbo, quod nobis praedicatur: Christus filius dei." WA 20:772,20-21. Cf. WA 17ᴵ:436,14-19; WA 19:490,31ff where this thought is repeated. — Luther probably played with the Latin words *credere = cedere*, as he did elsewhere with *credere = edere* (to believe is to eat), WA 12:582,10-11; WA 11:126,1ff; WA 15:471,4. See Bornkamm, *Luther in Mid-Career*, 224.

[59]"donum dei," WA 20:772,23-24.

[60]"Sic per gratiam purgatur cor, non per opera et studiis." WA 20:656,6-7.

[61]"Medicus, det gratiam", WA 20:636,31.

[62]WA 20:636,1-2.

[63]WA 20:638,22. With Emmanuel Hirsch, we may use Luther's concept of heart interchangably with "conscience." See E. Hirsch, Lutherstudien I (Gütersloh: C. Bertelsmann Verlag, 1954).

does not know Christ. This ignorance is Satan's reign.[64] There are those who ignore Christ and do not think of him in terms of reconciliation, and there are those who have heard of Christ's reign, and of his remission of sins through mercy without merits. But they only learned these words and preach them; they do not have a living, solid knowledge. In keeping with the Bernardine concept of *cognitio*, Luther referred to those who pay lip service as "foam over the water." They talk a lot, but they are make-believe. They do not walk in the light. In the core of their hearts, they do not have the light. Their *cognitio* is unfruitful.[65]

The first part of our *cognitio* is to believe in Christ who alone takes away sins. The other part is to love the brother. In other words, the first part is justification, the second part is the implementation of God's commandments.[66] Brotherly love is the sign that one knows Christ and that this *cognitio est salus*, this recognition is salvation.[67] This *cognitio* is identical with faith.[68] Such thoughts are soothing to the heart and they assist the weak. Christ in heaven is fight-

---

[64] WA 20:638,30-640,21 (line 21: "quae ignorantia est regnum Satanae," — on 1 John 2:3).

[65] "vivax, solida cognitio sed sicut spuma super aquam, est verbositas in linqua eorum. . . . vera cognitio. . . . infructuosa cognitio." WA 20:640,24-641,10.

[66] "Credere, quae est prima pars cognitionis nostrae, quod solus Christus auferat peccata. Altera pars est diligere fratrem. . . . Prima pars est iustificationis, altera, ut impleamus mandata dei." WA 20:641,11-14.

[67] WA 20:641,18.

[68] "ibi studendum, ut haec cognitio, fides augeatur in nobis," WA 20:756,1. Here *cognitio* and *fides* are synonymous. The young Luther, speaking in terms of Bernardine bridal mysticism, said that faith copulates the heart with the Word of God: "fides enim copulat cor et verbum dei." WA 4:695,35f.

ing for the weak ones. He is *propugnator*.[69] They are weak because they have been fed with the nausea of the monks.[70] They would talk differently and they would not be false brethren if they would have the (speaking here again as Bernard does) *cognitio dei*, which consists of faith in Christ as our Savior and Paraclete, who places his blood between God and man. But they are not "affected."[71] Luther distinguished their false knowledge from the central and ultimate concern of Christian faith, which they do not have: faith in Christ's divinity and humanity.[72]

In his lecture on September 4 Luther said that the true Christian is affected in his heart by the true knowledge of Christ, and therefore he does good works. In his subsequent lecture, on September 9, he picked up on the Johannine symbolism of light and darkness in terms of knowledge of old and new teachings. In this context, he derives the Christological title "Sun of Righteousness" from the Johannine light-symbolism — a symbol also found in the writings of Bernard.[73]

Christ, the Sun of Righteousness

The young Luther applied Malachi's metaphor, "Sun of Righteousness," to Christ.[74] Now again Lu-

---

[69]WA 20:642,4.

[70]WA 20:642,13.

[71]"Cognitio dei scire, quod Christus sit salvator et paracletus noster"; WA 20:643,5. — "adfecti," line 9.

[72]"negabunt eius divinitatem et humanitatem," WA 20:643,10-11. Here again, one may find Bernard's "humanitas dei" being transparent in Luther's words.

[73]Cf. J.-M. Déchanet, "la Christologie de Saint Bernard," 65.

[74]Cf. D. Vorländer, *Deus incarnatus*, 188. — On this motif also see the Chapter on Bernard.

ther employed it in his interpretation of 1 John 2:7-11. The problem for the Christian is that the devil imitates the light of Christ. The devil stirs up his own teachers by giving them new doctrines, with new commandments. The apostle's grave concern, that the church remain with the true doctrine, was shared by Luther: "So it is with our fight, to see to it that the true doctrine remains in them."[75] And he continued as follows:

> The foundation is laid, i.e., the Sun of Righteousness has risen. Now, so many new teachers stand up, that we have enough to do to preserve the dogma. . . . I want only "faith and love." Therefore I write about older things, in order to protect you from new ones. . . . I want to keep you in simplicity in Christ, against new teachers, so that you do not accept new dogmas, but remain. May God watch over us, for Satan does not sleep. . . . With great and divine counsel God let the gospel be the word of the cross, and he chases vainglory like a beast. . . . Jesus Christ is righteousness. This I know. If another opinion comes up, [I] will pounce on it; all the saturated ones despise the doctrine of justification and the fruit of the Spirit. . . . Christ shines through his word in you. . . . In you he shines. From them the darkness did not yet depart. . . . They transfigure themselves into "angel of light." It is horrible that they have the name "doctors of Christ."

---

[75]Cf. WA 20:646,16-647,3.

> But I will dare, nevertheless, to call myself a
> servant of God.[76]

Luther identified the lucifers to whom he alluded with the expression "angel of light." Later, on 1 John 5:10, Luther referred to the new and false teachers as *luciferi* who take away the divinity and make it into *diabolitas*.[77] The devil makes a smoke-screen before the truth, which is the sun, but the sun will survive the clouds of the sects.[78]

The sign and certainty for being in the light is love, Luther said, interpreting 2:10,[79] for the affected heart is reflecting the Sun of Righteousness. On 1:6 he said that the unaffected ones have a sinister and false heart, and therefore they are sons of darkness, but the affected ones have the light, and then works follow. When the light is present, it illuminates a person, so that he does good to others. If the true light is not present, it is a lost cause, whatever works may follow. If faith is false, no works follow.[80]

The sects rush in to "tear up" (*zertrennen*) the light, but it is apparent that they are in darkness; Christ is *unica lux*, the unique light, and therefore, "we must preach the 'simple light.' "[81]

---

[76]" ... ortus est sol iusticiae.... ut conservetur dogma.... Euangelium sit verbum crucis. . . . Iesus Christus est iusticia, das kan ich. . . . Christus lucet per verbum suum in vobis. . . . transfigurant se in angelum lucis. Horrendum est, quod nomen habent doctorum Christi. . . . Ego auderem me quidem vocare servum dei." WA 20:647,4-649,7.

[77]WA 20:785,17-786,11.

[78]Cf. the Chapter 9 on the German elements. Here, WA 20:680,15-20.

[79]"Signum et certitudo, quod sit in lumine, est charitas." WA 20:650,18-19.

[80]WA 20:616,22-617,4.

[81]" ... praedicamus simplicem lucem ... Neben dem liecht treten viel secten herein ... et wollen das liecht zertrennen ... Christus est unica lux, vestrae doctrinae sunt tenebrae." WA 20:614,14-19.

Christ as Exemplum

In the same crucial lectures on 1 John 3:9 in which he unraveled the question as to how a Christian was without sin, Luther also gave a further explanation of Christ's *adventus* in the flesh and of his entry into the heart of man. "Christ appeared in flesh in order to give us an example."[82]

The example which Christ gives, in connection with 1 John 3:9, has to do with removing sins. Luther found this expressed also in Ephesians 5, where it is said that Christ died and shed blood in order to cleanse his church. If someone does not want to produce the fruits of the spirit and to fight his own inclination to sin, he is against Christ.[83] The purpose of the incarnation is the purification of the church; On the individual level, through the presence of Christ in the heart. It is Christ's office [*negotium*] to take away sin.[84] As Christ fought sin in his earthly life, he continues to help us spiritually by his presence in the heart. As Christ fights sin with his teeth, so the Christian must follow his example and use his spiritual teeth in order not to let sin reign in his heart. "The Christian mortifies the flesh, as in Galatians 5. He does not let sin reign, but detests it and immediately begins to bite it with his spiritual teeth. Let us see to it that we are found among those who are removing sins as we serve our neighbors."[85]

---

[82]WA 20:701,20-21.

[83]WA 20:702,3-4.

[84]"ergo manet in eo negotio, quod est 'Tollit peccatum' "; WA 20:702,18.

[85]"ergo Christianus mortificat carnem, ut Gal 5. Non sinit peccatum regnare sed detestatur, morsus dentium spiritualium statim adest. Videamus, ut simus in numero, qui tollamus peccata et serviamus proximis nostris." WA 20:702,18-703,1.

At Christ's Advent on the Day of Judgment, We Will Appear Good by Nature Who Were Bad Before

Luther's concern was the Day of Judgment and how men would appear before God on that day. Luther knew very well the anxieties of a bad conscience. The professor addressed this issue when he interpreted 1 John 2:28-29 with its key word "confidence."[86] Luther first of all spoke of Christ's coming[87] and of man's frightened conscience because of this coming, if man should rely on his own works.[88] For Luther, 1 John 2 should end with verse 28; he takes verse 29 as belonging to the new chapter, which begins thus: "If you consider the holiness which is his, you can be sure that everyone who acts in holiness has been begotten by him. See what love the Father has bestowed on us in letting us be called children of God. Yet, that is what we are."[89]

Luther wanted this correction of the literary chapter division to preserve John's train of thought. We must stay confident, as John wants to confirm in us the doctrine that we are saved by faith, and not by works. At Christ's coming there will be no escaping condemnation unless we remain in this word and grace, because the whole world is engulfed in sin (cf. Romans 11:32). Otherwise we will be confounded and we will have fear (*pavebimus*) at his coming. Adam

---

[86]Greek: παρρησία; Vulgate: *fiducia*; Luther's German translation in his sermon on 1 John is "Freidigkeit," a word which did not enter the modern German language. Cf. "Freydickeit... Das ist die zuversicht," WA 36:470,13-14 (R).

[87]"Adventus Christi," WA 20:690,1.

[88]WA 20:691,9-11.

[89]Luther comments: "Here Chapter Three should begin." WA 20:691,13-14.

and Eve were in sin and death; "in the conscience" they were terrified. But soon the evangelical promise arrived for Adam and Eve, referring to Gen 3:15 (not *2.Mose 3:15* as the editors note, referring to R). Through this word they have remission of sins without any works at all. The only road is to remain in grace, without deviating from it to the right or to the left. Those who trust him will not be confused when he comes. This is the main part of the doctrine, the doctrine of grace, which makes a person good.[90] In other words, man becomes "good" by God's grace and that is what is needed on the Day of Judgment. Any goodness in man is totally God's work.

The train of thought includes 1 John 2:29-3:1. John disapproves of lazy persons, who do not bring forth fruit. John calls on us to do good works. Christ makes the tree into a good one, which is not idle. He then adds a temptation in order that the tree might produce fruit. The word of God is not just a nice sermon, otherwise one would be a Christian of words. We preach sound doctrine. We recognize its soundness by the fruit it produces. Whoever follows sound doctrine, namely, that we are justified by grace, is born of God. Therefore, we know who is a Christian and who is not. John "distinguished the birth from hearing. To be born of God is to acquire the nature of God."[91] Those born of God's *semen*, God's word, are

---

[90]" 'Fiduciam.' Vult confirmare nos. . . . Adam et Eva sic quoque erant in peccato et morte et in conscientia dei iudicis occidebantur et terrebantur. Sed mox sequitur Euangelica promissio . . . 'Semen,' etc. . . . Exhortatio pro principali parte doctrinae, quae est doctrina gratiae, quae personam facit bonam." WA 20:689,16-691,12.

[91]"Distinguit nativitatem ab auditu. Nasci ex deo est acquirere naturam dei," WA 20:692,4-5.

born of God and have the nature of God. Luther went on: "Therefore, we are not given a deceptive appearance, but we are born as Christians, so that we, who were bad before, are now by nature good."[92] Clearly, there is no *"simul"* of good and bad, but a change from "then" to "now," from bad to good. This is so because of the joyous exchange, by which our sinfulness is exchanged for Christ's sinlessness, as Luther alluded to in this text: "In him is no sin, because he liberates us from all sin."[93]

> Christ is the Lord, who shares with man his unction and the Holy Spirit, and so a man trusts in him and is one cake with him. I have the same righteousness which he has. Therefore, we become Christians by faith alone. I clothe myself with him, and he clothes me, and through him I put all my mischief on him, and he puts all good things on me.[94]

Luther commenting on 1 John 3:1, added this thought: "Baking-oven — so has Christ loved us."[95] Only confidence (faith) in Christ's love for us enables us to emerge as "good by nature," by his grace, on the Day of Judgment. We will be similar to God on that last day, not the same as God, but similar to him who

---

[92]"Ergo non adumbremur specie sed nascamur Christiani, ut simus iam natura boni, qui ante mali." WA 20:692,5-6.

[93]WA 20:692,2-3.

[94]WA 20:677,3-7. Two years earlier, in a sermon in 1525, the same idea of the joyous exchange is combined with the image of baking. "Christ and I will be baked into each other, so that my sin and death become his and his justice and life become mine."

[95]"Caminus, sic dilexit nos Christus." WA 20:693,6-7, referring then to Romans 8:32.

is the Life, the Justice.... Then it will become apparent that we are saints.[96] When commenting on 2:25,
Luther declared that "we become divine, because he
who is in the Father, remains in God, therefore,
through his word we become gods.... " He continued
to qualify this statement by interpreting it according
to 1 Peter 2:9, "i.e., priests and kings."[97]

---

[96]" ... in extremo die, erimus similes, non idem quod deus, sed similes
ei, qui vita.... apparebit nos esse sanctos." WA 20:698,12-15.

[97]"Est fieri divinum, quia qui in patre, in deo, ergo per illud verbum
efficimur dii i.e. sacerdotes et reges, 1 Pet. 2." WA 20:687,2-3.

CHAPTER 11

CHRISTOCENTRISM AS USED TO CLARIFY LUTHER'S POSITION IN CONTEMPORARY DEBATES

The Blood of Christ

Luther used the expression that Christ came "through the blood" as a parallel to the expression "into the flesh." In an allusion to 1 Peter 1:2, Luther said, when commenting on 1 John 5:6, that this is what he meant by "through the blood."[1] Incarnational theology and the theology of the cross must not be separated. And both theologies must not be separated from the theology of the Word, because first comes the actual matter of the cross, which is the corporal suffering. The spiritual spreading and sprinkling follows as the application of the corporal diffusion of the blood. Only through preaching does this blood come to me. The application of the blood is there when I believe. Is the crucified Christ, as such, any good for us? Luther answered: Only when Christ

---

[1]The editor notes that over the word *accomodare* in WA 20:777,19 is written in the manuscript of R: "das heis ich venire per sanguinem." Cf. on 1 John 1:7: "Sanguis est cum illis, qui manent in suo verbo, habent remedium sanguinem qui non sinit Christianos desperare." WA 20:618,23; 619,4.

and his cross are "vulgarized," or "popularized," is he
any good for me. He comes to us as the preached one.[2]

Christ shed his blood as one who is innocent, holy,
just, immaculate — the physician; he is without sin.[3]
The monks, however, with their works, fight against
God's mercy and they "mistreat the blood." They
reckon Christ among the offenders, i.e., Christ with
his blood is not enough. They want to find a better
way than this to heaven. If anyone seeks as they do,
he helps them show Christ to be a sinner, crucified
between the robbers. Here Luther did not call Christ
a sinner, but he said that the Carthusians make him
into nothing more than a sinner crucified between
the robbers: Fatal lapse.[4]

Luther went on to say, "When I know Christ as the
Lamb of God, I know nothing about sin." And yet, he
continued, "If I have [sin], Christ has [sin]."[5] My sin

---

[2]"Sanguis quidem effusus in cruce, nisi vero aspergeretur per praedi-
cationem, non veniret ad me usus istius sanguinis, qui est, quando per
verbum venit ad nos recipitur per fidem, et sic spiritus mundat me. Si
solum Christus crucifixus, cui prodesset? sed quia invulgatur in orbem
terrarum, etc." WA 20:777,19; 778,4. "Euangelium venit per Christum
et disperguit aquam et sanguinem per verbum suum i.e. praedicatus
venit." WA 20:779,7-9. — Two years before this, Luther spoke against
the heavenly prophets as follows: "Das wort, das wort, das wort, hörest
du lügen geyst auch, das wort thuts, Denn ob Christus tausendmal fur
uns gegeben und gecreutzigt würde, were es alles umb sonst, wenn
nicht das wort Gottes keme." WA 18:202,37-39.

[3]"Est sine peccato. . . . quia innocens, sanctus, iustus, immaculatus,
medicus." WA 20:636,29-31.

[4]"Interim orta Carthusianorum religio. . . . Tum dicunt: quare sum in
Carthusia? Ita cum istis operibus pugnant contra misericordiam dei et
concultant sanguinem et reputant Christum inter sceleratos i.e. Christus non est satis cum suo sanguine, meliore via eam ad coelum. . . . ergo
idem est Christus peccator, et inter latrones depictus crucifixus. Fata-
lis lapsus . . . " WA 20:670,14-19.

[5]" . . . Quod scio Christum agnum dei, nescio de peccato. Si habeo,
Christus habet." WA 20:672,4-5.

is carried by Christ, the Lamb of God. In this respect Christ has my sin, and I have his righteousness. Luther did not know what else to add to what he already had said.[6] Thus Luther retained the idea of the joyous exchange by which Christ takes our sins and gives us his righteousness. Christ was made sin for us metaphorically, Luther said in 1521,[7] but not according to the understanding of the Carthusians. Although they see Christ between the offenders as *peccator*, they mistreat the effectiveness of the blood of Christ by insisting on their own works for salvation. When lecturing on Isaiah, Luther maintained the metaphorical title of "sinner" for Christ.[8]

Christ's blood is of great value, because it absorbs sin, hell and God's judgment.

> Satan wants us to hold Christ's blood in contempt, [but] Scripture [calls it] most precious;
> . . . and we are used to our works and statutes, which permeate the heart, so that we could know nothing about the blood, etc. It is a blood of great value, it absorbs sin, hell, judgment. Here Satan fights uniquely; he holds up sin, the world, the judgment of God, hell, before us in order to cloud things up, so that we may not see Christ's blood. A Christian, how-

---

[6]"Ego peccatum tuum, tu iusticia mea, olim dicere solebam, nescio quid iam." WA 20:671,13.

[7]"Christus dum offenetur pro nobis factus est peccatum metaphorice." WA 8:86,31-32 (LW 32:200).

[8]"wir mussen den text lassen sthen Ex Esaia, quod fuerit Christus peccator, peccatum habuit . . . Christus est verus peccator qui nullum fecit et tamen reus omnium." WA 27:109, 1-12. See E. Vogelsang, *Der angefochtene Christus bei Luther*, 28-30.

ever, should always say in such situations: Christ's blood is mightier, for it is not of goats, etc.[9]

This comparison of Christ's blood with goats' blood is a reference to Hebrews 9:12. When interpreting 1 John 4:3, Luther said the Christian must remain with this: to do good, but not to expect justification from works, but "gratis, through the blood of Jesus Christ."[10]

Christ's blood is the ground on which Christ, the advocate before God, rests his case when he argues with the Father. He says, "Father have mercy on him, because I have shed my blood for him."[11] Still interpreting 2:1, Luther employed Romans 8:34. Christ has shed his blood for us and not against us,[12] in contrast to Marian piety. When we most fear God's judgment, Christ is there before the Father in heaven. "But another one is there, who speaks better for us, whose blood cries: remission!"[13] Then follows a reference to Abel's blood.[14] The innocent blood of

[9]"Satan vult nobis contemptum facere sanguinem Christi . . . Est magni valoris sanguis, absorbet peccatum, ingernum, iudicium. . . . ut obnubilet nobis, ne videamus Christi sanguinem. . . . potentior est Christi sanguis, non enim est hircorum, etc." WA 20:758,3-10. Cf. on 1 John 1:7, WA 20:618,20; 619,9.

[10]" . . . sed inde non iustificemur sed per sanguinem Iesu Christi gratis"; WA 20:730,5-6.

[11]WA 20:634,18-19.

[12]"Christus est autem, qui fudit sanguinem pro nobis, 8 Ro., non contra nos." WA 20:636,13.

[13]"Sed alius quisquam adest, qui pro nobis loquitur meliora cuius sanguis clamat: remissio." WA 20:636,24-26.

[14]"Abel pronominavit iam Christi misericordiam et gratiam." WA 20:636,26, but in S we read quite differently: Sanguis quidem Abel clamat vindictam, sanguis vero Christi gratiam et remissionem peccatorum." WA 48:321,17-18. Cf. Hebrews 12:24, on the speaking blood.

Abel is a type of Christ's innocent blood. This innocence is essential because it is the sinlessness of Christ, the immaculate one, who makes possible the joyous exchange. From the innocent Lamb of God we receive innocence and righteousness in exchange for our sins.[15] His blood absorbs even hell.

While John the Baptist came with water, Christ came with water and blood, because the water of baptism is sanctified by the blood of Christ. Because of this, the baptismal water is not pure but colored with blood through the Word which joins the blood of Christ saying: through the blood of Christ you are redeemed from sins, when you are baptized. According to Luther, this is the very simple understanding of 1 John 5:6,[16] that the blood colors the baptismal water, and therefore it is not a mere water bath, but a "blood bath."[17] Because of the coming of Christ in

---

[15]"In der Sündlosigkeit Christi ruht doch gerade der Grund für den 'fröhlichen Wechsel und Streit,' dass wir seine lautere Gerechtigkeit empfangen und er unsere Sünde trägt." E. Vogelsang, *Der angefochtene Christus bei Luther*, 75.

[16]"Sic non pura aqua sid cruentata cruore sanguineo per verbum ... Sic ego hunc locum intelligo simplicissime," WA 20:778,15-18.

[17]Luther said in 1544, on 1 John 5:4-12: it is not a bath in water, but in blood: "*Blutbad*" (blood bath). In 1544, Luther writes that Christ's blood is strongly mixed with the baptismal water which should not be considered as being water, but colored and reddened with the dear rose-colored blood of the dear Savior, Christ. This is not a common bath of water as Moses or an attendant at the baths can give, but it is salutary baptism of blood or a "blood bath," which Christ alone as God's Son himself has prepared through his own death: "Und wird also das Blut Christi krefftiglich in die wasser Tauffe gemenget, das man sie nu also nicht sol ansehen noch halten fur schlecht lauter wasser, sondern als schon geferbet und durch rötet mit dem tewren rosenfarben Blut des lieben Heilands Christi. Das es nicht heisse ein gemein Wasserbad, wie Mose oder der Bader geben kan, sondern eine heilsame Bluttauffe oder Blutbad, welches allein Christus Gottes Son selbs durch seinen eigen tod zugericht hat." WA 21:286,11-20 (Cruciger's Summer Postil, 1544).

water and blood to us in the sacrament, the verbal form of the biblical expression of 5:6 is to be taken in the present tense, not the past tense. Therefore, Luther translated "he is coming" and not "he has come," making use of the German at this point,[18] because the Latin *venit* of the Vulgate could be either present or past tense. The Greek text has ἐλθών, the aorist participle.

Luther's preference for the present tense of *venit* in the Vulgate[19] concurred with Luther's conviction that the preached word, the preached Christ, is of greatest significance, because this is the manner in which he comes to us today: in blood-colored water of baptism via the word. On another occasion Luther said that the proclaimed word, the preached Christ, insofar as it affects us, has far greater direct value for us than his humanity as such.[20] Ten years after the lectures on 1 John, Luther again interpreted baptism Christologically as he did in the lectures: By Christ's blood the person to be baptized has his dirt washed out from the inside as with a sharp soap which eats through the skin, so that the heart is pure for God.[21] All this is accomplished by the power of

---

[18] " 'Qui venit' praesentis temporis, scilicet ad nos. 'Per aquam' so khombt er zu uns." WA 20:777,13-14.

[19] Cf. Part One on Luther's use of the Vulgate.

[20] Cf. above 166, n. 58 and 228, n. 2.

[21] "Darumb ist nu auch in der Tauffe solche krafft des Blutes Christi, Das ist die rechte scharffe Seiffen, so nicht allein den unflat von der Haut am Leibe abwescht, sondern hindurch frisset und den inwendigen unflat heraus beitzet und wesscht, das das hertz fur Gott rein wird." WA 21:286,11-12. See C. Windhorst, *Täuferisches Taufverständnis: Balthasar Hubmaiers Lehre zwischen traditioneller und reformatorischer Theologie*, Studies in Medieval and Reformation Thought 16 (Leiden: E. J. Brill, 1976), 175.

Christ's blood, which, because of the *communicatio idiomatum*, is "God's blood."[22]. Therefore Luther exclaimed in his lecture of August 21, 1527, "See, what a treasure — the blood of the Son of God!"[23]

In 1527 the activity of the radical wing of the Reformation strongly provoked Luther to anger, because they referred to baptism as a "dog's bath."[24] Therefore when Luther lectured on 1 John 5:6, he took this verse as if John himself had directed his letter against these *hypocritas*.[25] Luther, who remained with the Bernardine terminology of *adventus Christi*,[26] continued his lecture by saying that through the advent of the word the Holy Spirit creates faith in Christ, and that it is this word "which preaches the baptism and the blood." And when Christ is preached, he is preached in such a way that he redeems through baptism and blood, and that he is distributed through the word. When this word is heard, faith comes through the Holy Spirit. "It is the Holy Spirit in the water."[27]

Christ as War Lord, Victor and Savior of the World

Luther employed in his interpretation not only medical language, but also military language. We touched upon this kind of language when dealing

---

[22]WA 50:590,19. See J. von Walter, "Luthers Christusbild," 5.

[23]"Vide, quantus thesaurus: filii dei sanguis." WA 20:619,9. See Carl Stange, "Das Heilswerk Christi nach Luther," *ZST* 21 (1950):201.

[24]"Caninum balneum," WA 20:780,4. Cf. P-version in German: "Sie heissen es ein hundsbad." WA 20:779,26. Cf. S-version in Latin: "baptismum caninum balneum vocant."; WA 48:323,23.

[25]WA 20:780,6.

[26]WA 20:780,8.

[27]WA 20:780,13-19.

with the smoke-screen tactics which Satan uses to obscure the truth. Paul Althaus has observed that Christ's work is understood by Luther as a battle with demonic powers.[28] Although Althaus did not draw upon the lectures on 1 John, we find his observation true when studying Luther's mid-career lectures on 1 John. Luther in times of temptation, as in the year 1527, understood the Christian life as a battle under Christ against the devil. A recent biography describes Luther's life in terms of struggle with the devil.[29] In the lecture on 1 John 5:1-4 Luther related to his students a personal experience of demonic temptation with regard to fictitious sins: "So it has happened to me." Satan causes troubles for us externally through the hypocrites around us, and internally through unbelief. Satan fights, most of all, our trust (*fiducia*); he makes the heart fearful as if it does not believe that one is born of God and that one has this trust. Satan is an artist capable of painting fictitious sins. Luther knew this from experience.[30] He invents sins. All this happened to Luther. After having mentioned this satanic tool of temptation, Luther returned at the end of this lecture to another personal experience. Earlier in his life he had hated Christ as a judge:

---

[28]Cf. *The Theology of Martin Luther*, 208-11, with special consideration given to Luther's commentary on Galatians (1531-35).

[29]Cf. H. A. Oberman, *Martin Luther: Mensch zwischen Gott und Teufel*.

[30]"Quando hoc sentio . . . Contra hoc maxime pugnat Satan, . . . ut redderet cor pavidum, quasi non credat hoc, quia est artifex fingendorum peccatorum, quae non sunt: Ah, tu non credis . . . Ita mihi factum." WA 20:767,10-17.

I had believed that Christ is like a tax collector and, even more, I had become pale at the mention of Christ's name, as of Moses' and of Satan's, because I sensed that their laws were impossible. So the heart was wounded by this prolonged craziness. So I truly tell you: You do not have to comprehend Christ as a tax collector, but as the Savior, the liberal Giver. . . .[31]

This is another description of Luther's so-called tower experience. This was indeed a spiritual struggle, and that is why he mentions it again in this context of spiritual warfare. Luther had carefully evaluated the traditions of the church and what the authorities had recommended in order to achieve the victory in this spiritual warfare:

You have read many sermons in which devotionalists liked Bernard gave us remedies against vices; and like Erasmus's *Miles*, which arms us against diverse kinds of vices but never deals with faith. Eyes are to be turned away, so that you do not see a woman; be

---

[31]"putavi Christum exactorem et magis expallui ad nomen Christi quam Mosi et Satanae. . . . Oportet te Christum non intelligere exactorem sed salvatorem, largitorem." WA 20:770,22-25. Luther's notion of Christ as "liberal Giver" is found already in the conclusion of Staupitz's Advent sermon 18 (1516), where Christ is called "most liberal Giver": *Darumb haben sie Christum nit einen schuldner, sunder einen mildesten begaber*: the Latin version by Scheurl has . . . *sed liberalissimum datorem*. See Johann von Staupitz, *Libellus De Exsecutione Aeternae Praedestinationis*, 226/227 (no. 161). Rörer's lectures stenogram gives the Latin expression of *largitor* for "liberal giver." The congeniality of Staupitz and Luther is evident at this point; and under this perspective then it comes as no surprise when in a table talk Luther says that he has everything from Staupitz and nothing from Erasmus, WA TR 1: 80,6-7 (no. 173).

abstinent of food, have self-discipline. I tried it! Jerome also arms us against sinning with our works. But did the treatment help Jerome? So when I fasted the most, the flesh went crazy the most and a pollution followed, because with these rules we wanted to fight against vices, against the absurdity of vice, the bad smell of sin, the burdens of punishments.[32]

All one needs is to be born of God through justifying faith. Although this text, 1 John 5:4, is read every year, it is not understood. Luther gave this reason: those who do not understand it are those who are not tempted. Here the professor of the Bible again explicitly introduces *tentatio* as a hermeneutical principle:

This text should be written with golden letters: one needs to be born of God. "And this is the victory" is read every year but not, etc., because they are not tempted. If you want to be so [i.e., victorious], it will not be through any work, like the cowl, etc. If *libido* tempts you and you look at a woman and you are enflamed with *libido*, then take Christ's word. Faith in him is victorious, and then the greatest concupiscence will be dirt.[33]

---

[32]WA 20:773,18-26.

[33]WA 20:773,28-774,4. See above Chapter 8, especially n. 5, on Luther's hermeneutics. Only those who are tempted and who employ meditation will be able to understand the Bible. Cf. WA 3:549,32-35 (LW 11:37), where Luther said about Psalm 77 that one cannot interpret it if one has not experienced this *compunctio* and *meditatio*: "Unde qui non est expertus hanc compunctionem et meditationem: nullis verbis potest hunc psalmum docere. Inde enim et mihi difficilis, quia extra compunctionem sum et loquor de compunctione."

At the end of his lecture on October 29 Luther made a remark about temptation by women by referring to 1 John 5:5:

> One needs to believe that Jesus [died], etc., so that we may have the true and sincere faith, not in any way corrupted by heretical opinions. . . . Occupy yourself with the Word and faith in Jesus. There is no other kind of weapon or remedy, except faith alone.[34]

In the face of his own temptations Luther concluded that the remedies offered by traditional monastic spirituality did not help. At this time, one of the most popular books on the spiritual warfare of a Christian was Erasmus' *Handbook of a Christian Soldier*. This book had made Erasmus the mouthpiece of what Bainton called the liberal Catholic Reformation movement, the counselor of popes and the mentor of Europe.[35] Between 1518 and 1530 no fewer than thirty-seven editions had been printed.[36]

Luther especially disliked Erasmus's *Miles*, because in it he did not find anything on faith,[37] which was Luther's main concern. Without mentioning Erasmus by name, Luther pointed this out in reference to 1 John 5:4:

> This verse should be written down, that faith in the mercy of God is to be pictured. Believe:

---

[34]WA 20:776,13-18.

[35]Cf. *Erasmus of Christendom*, 65.

[36]Cf. Cornelius Augustijn, art. Erasmus, *TRE* 10:8.

[37]" . . . ut Erasmi Miles, armat nos contra diversa genera vitiorum et nunquam tractat fidem"; WA 20:773,20-21 (i.e. *Enchiridion Militis Christiani*).

> Christ is mercy, not death and poison, but life,
> grace, salvation and light. Whoever, therefore,
> believes . . . is an instructed soldier who by
> faith in Christ supercedes everything, etc. St.
> Thomas, Scotus — Satan is content that they
> write innumberable books of this kind — also
> Lactantius. The old and the young, all of them
> are insane, especially Jerome [when writing]
> to Paula and Eustochium, and Bernard. . . .[38]

Luther had no use for the Erasmian "dagger" of a Christian soldier. He pointed his students to faith alone as the remedy.

The Christian tradition, from Jerome through Bernard and to Erasmus, has failed, since it failed to focus on faith in Christ. Therefore Luther turned away from Erasmus's "Christian soldier" and pointed to the Christian's War Lord, i.e., Christ himself. He is the only help in the spiritual warfare, and Christianity means warfare.[39]

Twice in the Johannine lectures Luther referred to Christ as the Leader, or War Lord: "God has placed us in the midst of wolves and devils." With this he again picked up on what he had said in his first lecture in regard to the contemporary scene. "Therefore, the War Lord says, 'I will be with you,' because he gave his weaponry, i.e., the Word and the Holy Spirit, to 'fight against death and all sins.' "[40] It is not the Christian soldier by virtue of his own forces that

---

[38] WA 20:775,13-19.

[39] "Christianismus est pugna." WA 20:684,21-22.

[40] "Constituit nos in medio luporum et diabolorum. Ergo dux belli: adero vobis, quia dedit sua arma i.e. verbum et spiritum sanctum, pugnate contra mortem, peccata omnia." WA 20:773,14-16.

wins the victory, but it is Christ who conquers the devil, with his powers of leadership.[41] This military Christology fit into the religious scenery of the times and picked up on Erasmus's "Dagger of a Christian Soldier" terminology, but Luther departed from it decisively with his Christocentric emphasis. Only with the Leader's forces will one conquer the devil.

In one early sermon Luther spoke of Christ as the "Duke" who leads us out from death.[42] In 1536 Luther called Christ the true "Captain." In German Luther used the term *heubtman*,[43] as also did Zwingli.[44] Luther used also the title "our King"[45] in the Johannine lectures.

The exposition of 1 John 4:18 provided an opportunity to lecture on fear and love and on the "spiritual battles" which are fought in the "war of fear":

> As it happens in war, those are more likely to win who have been most desperate; the presumptuous ones are as good as pierced. So it is in spiritual wars. Unbelief is presumptuous and is conquered. It is the opposite with faith.[46]

Luther continued by making a differentiation between two kinds of fear, the Vulgate term *timor* and

---

[41]"Sic Christus vicit diabolum, sic Christianus, non in suis viribus sed ducis." WA 20:775,21-22.

[42]"Ita Christus: Herczog von toten." WA 9:407,15.

[43]"Praesertim habeamus verum heubtmann, qui praecessit," WA 41:577,10. Cf. WA 20:427,8-9 about Christ who is the first, the Captain who leads the way: "der erste, . . . der heubtmann, der die pan bricht und den Weg macht."

[44]Cf. Gottfried W. Locher, *Christus unser Hauptmann. Ein Stück der Verkündigung Huldrych Zwinglis in seinem kulturgeschichtlichen Zusammenhang* (Zurich: Zwingliana, 1950).

[45]"Tu, Christe, es noster rex." WA 20:625,1.

[46]" . . . sic in spiritualibus bellis"; WA 20:761,13-15.

his own term *pavor*; fear as *pavor* cannot be in love or faith; therefore, if one has it, one is not a Christian. Yet, those are not to be rejected who fight in the war. Even the most holy people are weakened by the "war of fear."[47] This is so and happens "because God suspends the great Spirit of blasphemy. . . . "[48]

In these spiritual wars one will either despair or win. Despairing is blasphemy.[49] Faith is victory, faith in Christ, the Savior of the world, who shed the blood for us.[50] Having heard this word about Christ and his blood, we are born as God's sons, and faith is the victor. Faith is acquired through the gospel, as Christ comes as the preached one. This is so only because the Holy Spirit is there, and the preaching has the glory of being the "vehicle of the Spirit."[51]

Not only is faith called the winner (*victrix*), but Christ himself is the *victor* and the *rex*; thus the Christians rightly may call themselves kings.[52] Christ is the conquerer of death and sin because of his resurrection.[53]

For Erasmus, the Christian soldier's weapon is prayer, his armament is the Scripture[54]; so it is for

---

[47]"Bellum pavoris infirmat etiam sanctissimos." WA 20:762,5-6.

[48]"Quia deus suspendit magnum Spiritum blasphemiae. . . . " WA 20:762,6-7.

[49]"Ergo desperare est blasphemare." WA 20:774,22-23.

[50]Cf. WA 20:775,9-10.

[51]" . . . Isto verbo audito nascimur filii dei et victrix fides acquiritur. Ergo fides per Euangelium acquiritur . . . i.e. praedicatus venit. . . . Egregia consolatio: Ista unica praedicatio, et nulla, habet gloriam, quod sit vehiculum spiritus. . . . " WA 20:779,7-21.

[52]WA 20:683,1-3.

[53]" 'Et vidimus' hanc manifestatam vitam, quia Christus resurrexit a mortuis victor mortis. . . . ubi declaratus Christus victor mortis, peccati." WA 20:607,17-19.

[54]Cf. R. H. Bainton, *Erasmus of Christendom*, 68.

Luther's Christian in the struggle with the devil.[55] Unlike Erasmus, however, Luther pointed to Christ as the War Lord and the Victor. Here, in Luther's Johannine lectures, we find Erasmus's Christian soldier rewritten in Christocentric terms. Furthermore, Luther's hermeneutics is interwoven here with his military Christology. The struggle with temptations, with the devil, gives a Christian soldier experience under the War Lord, Christ. Only because of this can the Christian understand Christ as Victor.

In a table talk, dated between 1540-44, Luther said, "Whoever has not been tempted does not know anything."[56] In the preface to the Wittenberg edition of Luther's works, published in 1539, Luther wrote, "The devil will visit you once the word of God blossoms through you. Thus the devil will make you a good teacher, and by his temptations he will lead you to seek and love the word of God." Also because of the papist's attacks he was forced, by their help and the help of the devil, to become a rather good theologian, which otherwise would not have been.[57]

Luther and Erasmus agreed that the Christian lives in a battle zone. Luther, however, put his emphasis and trust in the War Lord, Christ, rather than

---

[55]Cf. above on "remedy," which is faith and prayer, as well as the meditation of Scriptures.

[56]"Qui non est tentatus, nihil scit." WA TR 5:592,25 (no. 6305). — See the section above, on Luther's "orational approach."

[57]"Denn so bald Gottes wort auffgehet durch dich, so wird dich der Teuffel heimsuchen, dich zum rechten Doctor machen, und durch seine anfechtunge leren, Gottes wort zu suchen und zu lieben. Denn ich selber habe seer viel meinen Papisten zu dancken, das sie mich durch des Teufels toben so zuschlagen, zudrenget und zuengstet, das ist, einen ziemlichen guten Theologen gemacht haben, dahin ich sonst nicht komen were." WA 50:660,8-14.

in the soldier's reason, free will, wisdom, virtues and works, as Erasmus did. Luther's biblical basis for this Christocentric view is 1 John 4:14. He said that one should keep this verse at hand when entering the battle against the enemy.[58] It is obvious that Luther, in mid-career, saw Erasmus as his theological adversary. As it was pointed out above in the chapter on the German fragments of the lecture notes, Luther was critical of the Erasmian retranslation of *servator*[59] instead of the Vulgate's *salvator*. R has *redemptor mundi*,[60] while P gives the Vulgate version.[61]

Now we will leave the linguistic and textual critical aspect aside and will turn to Luther's theological interpretation of 1 John 4:14. In order to see the Christocentrism at work in Luther's criticism of Erasmus, we must first of all note the brevity of Luther's exposition of this verse which contains this most significant Christological title, "Savior of the world." Again, we must realize that we are dealing with student lecture notes,[62] and this means that we probably have just the bare essentials. Thus, this brevity becomes even more significant, because in this very brevity lies the spice.[63]

With polemical spice and precision, but without mentioning any names, Luther interpreted verse 14

---

[58]"Hos locos congerite et instruite tanquam in aciem contra huiusmodi impugnatores." WA 20:751,20-21.

[59]See above p. 197, also 82-84.

[60]WA 20:751,13.

[61]WA 20:751,33.

[62]See above Chapter 1.

[63]"In der Kürze liegt die Würze," says a German proverb. — P-notes devote only four and one half lines of the WA to verse 14, while R has three times as many, WA 20:751,31-35(P), 751, 10-23(R).

in an anti-Erasmian way, with a loud rejection of work-righteousness. On the basis of this verse Luther summarized once more his theological position contrary to that of Erasmus. Luther saw his position as the *inevitabilis consequentia*[64] of 1 John 4:14. Here is what Luther had to say:

> "That the Father has sent the Son as Redeemer of the world" [4:14], I expound as above.[65] "So that we live through him." Pure thunder, which destroys our efforts and good works, because if the world is saved through Christ, then it first will have to be damned, cursed. An inevitable consequence. If it is a damned world, then reason, free choice, will, wisdom, virtue, works and all which is in the world are damned, because it needs the Savior. Therefore, it is impiously taught that through them salvation is prepared.[66]

Luther interpreted the "world" (as this word is part of the Christological title "Savior of the world") with

---

[64]WA 20:751,15-16.

[65]Luther was referring to 4:9, WA 20:741,18-742,26, where Luther interpreted John's verse polemically against the monastic work-righteousness, specifically against Augustine's rule. WA does not give us any editorial help here.

[66]" 'Quod pater miserit filium redemptorem mundi.' Hoc expono ut supra. 'Ut vivamus per eum.' Mera tonitrua, quae destruunt nostra studia et bona opera, quia, si mundus per Christum salvus factus, ergo fuerit damnatus, maledictus. Inevitabilis consequentia. Si est damnatus mundus, ergo ratio, liberum arbitrium, voluntas, sapientia, virtus, opera et quae in mundo, sunt damnata, quia indiget salvatore. Ergo impie docetur per ea parari salutem." WA 20:751,12-18.

[67]For *ratio*, see above on the "orational approach" as being in contrast to the "*ratio*-nal" approach. For Luther, reason is *ratio frigida*. WA 20:658,6. Those who use this kind of "ratio" are frigid lectors, according to Luther cf. WA 20:607,6 ("frigidus lector").

terms which are in themselves in need of interpretation: *ratio*,[67] *liberum arbitrium*,[68] *voluntas, sapientia,*[69] *virtus, opera*. It is clear that Luther worked with these notions in an anti-Erasmian way, as he accused the humanist of not having understood the Johannine notion of the "world."[70]

Luther's theological logic is this: his starting point in verse 14 (the Father has sent the Son to be Savior of the World). If this "world" of human reason, free will, philosophers' wisdom and monastic works is saved through Christ, the Savior, then this "world" first has to have been damned. It is a damned "world" precisely because it needs the Savior. For Luther this is the Christocentric and inevitable consequence. His Christocentrism demands a concept of "world" as a cursed place.

Luther continued to interpret 1 John 4:14 by following his hermeneutical principle of "Scripture interprets Scripture." Thus he interpreted this verse according to Matthew 9:13: "Christ is not the savior of those who are saved already. 'I have come to call, not the self-righteous, but the sinners.' Therefore, sin belongs to the

---

[68]For "free will," see the lecture notes within the commentary on 1 John 4:5: WA 20:734,23-24, where "free will" is identified as *inventum Satanae* (invented by Satan). Cf. on 4:9, "Hoc apostoli inculcant contra liberum arbitrium." WA 20:741,16.

[69]" . . . ut Erasmus infensus: crepat meros mundos. Sapientia debet offendi in simplicitate Christiana. Si scirent, quid esset mundus, in maiore honore Iohannis verbum haberent Ergo ignorant, quid sit mundus." WA 20:661,1-4.

[70]For Luther, worldly wisdom and reason are expressed in the *sapientia* of the philosophers, who become more stupid the more they study. In this context, Luther referred to *humana ratio* and the myths of the pagans, about which Augustine had reported, e.g., on the sex-God Priapus. Cf. WA 20:734,5-24.

whole world."[71] The sinful world is in need of the Savior, who is "alien righteousness" personified;[72] with this thought Luther concluded his exposition on verse 14 about the "Savior of the world."

---

[71]"Christus non est salvator eorum, qui salvi sunt. 'Non veni, inquit, iustos' (cf. Mt 9:13). Ergo totius mundi est peccatum etc." WA 20:751,18-20.

[72]"Maximus articulus aliena iusticia salvari." WA 20:751,21. However, Luther added obscurely, "ut alieno peccato damnari" (line 22), which requires further detailed study of Luther's concept of sin and of his contention that "all good works are sins" (WA 20:739,11 — on 1 John 4:8), or that the nature of the sin unto death (1 John 5:16) "is to fight against grace" (WA 20:795,9). It would also explain Luther's notions of *peccatum naturale* and *peccatum grande* (WA 20:794,24), and his concept of concupiscence. Furthermore, Luther's distinction of *peccare* and *peccatum habere* would have to be investigated (WA 20:627,18 —on 1 John 1:10).

SUMMARY IN CONCLUSION

Following the historical-critical method, we dealt with Luther's lectures on 1 John first in a textual-critical way in order to clarify the source material which is available for the investigation of Luther's mid-career understanding of Christ. It was concluded in Part One that, among the textual sources edited in WA 20 and 48, Chaplain Rörer's lecture notes are the most reliable and complete. These notes are to be preferred over the printed version of the year 1708, which is based upon another student's notes. When the English translation used this printed version as textual basis, it gave this source more credit than it deserved. Connected with the textual criticism is the question as to which Bible version Luther used in his academic work. It seems likely that he consulted Erasmus's edition of the New Testament in Greek with a fresh Latin translation, while at the same time he used the Vulgate as his starting point.

Following the aforesaid method, we dealt secondly with the context of Luther's lectures on 1 John. We covered four major aspects of this historical context: The *academic* context; the *biographical* one, with Luther's "mid-life crisis" in the tenth year of the Reformation; the *international and local political* scene, symbolized in the imperial Sack of Rome and in the fortification of Wittenberg; and finally, the *theological* background, within which we concentrated on Bernard's influence on Luther in his lectures on 1 John. We could show that Bernard's and Luther's theology are congenial, and that specifically in regard to their Christology there are apparent parallels. In his Johannine lectures Luther critically evaluated the Bernardine tradition in a Christocentric and evangelical way.

Remaining with the indicated method, we dealt in Part Three with the Christological content of the lectures. First, however, the assumption had to be verified that Luther had a preference for the Johannine tradition and that he was not a "subjectivist" in his Christology. We saw Luther admiring the Johannine form of language (*simplex forma loquendi*), and we saw with Luther that John is not a Platonist, but an Evangelist. After 1527, the year of the Johannine lectures, we found Luther's esteem of John reinforced when Luther called John *summus evangelista* and highest authority among Christians after Christ. To Luther it was without question that John's theology propels the doctrine of Christ as natural Son of God and man in one person, and that his understanding is identical with the Christology of the early councils of Christianity. After this we could demonstrate that Luther's opening lecture on 1 John 1:1 rested squarely on this "dogmatic foundation" of the doctrine of Christ's *person* with two natures. This led us to speak of Luther's Christology as catholic and, consequently, of Luther as *doctor catholicus*. In order to remain on historically responsible ground, we continued by focusing on Luther's Saxon-German phrases. The "German Cicero's" understanding of Christ's person and work, as he expressed it in his native tongue, was clothed in colorful, forceful language with impressive images.

We then moved on to present Luther's doctrine of Christ's *work*. We elaborated on Luther's employment of Christological titles and images as found in the rich medieval tradition, mainly that of Augustine and Bernard. Luther saw Christ as resident in the heart of the believer and with his teeth defending man against temptation. Luther was led by 1 John 3:9 to lecture on the *non stant simul* of sin and being born of God. Thus he put into perspective the paradox that the Christian man is *simul* saint and sinner. The *status Christianitatis* cannot be understood by *ratio*, but is believed *sola fide*, namely, that the same man is saint and sinner (*idem homo sit sanctus et peccet*). That which is born of God *non potest peccare*. And that which is born of flesh is flesh *non potest non peccare*. Hence the constant, daily battle which rages within the Christian. But Christ, as the Savior and "War Lord," remains the "Victor" and gives the victory to his people, in whose hearts he dwells by faith.

The Christian's heart makes room for Christ through faith, which is synonymous with *cognitio*. Ignorance, on the other hand, belongs to the devil's realm. Besides the Bernardine motif of *cognitio*, the Christological title for the Son of God as "Sun of Righteousness" points to the ongoing struggle against darkness and the perverted light-bearers, Satan and his evil angels.

Since Christ removed our sins once and for all on the cross, the new-born man of faith has the strength to fight temptation. As Christ is fighting with his teeth against the murmuring sins of man's heart, so also the Christian is expected to bite sin to death with his spiritual teeth.

Luther's main concern is how man will appear before God on the Day of Judgment, the day of Christ's final advent. Luther pointed out that on this last day those who are born of God will survive. They will appear "by nature good who were bad before." On that day it will be apparent that we are saints (*nos esse sanctos*).

The main interest of this study is not so much to refute current interpretations by Catholic scholars, as to demonstrate that Luther's Christology is built on the framework of the Christological dogma of Chalcedon and of the medieval tradition of Augustine and Bernard of Clairvaux. Certainly, some of Luther's Christological reflections, if viewed in isolation, invite misunderstanding — such as when he describes the two natures in Christ as a solution of sugar in water (which imagery did not occur, however, in the lectures on 1 John, but elsewhere [WA 33]). When taken, however, in its context as a polemic against Zwingli, it becomes obvious that this image of sugar-water was meant to illustrate the unity of the person of Christ against Zwingli's efforts to separate the two natures in Christ. Any interpretation of Luther's doctrine which overlooks references to the *communicatio idiomatum* (which Luther thoroughly championed) is destined to misunderstand and to misrepresent Luther's Christology.

Luther, toward the end of the course on 1 John, attacked the contemporary monastic mistreatment of the precious blood of Christ, which is so powerful that it cannot tolerate and does not depend upon monastic merits as a means of salvation. Luther also attacked the Anabaptists and their depreciation of the blood of Christ with respect to their erroneous view of baptism. The advent of Christ in the flesh means, at the same time, his coming "in the blood," which renders the baptismal water a "blood bath," and not a "dogs' bath," as the radical reformers had called it. Luther also reevaluated in Christocentric terms, on the basis of 1 John, the contemporary and dominant Erasmian piety, as it was expressed in the humanist's "Handbook of a Christian Soldier." Luther, in contrast to Erasmus's "Soldier," pointed to his "War Lord," Christ, and to faith in him as the "Victor." Thus Luther Christocentrically criticized Erasmus, and with him Bernard, as being *devotuli* who recommended useless remedies against vices and who had forgotten that all that counts in spiritual warfare is faith in Christ.

When looking back at the young Luther in the monastery we see a man contemplating a harsh image of Christ sitting on a rainbow as the judge of the world. At that time Luther did not recognize Jesus as the Lamb of God who bears the world's sins.[1] After the Reformation breakthrough, however, we observe no deviation from the ancient creeds and councils in Luther's Christology. Luther's doctrine of Christ in mid-career is that of the young Luther and also that of the old Luther, who demonstrated his *fides catholica* in his Christological disputations of 1535-1540. Luther unfolded his orthodox Christology along the lines of the Johannine text and the dogmatic tradition of Augustine and Bernard.

It is necessary to liberate Luther from false perception of his "effectiveness in history" by making full

---

[1]Cf. H. Boehmer, *Martin Luther*, 91.

use of the critical edition of Luther's works in the *Weimarer Ausgabe*.[2] On the basis of this critical edition, further studies on Luther's Christology are a desideratum, as was expressed in the journal *Una Sancta*.[3] The question as to whether Luther interpreted the Scriptures "subjectively," and whether or not he was a "full hearer" of the Word, should not be posed from a biographical-psychological perspective, but rather as a hermeneutical question regarding the central meaning of the Scriptures.[4]

In his commentary on 1 John, Luther constantly and necessarily interwove his hermeneutical principles (*solus Christus, was Christum treibet, Scriptura sua ipsius interpres,* and *oratio, meditatio, tentatio*) with the "dogmatic" Christological principle of Christ in one person with two natures which are in communication. As we can see from his comments on 1 John, Luther's own principles of interpretation prevented him from being a subjectivist. If there ever existed (or exists) a non-subjectivistic interpretation, it is Luther's, with his central concern that the article of *fides Christi* should reign in the heart. This is the article from which, through which and to which all his theological thoughts flowed and returned day and night. It is this Luther, with his Christocentric

---

[2]Cf. Gerhard Ebeling, *Umgang mit Luther* (Tübingen: J. C. B. Mohr [Paul Siebeck] 1983), 221.

[3]Cf. G. Kretschmar, "Luther und das altkirchliche Dogma," *Una Sancta* 37 (1982), 301.

[4]Cf. *Luther's Ecumenical Significance: An Interconfessional Consultation,* edited by Peter Manns and Harding Meyer in collaboration with Carter Lindberg and Harry McSorley (Philadelphia: Fortress Press, 1984), 48.

faith, who is a "father in faith" — faith in the God-man Jesus Christ — and who, therefore, deserves to be called *doctor communis* and *doctor catholicus*.

BIBLIOGRAPHY

Primary Sources

Biblia Hebraica. Edited by Rud. Kittel. Stuttgart: Württembergische
Bibelanstalt, 1937.
Novum Testamentum Graece et Latine. Edited by Erwin Nestle and
Kurt Aland. Stuttgart: Württembergische Bibelanstalt, 1963.
Novum Testamentum cum annotationibus. Edited by Desiderius Eras-
mus. Basel: Johann Froben, 1519 and 1522.
D. Martin Luthers Werke: Kritische Gesamtausgabe. Weimar: Her-
mann Böhlaus Nachfolger; Graz: Akademische Druck u. Verlag-
sanstalt, 1883-1983.
Luther's Works. Edited by Jaroslav Pelikan and Helmut T. Lehmann.
St. Louis: Concordia Publishing House; Philadelphia: Fortress
Press, 1955-.
Concilium Tridentinum. Edited by Societas Goeresiana. Freiburg:
Herder, 1950-1967.
Corpus Reformatorum. Edited by Carolus Gottlieb Bretschneider. Ha-
lis Saxonum: C. A. Schwetschke, 1834-.
Migne, J. P. *Patrologia Latina.* Paris, 1844-1864.

Secondary Sources

Althaus, Paul. "Die Bedeutung des Kreuzes im Denken Luthers," *Lu-
ther* 8 (1926):97-107.
_____. *The Theology of Martin Luther.* Translated by R. C. Schultz.
Philadelphia: Fortress Press, 1966.
Arbesmann, Rudolph. "Christ the *Medicus humilis* in St. Augustine."
Augustinus Magister. Congrès International Augustinien Paris,
21-24 September 1954, vol. 2. Paris: Etudes Augustiniennes, 1954,
623-629.
Augustijn, Cornelius. "Erasmus." *TRE 10:8.*
St. Augustine. *On Christian Doctrine.* Translated and introduced by
D. W. Roberston, Jr. Indianapolis: The Bobbs-Merrill Company,
Inc., 1976.
Aulén, Gustaf. *Christus Victor.* New York: Macmillan, 1969.
Asendorf, Ulrich. *Gekreuzigt und Auferstanden. Luthers Herausfor-
derung an die moderne Christologie. Arbeiten zur Geschichte und
Theologie des Luthertums,* 25. Hamburg: Lutherisches Verlags-
haus, 1971.
Atkinson, James. *Martin Luther: Prophet to the Church Catholic.*
Exeter: The Pater Noster Press; Grand Rapids: William B. Eerd-
mans Publishing Company, 1983.

Bibliography

_____ . "Luthers Einschätzung des Johannesevangeliums. Erwägungen zu Luthers Schriftverständis." *Lutherforschung heute.* Edited by Vilmos Vajta. Berlin: 1958.

Bainton, Roland H. *Erasmus of Christendom.* New York: Crossroad, 1982.

_____ . *Here I Stand: A Life of Martin Luther.* New York: Abingdon-Cokesbury Press, 1950.

Baur, Jörg. "Lutherische Christologie im Streit um die neue Bestimmung von Gott und Mensch." *EvTh 41* (1981):423-439.

Bedouelle, Guy. "Lefevre d'Etaples et Luther. Une recherche de frontières 1517-1527." *Revue de theologie et de philosophie 33* (1983):17-31.

Beer, Theobald. *Der fröhliche Wechsel und Streit. Grundzüge der Theologie Martin Luthers.* Second revised edition. Einsiedeln: Johannes Verlag, 1982.

Bigane, Jack and Hagen, Kenneth. "Annotated Bibliography of Luther Studies 1967-1976." *Sixteenth Century Bibliography 9.* St. Louis: Center for Reformation Research, 1977.

Bihlmeyer, Karl and Tüchle, Hermann. *Church History, Vol. 2.* Translated by Victor E. Mills and Francis J. Muller. Westminister, MD: The Newman Press, 1963.

Bludau, August. *Die beiden ersten Erasmus-Ausgaben des Neuen Testaments und ihre Gegner.* Freiburg: Herder, 1902.

_____ . "Das Comme Ioanneum (1 Io 5,7) im 16.Jahrhundert." *Biblische Zeitschrift 1* (1903): 280-302 and 378-407.

Boehmer, Heinrich. *Martin Luther: Road to Reformation.* Translated by John W. Doberstein and Theodore G. Tappert. New York: Meridian Books, 1960.

Bornkamm, Heinrich. *Martin Luther in Mid-Career 1521-1530.* Edited and with a Forward by Karin Bornkamm. Translated by E. Theodore Bachmann. Philadelphia: Fortress Press, 1983.

_____ . *Luther's World of Thought.* Translated by M. H. Bertram. St. Louis: Concordia Publishing House, 1958.

Bott, Gerhard, Ebeling, Gerhard; and Moeller, Bernd. *Martin Luther: Sein Leben in Bildern und Texten.* Frankfurt: Insel Verlag, 1983.

Brandenburg, Albert. *Die Zukunft des Martin Luther: Luther, Evangelium und die Katholizität. Eine These.* Münster: Aschendorff; Kassel: Johannes Stauda Verlag, 1977.

Brandi, Karl. *The Emperor Charles V. The Growth and Destiny of a Man and of a World-Empire.* Translated by C. V. Wedgwood. Oxford: Alden Press, 1939.

Brecht, Martin. *Martin Luther: Sein Weg zur Reformation 1483-1521.* Second edition. Stuttgart: Calwer Verlag, 1983.

_____ . "Zum Verständnis von Luthers Lied 'ein fest Burg.' " *ARG 70* (1979):106-121.

Breymayer, Reinhard. "Bibliographie zum Thema 'Luther und die Rhetorik.' " *Linguistica Biblica 21-22* (1973):39-44.

Brooks, Peter Newman, editor. *Seven-Headed Luther. Essays in Commemoration of a Quincentenary 1483-1983*. Oxford: Clarendon Press, 1983.

Brosseder, Johannes. "Martin Luther (1483-1546)." *Klassiker der Theologie, Vol. 1*. Edited by Heinrich Fries and Georg Kretschmar. Munich: C. H. Beck, 1981.

Chadwick, Owen. *The Reformation. The Pelican History of the Church 3*. Revised edition. Middlesex: Penguin Books, Ltd., 1982.

Chastel, André. *The Sack of Rome, 1527*. Princeton: University Press, 1983.

Congar, Yves. *Martin Luther: Sa foi, sa réforme. Etudes de théologie historique*. Paris: Les Editions Du Cerf, 1983.

————. "Regards et réflexions sur la christologie de Luther." *Das Konzil von Chalcedon: Geschichte und Gegenwart*. Edited by Aloys Grillmeier and Heinrich Bacht. Würzburg: Echter Verlag, 1954, 457-486. "Considerations and Reflections on the Christology of Luther." *Dialogue between Christians*. Westminister: 1966, 372-406.

Daniel-Rops, Henri. *Bernard of Clairvaux*. With a foreword by Thomas Merton. Translated by Elizabeth Abbott. New York and London: Hawthorn Books, Inc., 1964.

Dippelt, Hermann. "Hatte Luthers Verdeutschung des Neuen Testaments den griechischen Text zur Grundlage?" *ARG 38* (1941):300-330.

Diwald, Hellmut. *Luther: Eine Biographie*. Third edition. Bergisch Gladbach: Gustav-Lübbe-Verlag, 1982.

Dockhorn, Klaus. "Luthers Glaubensbegriff und die Rhetorik. Zu Gerhard Ebelings Buch 'Einführung in die theologische Sprachlehre.' " *Linguistica Biblica 21-22* (1973):19-38.

Duden Ethymologie. Herkunftswörterbuch der deutschen Sprache. Der Grosse Duden 7. Mannheim: Dudenverlag, 1963.

Düfel, Hans. *Luthers Stellung zur Marienverehrung*. Göttingen: Vandenhoeck & Ruprecht, 1968.

Ebeling, Gerhard. *Evangelische Evangelienauslegung. Eine Untersuchung zu Luthers Hermeneutik. Forschungen zur Geschichte und Lehre des Protestantismus 10/1*. Reprint Darmstadt: Wissenschaftliche Buchgesellschaft, 1962 (first printing, 1942).

————. *Luther: Einführung in sein Denken*. Tübingen: J. C. B. Mohr (Paul Siebeck), 1964. *An Introduction to His Thought*. Philadelphia: Fortress Press, 1970.

————. *Lutherstudien II. Disputatio de homine*. Two volumes. Tübingen: J. C. B. Mohr (Paul Siebeck), 1977 and 1982.

————. *Umgang mit Luther*. Tübingen: J. C. B. Mohr (Paul Siebeck), 1983.

Eck, John. *Enchiridion of Common Places of John Eck against Martin Luther and other Enemies of the Church*. Translated by Ford Lewis Battles. Grand Rapids: Calvin Theological Seminary, 1978.

Eckermann, Karl W. "Luthers Kreuzestheologie." *Catholica 37* (1983):306-317.

Bibliography

Ellwein, Eduard. *Summus Evangelista. Die Botschaft des Johannesevangeliums in der Auslegung Luthers.* Munich: Kaiser Verlag, 1960.

Evans, G. R. *The Mind of St. Bernard of Clairvaux.* Oxford: Clarendon Press, 1983.

Frick, R. "Luther's Christusbild in der Hauspostille." *Monatsschrift für Pastoral Theologie 26* (1930):16-19 and 76-82.

Friedenthal, Richard. *Luther: His Life and Times.* Translated by G. J. Nowell. New York: Harcourt, Brace, Jovanovich, 1970.

Gadamer, Hans Georg. *Truth and Method.* Translated by Garrett Barden and John Cumming. New York: The Seabury Press, 1975.

Gebrehiiwet, Mihreteab. *Christ-Mysticism in the Theology and Spirituality of Martin Luther.* Dissertation, Lutheran School of Theology at Chicago. Chicago: 1976.

Gennrich, Paul Wilhelm. *Die Christologie Luthers im Abendmahlsstreit 1524-1529.* Inaugural-Dissertation Berlin. Königsberg: Otto Kümmel Druckerei, 1929.

Grane, Leif. "Divus Paulus et S. Augustinus, interpres eius fidellissimus: über Luthers Verhältnis zu Augustin." *Festschrift für Ernst Fuchs.* Edited by Gerhard Ebeling et al. Tübingen: J. C. B. Mohr (Paul Siebeck), 1973.

Günther, Hartmut and Volk, Ernst, editors. *D. Martin Luthers Epistelauslegung, Vol. 5.* Göttingen: Vandenhoeck & Ruprecht, 1983.

Hagen, Kenneth G. *A Theology of Testament in the Young Luther: The Lectures on Hebrews, Studies in Medieval and Reformation Thought, 12.* Leiden: E. J. Brill, 1974.

_____. *Hebrews Commenting from Erasmus to Bèze 1516-1598. Beiträge zur Geschichte der Biblischen Exegese, 23.* Tübingen: J. C. B. Mohr (Paul Siebeck), 1981.

_____. "The Testament of a Worm: Luther on Testament and Covenant." *Consensus 8/1* (1982),12-20.

Hagen, Kenneth, and Posset, Franz. "Annotated Bibliography of Luther Studies 1977-1983." *Sixteenth Century Bibliography 24.* St. Louis Center for Reformation Research, 1985.

Hausherr, Irénée. *Penthos: The Doctrine of Compunction in the Christian East,* trans. Anselm Hufstader. Kalamazoo: Cistercian Studies 53, 1982.

Hendrix, Scott. *Luther and the Papacy. Stages in a Reformation Conflict.* Philadelphia: Fortress Press, 1981.

Herrmann, Horst. *Martin Luther: Ketzer wider willen.* Munich: Bertelsmann, 1983.

Hirsch, Emmanuel. *Lutherstudien 1.* Gütersloh: Gütersloher Verlagshaus, 1954.

Hoffman, Bengt Runo. *Luther and the Mystics: a Reexamination of Luther's Spiritual Experience and His Relationship to the Mystics.* Minneapolis: Augsburg Publishing House, 1976.

Hofmann, Hans-Ulrich. *Luther und die Johannesapokalypse. Beiträge zur Geschichte der biblischen Exegese, 24.* Tübingen: J. C. B. Mohr (Paul Siebeck), 1982.

Holl, Karl. *Gesammelte Aufsätze zur Kirchengeschichte, Vol. 1: Luther.* Seventh edition. Tübingen: Mohr Verlag, 1948.

──────. *What Did Luther Understand by Religion?* Edited by J. L. Adams and W. Bensel. Philadelphia: 1977.

Huck, Friedrich. "Die Entwicklung der Christologie Luthers von der Psalmenvorlesung zur Römerbriefvorlesung," *ThStKr 102* (1930):61-142.

Iserloh, Erwin. *Johannes Eck (1486-1543): Scholastiker, Humanist, Kontroverstheologe. Katholisches Leben und Kirchenreform im Zeitalter der Glaubensspaltung, 41.* Münster: Aschendorff, 1981.

Iwand, Hans Joachim. *Rechtfertigungslehre und Christusglaube. Eine Untersuchung zur Systematik der Rechtfertigungslehre in ihren Anfängen.* Third edition, reprint. Darmstadt: Wissenschaftliche Buchgesellschaft, 1966.

Jarrott, C. A. L. "Erasmus In principio erat sermo: A Controversial Translation." *Studies in Philology 61* (1964):35-40.

Jedin, Hubert. *A History of the Council of Trent.* Translated by E. Graf. New York: Thomas Nelson and Sons, 1957.

Jonge, H. J. de. "Erasmus and the Comma Johanneum." *Ephemerides theologiae lovanienses 56* (1980):381-89.

Junghans, Helmar, editor. *Leben und Werk Martin Luthers von 1526 bis 1546. Festgabe zu seinem 500. Geburtstag.* Berlin: Evangelische Verlagsanstalt; Göttingen: Vandenhoeck & Ruprecht, 1983.

──────. "Rhetorische Bemerkungen Luthers in seinen 'Dictata super Psalterium.' " *Theologische Versuche, 8.* Edited by Joachim Rogge and Gottfried Schille. Berlin: Evangelische Verlagsanstalt, 1977, 97-128.

──────. "Interpreting the Old Luther (1526-1546)." Translated by Inge Forssmann. *Currents in Theology and Mission, 9* (1982):271-81.

──────. "Wittenberg und Luther — Luther und Wittenberg." *Freiburger Zeitschrift für Philosophie und Theologie, 25* (1978):104-119.

Klaus, Bernhard. "Georg Rörer, ein bayerischer Mitarbeiter D. Martin Luthers." *Zeitschrift für bayerische Kirchengeschichte, 26* (1957):113-145.

Kleineidam, Erich. "Ursprung und Gegenstand der Theologie bei Bernhard von Clairvaux und Martin Luther." *Dienst der Vermittlung. Festschrift zum 25-jährigen Bestehen des philosophisch-theologischen Studiums im Priesterseminar Erfurt.* Edited by Wilhelm Ernst et al. Leipzig: St. Benno Verlag, 1977, 221-247.

Kleinig, John W. "The Kindred Heart: Luther on Meditation," *Lutheran Theological Journal* 20(1986):142-54.

Bibliography

Köpf, Ulrich. *Religiöse Erfahrung in der Theologie Bernhards von Clairvaux. Beiträge zur Historischen Theologie, 61.* Tübingen: 1980.

Koopmans, J. *Das altkirchliche Dogma in der Reformation. Beiträge zur evangelischen Theologie, 22.* Munich: Kaiser Verlag, 1955.

Kratzsch, Irmgard. "Quellenmaterial zu Martin Luthers Leben und Werk in der Universitätsbibliothek Jena." *Wissenschaftliche Zeitschrift der Friedrich-Schiller-Universität Jena, Gesellschaft-und Sprachwissenschaftliche Reihe, 32* (1983):229-248.

Krauth, Charles Porterfield. *The Conservative Reformation and Its Theology.* Reprint, Minneapolis: Augsburg Publishing House, 1978.

Kretschmar, Georg. "Luther und das altkirchliche Dogma." *Una Sancta 37* (1982):293-303.

Küng, Hans. *The Council, Reform, and Reunion.* Translated by Cecily Hastings. New York: Sheed and Ward, 1961.

_____ *Menschwerdung Gottes. Eine Einführung in Hegels theologisches Denken als Prolegomena zu einer künftigen Christologie. Ökumenische Forschungen, Vol. 2 (Soteriologische Abteilung 1).* Freiburg: Herder, 1970.

Landgraf, Wolfgang. *Martin Luther: Reformator und Rebell.* Second edition. Berlin: Verlag Neues Leben, 1982.

Läpple, Alfred. *Martin Luther: Leben, Bilder, Dokumente.* Aschaffenburg: Pattloch; Zurich: Delphin, 1982.

Lausberg, Heinrich. *Handbuch der literarischen Rhetorik: Eine Grundlegung der Literaturwissenschaft.* Munich: M. Hueber Verlag, 1960.

Leclercq, Jean. *Bernard of Clairvaux and the Cistercian Spirit.* Translated by Claire Lavoie. Kalamazoo: Cistercian Publications, 1976.

Leder, Hans-Günter. *Ausgleich mit dem Papst? Luthers Haltung in den Verhandlungen mit Miltitz 1520. Arbeiten zur Theologie, 1,38.* Stuttgart: Calwer Verlag, 1969.

Lehmann, Karl, editor. *Luthers Sendung für Katholiken und Protestanten.* Freiburg: Katholische Akademie; Zurich: Schnell und Steiner, 1982.

Lieball, Josef. *Martin Luthers Madonnenbild.* Stein am Rhein: Christiana-Verlag, 1981.

Lienhard, Marc. *Luther: Witness to Jesus Christ. Stages and Themes of the Reformer's Christology.* Translated by Edwin H. Robertson. Minneapolis: Ausburg Publishing House, 1982.

_____ *Un temps, une vie, un message.* Paris: Le Centurion; Geneva: Labor et Fides, 1983.

Lilje, Hanns. *Martin Luther: In Selbstzeugnissen und Bilddokumenten.* Reinbek: Rowohlt, 1981 (first printing, 1965). *Luther and the Reformation: an illustrated Review.* Philadelphia: Fortress Press, 1967.

Locher, G. W. "Christus unser Hauptmann." *Ein Stück der Verkündigung Huldreych Zwinglis in seinem Kulturgeschichtlichen Zusammenhang. Zwingliana no. 1.* Zurich: 1950.

Loewenich, Walther von. *Die Eigenart von Luthers Auslegung des Johannes-Prologes.* Bayerische Akademie der Wissenschaften, Philosophisch-Historische Klasse, Sitzungsberichte. Munich: Verlag der Bayerischen Akademie der Wissenschaften, 1960, 1-54.

————. *Luther und das Johanneische Christentum.* Munich: Kaiser-Verlag, 1982.

————. *Martin Luther: Der Mann und das Werk.* Munich: List-Verlag, 1935.

Lohse, Bernhard. *Martin Luther: Eine Einführung in sein Leben und sein Werk.* Munich: C. H. Beck, 1982.

————. "Luthers Christologie im Ablasstreit." *Lutherjahrbuch 27* (1960):51-63.

Lortz, Joseph. *The Reformation in Germany.* Translated by Ronald Wulfs. London: Darton, Longman & Todd; New York: Herder and Herder, 1968.

————, editor. *Bernhard von Clairvaux: Mönch und Mystiker.* Internationaler Bernhardkongress Mainz 1953. Wiesbaden: Franz Steiner Verlag, 1955.

Lumpe, Adolf. "Zur Bedeutungsgeschichte des Verbums 'reformare' und seiner Ableitungen." *Annuarium Historiae Conciliorum 14* (1982):1-12.

Mackinnon, James. *Luther and the Reformation.* New York: Russell & Russell, Inc., 1962.

Manns, Peter. "Ketzer oder Vater im Glauben?" *Vorlagen no. 4.* Hannover: Lutherhausverlag, 1980.

————. and Loose, Helmut Nils. *Martin Luther: An Illustrated Biography.* Text by P. Manns, photographs by H. N. Loose. Introduction by Jaroslav Pelikan. Translated by Michael Shaw. New York: Crossroad, 1982.

————. and Meyer, Harding, editors. *Luther's Ecumenical Significance: An Interconfessional Consulation.* In collaboration with Carter Lindberg and Harry McSorley. Philadelphia: Fortress Press, 1984.

Maron, Gottfried. *Das Katholische Lutherbild der Gegenwart. Bensheimer Hefte.* Edited by Evangelischer Bund, vol. 58. Göttingen: Vandenhoeck & Ruprecht, 1982.

Maurer, Wilhelm. *Die Anfänge von Luthers Theologie. Eine Frage an die Lutherische Kirche. ThLZ 77* (1952):1-12.

————. "Cisterciensische Reform und reformatorischer Glaube." *Cisterciensische Chronik 84* (1977):1-13.

Mayer, Hans. *Martin Luther:Leben und Glaube.* Gütersloh: Gütersloher Verlagshaus, 1982.

Meisner, Michael. *Martin Luther: Heiliger oder Rebell.* Lübeck: 1981.

Bibliography

Meyer, C. S., editor. *Luther for an Ecumencial Age*. St. Louis: Concordia Publishing House, 1967.

Moeller, Bernd and Stackmann, Karl. *Luder- Luther- Eleutherius: Erwägungen zu Luthers Namen.* Nachrichten der Akademie der Wissenschaften in Göttingen I. Philosophisch-Historische Klasse no. 7. Göttingen: Vandenhoeck & Ruprecht, 1981.

Mostert, Walter. *Scriptura sacra sui ipsius interpres. Bemerkungen zum Verständnis der Heiligen Schrift durch Luther.* Lutherjahrbuch 46 (1979):60-96.

Mühlen, Karl Heinz zur. "Luthers deutsche Bibelübersetzung als Gemeinschaftswerk." *Die Bibel in der Welt 18* (1978):90-97.

_____. "Mystik des Wortes: Über die Bedeutung mystischen Denkens für Luthers Lehre von der Rechtfertigung des Sünders." *Zeitwende 52* (1981):206-225.

Mülhaupt, Erwin. *Luther im 20.Jahrhundert.* Göttingen: Vandenhoeck & Ruprecht, 1982.

Müller, Gerhard. "Der Katholizismus als Heimat Martin Luthers," *Luther 52* (1981):78-80.

Nicol, Martin. *Meditation bei Luther.* Göttingen: Vandenhoeck & Ruprecht, 1984.

Nilsson, K. O. *Simul: Das Miteinander von Göttlichem und Menschlichem in Luthers Theologie.* Forschungen zur Kirchen- und Dogmengeschichte 17. Göttingen: Vandenhoeck & Ruprecht, 1966.

Oberman, Heiko, A. " 'Immo.' Luthers reformatorische Entdeckungen im Spiegel der Rhetorik." *Lutheriana. Zum 500. Geburtstag Martin Luthers von den Mitarbeitern der Weimarer Ausgabe* (Archiv der Weimarer Ausgabe, Vol. 5). Cologne: 1984,17-38.

_____. *Martin Luther: Mensch zwischen Gott und Teufel.* Berlin: Severin und Siedler, 1982.

_____. "Martin Luther: Vorläufer der Reformation." *Verifikationen.* Festschrift Gerhard Ebeling zum 70. Geburtstag. Edited by Eberhard Jüngel, Johannes Wallmann, Wilfried Werbeck, Tübingen: J. C. B. Mohr (Paul Siebeck), 1982.

Olson, Oliver. "Flacius Illyricus, Matthias (1520-1575)." *TRE 11*:206-214.

O'Malley, John W. "Developments, Reforms and Two Great Reformations: Toward a Historical Assessment of Vatican II," *Theological Studies 44* (1983):373-406.

Parker, Thomas Henry Louis. *John Calvin: A Biography.* Philadelphia: The Westminster Press, 1975.

Pauck, Wilhelm. *The Heritage of the Reformation.* Glencoe, Illinois: The Free Press, 1961.

Pesch, Otto Hermann. *Hinführung zu Luther.* Mainz: Matthias Grünewald-Verlag, 1982.

_____. "Neuere Beiträge zur Frage nach Luthers 'Reformatorischer Wende.' " *Catholica 38* (1984):66-133.

_____. " 'Um Christi willen.' Christologie und Rechtfertigung in der katholischen Theologie: Versuch einer Richtigstellung." *Catholica 35* (1981):17-57.

Peters, Albrecht. "Luthers Christuszeugnis als Zusammenfassung der Christusbotschaft der Kirche," *KD 13* (1967):1-26,73-98.

Pfitzner, Victor C. "Luther as Interpreter of John's Gospel with Special Reference to His Sermons on the Gospel of St. John." *Lutheran Theological Journal 18* (1984):65-73.

_____. "Das Christuszeugnis Luthers." *Jesusbilder in Theologischer Sicht*. Edited by K. Drescher. Munich: 1966,261-298.

Posset, Franz. "John Bugenhagen and the *Comma Johanneum*", *Concordia Theological Quarterly* 49(1985):245-51.

_____. "*Bernardus Redivivus:* The *Wirkungsgeschichte* of Medieval Sermon in the Reformation of the Sixteenth Century," *Cistercian Studies, fasc. 3* (1987):239-49.

_____. "Bible Reading "With Closed Eyes" in the Monastic Tradition: An Overlooked Aspect of Martin Luther's Hermeneutics," *The American Benedictine Review* 38(1987):293-306.

Prenter, Regin. *Spiritus Creator*. Translated by John M. Jensen. Philadelphia: Muhlenberg Press, 1953.

Randenborgh, Gottfried van. "Die Eigenart der Christologie Luthers." *Kirche in der Zeit 13* (December 1958):397-403.

Ratschow, Carl Heinz. "Christologie und Rechtfertigung: Luthers Christologie nach seinen Disputationen." *Iustificatio Impii*. Festschrift für Lauri Haikola zum 60. Geburtstag am 9.2.1977. Edited by Jussi Talasniemi. Helsinki: 1977,204-226.

Ratzinger, Joseph. *Introduction to Christianity*. Translated by J. R. Foster. New York: The Seabury Press, 1979.

Reardon, Bernard M. G. *Religious Thought in the Reformation*. London and New York: Longman, 1981.

Reinke, Darrel R. "Martin Luther: Language and Devotional Consciousness." *The Spirituality of Western Christendom*. Edited by E. Rozanne Elder. *Cistercian Studies Series 30*. Kalamazoo: Cistercian Publications, Inc. 1976, 152-168.

Rogge, Joachim. *Martin Luther: Sein Leben — Seine Zeit — Seine Wirkungen. Eine Bildbiographie*. Gütersloh: Gütersloher Verlagshaus, 1982.

Russell, Francis. *The Word of Dürer 1471-1528*. New York: Time Inc., 1967.

Rust, J. A. "Luthers Christusglaube." *ZST 1* (1923):452-467.

Sasse, Hermann. *This is my Body. Luther's Contention for the Real Presence in the Sacrament of the Altar*. Minneapolis: Augsburg Publishing House, 1959.

Sauer, Waltraut Ingeborg. "Bibelübersetzung III, 1." *TRE 6*:239-244.

Schlingensiepen, Hermann. "Erasmus als Exeget Auf Grund seiner Schriften zu Matthäus." *ZKG 48* (1929):16-57.

261

Schmauch, Werner, editor. *In Memoriam Ernst Lohmeyer.* Stuttgart: Evangelisches Verlagswerk, 1951.

Schnackenburg, Rudolf. "Paulinische und johanneische Christologie. Ein Vergleich." *Das Johannesevangelium IV. Teil. Ergänzende Auslegungen und Exkurse.* (Freiburg: Herder, 1984), 102-118.

Schwager, Raymund. "Der fröhliche Wechsel und Streit. Zur Erlösungs-und Rechtfertigungslehre Martin Luthers." *ZThK 106* (1984):27-66.

Schwarz, Reinhard. "Gott ist Mensch. Zur Lehre von der Person Christi bei den Ockhamisten und bei Luther." *ZThK 63* (1966):289-351.

_____. "Mystischer Glaube — die Brautmystik Martin Luthers." *Zeitwende 52* (1981):193-205.

Schwiebert, E. G. *Luther and His Times. The Reformation from a New Perspective.* St. Louis: Concordia Publishing House, 1950.

Seeberg, Erich. *Luthers Theologie, Vol. 2. Christus: Wirklichkeit und Urbild.* Reprint, Darmstadt: Wissenschaftliche Buchgesellschaft, 1969 (first printing, 1937).

Seeberg, Reinhold. "Die Sünden und die Sündenvergebung nach dem ersten Brief des Johannes." *Das Erbe Martin Luthers und die gegen-wärtige theologische Forschung.* Festschrift L. Ihmels. Edited by R. Jelke. Leipzig: Dorffling und Franke, 1928,19-31.

Siggins, Jan D. Kingston. *Martin Luther's Doctrine of Christ. Yale Publications in Religion, 14.* New Haven: Yale University Press, 1970.

Stange, Carl. *Bernard von Clairvaux. Studien der Luther-Akademie 3.* Berlin: Verlag Alfred Töpelmann, 1954.

_____. "Das Heilswerk Christi nach Luther." *ZST 21* (1950):183-211.

_____. "The Johannine Character of Luther's Doctrine of Salvation." *Lutheran World Revue 2* (October 1949):65-77.

_____. "Die Person Jesu Christi in der Theologie Luthers." *ZST 6* (1926):449-483.

Stauffer, Richard. *Luther as seen by Catholics.* Translated by Mary Parker and T. H. L. Parker. London: Lutterworth Press, 1967.

Stolt, Birgit. *Die Sprachmischung in Luthers Tischreden. Studien zum Problem der Zweisprachigkeit.* Uppsala: Almquist & Wiksell, 1964.

Stupperich, Robert. *Melanchthon.* Translated by Robert H. Fischer. Philadelphia: Westminster Press, 1966.

Todd, John Murray. *Luther: A Life.* New York: Crossroad, 1982.

Turner, Cuthbert Hamilton. *The Early Printed Editions of the Greek Testament.* Oxford: Clarendon Press, 1924.

Vercruysse, J. E. "Luther's theology of the cross in the time of the Heidelberg Disputation." *Gegorianum 57* (1976):523-48.

Vogel, Heinrich J. *Vogel's Cross Reference and Index to the Contents of Luther's Works.* A cross reference between the American Edition and the St. Louis, Weimar and Erlangen Editions of Luther's Works. Milwaukee: Northwestern Publishing House, 1983.

Vogelsang, Erich. *Christusglaube und Christusbekenntnis bei Luther*. Munich: 1935.

————. *Die Anfänge von Luthers Christologie nach der ersten Psalmenvorlesung insbesondere in ihren exegetischen und systematischen Zusammenhägen mit Augustin und der Scholastik dargestellt*. Berlin and Leipzig: Verlag von Walter de Gruyter & Co., 1929.

————. *Der angefochtene Christus bei Luther, Arbeiten zur Kirchengeschichte, 21*. Berlin and Leipzig: Verlag von Walter de Gruyter & Co., 1932.

Volz, Carl. "Martin Luther's Attitude Toward Bernard of Clairvaux." *Studies in Medieval Cistercian History*. Presented to Jeremiah F. O'Sullivan. Spencer, MA: Cistercian Publications, 1971, 186-204.

Volz, Hans D. *Martin Luther: die gantze Heilige Schrift Deutsch. Wittenberg 1545*. Munich: Kaiser Verlag, 1972.

————. *Martin Luthers deutsche Bibel. Entstehung und Geschichte der Lutherbibel*. Introduction by Friedrich Wilhelm Kantzenbach, edited by Henning Wendland. Hamburg: Friedrich Wittig Verlag, 1978.

Vorländer, Dorothea. *Deus incarnatus. Die Zweinaturenchristologie Luthers bis 1521. Untersuchungen zur Kirchengeschichte, 9*. Witten: Luther-Verlag, 1974.

Walter, J. von. "Luthers Christusbild." *Lutherjahrbuch 6* (1939):1-27.

Wendelborn, Gert. *Martin Luther: Leben und reformatorisches Werk*. Vienna: Hermann Böhlaus Nachf., 1983.

Wicks, Jared, editor. *Catholic Scholars Dialogue with Luther*. Chicago: Loyola University Press, 1970.

————. *Luther and His Spiritual Legacy. Theology and Life Series 7*. Wilmington: Michael Glazier, Inc., 1983.

Windhorst, Christof. "Luther and the 'Enthusiasts.' Theological Judgments in his Lecture on the First Epistle of St. John (1527)." Translated by Dorothea Woydaek. *Journal of Religious History* (1977):339-348.

————. *Täuferisches Taufverständnis. Balthasar Hubmaiers Lehre zwischen traditioneller und reformatorischer Theologie. Studies in Medieval and Reformation Thought, 16*. Leiden: E. J. Brill, 1976.

Winkler, Gerhard B. *Erasmus von Rotterdam und die Einleitungschriften zum Neuen Testament. Formale Strukturen und theologischer Sinn*. Münster: Aschendorff, 1974.

Wolf, Ernst. *Peregrinatio: Studien zur reformatorischen Theologie und zum Kirchenproblem*. Second edition. Munich: Kaiser Verlag, 1962, 30-80.

Zahrnt, Heinz. *Martin Luther in seiner Zeit für unsere Zeit*. Ulm: Süddeutscher Verlag, 1983.

Zeller, Winfried. *Das Christusverständnis im Wandel der Zeiten: Eine Ringvorlesung der Theologischen Fakultät der Universität Marburg*. Edited by Hans Grass and Werner Georg Kümmel. Marburg: N. G. Elwert-Verlag, 1963.

INDEX OF NAMES
(without Luther or Biblical Authors)